POLITICS & GOVERNMENT *in* MICHIGAN

FOURTH EDITION

James P. Hanley, Jr.

Paul A. Rozycki

Charles Stewart Mott Community College

Custom Publishing

Boston   Burr Ridge, IL   Dubuque, IA   Madison, WI   New York
San Francisco   St. Louis   Bangkok   Bogotá   Caracas   Kuala Lumpur
Lisbon   London   Madrid   Mexico City   Milan   Montreal   New Delhi
Santiago   Seoul   Singapore   Sydney   Taipei   Toronto

The McGraw·Hill Companies

Politics and Government in Michigan

McGraw-Hill's Custom Publishing consists of products that are produced from camera-ready copy. Peer review, class testing, and accuracy are primarily the responsibility of the author(s).

1 2 3 4 5 6 7 8 9 0   QSR QSR   0 9 8 7 6 5 4 3 2

ISBN 0-07-286616-0

Editor: Tammy Immell
Production Editor: Susan Culbertson
Printer/Binder: Quebecor World

PREFACE

We have used many versions of this book in our American Government courses at Mott Community College since the early 1980s, updating it along the way. The study of Michigan's politics and governance has acquainted our students with the many interesting comparisons and contrasts of the state's features with those of the nation.

No effort like this can proceed without the encouragement assistance and support of many people. We thank our families, Mott Community College, our colleagues, many officials of organizations and governments, faculty at other colleges who've used the book, and McGraw-Hill publishers. Thanks also to Andrea Meizlish, Michael Tews and Rich Thompson for the computer expertise and assistance in producing this edition.

Above all, we thank our Mott students who have read this book, digested it, criticized it and suggested both minor and major improvements.

As we enter the new century, Michigan's political scene is undergoing some significant changes. We have done our best to incorporate up-to-date information and analysis in this book. Naturally, we bear responsibility for any errors, omissions or misinterpretations.

We would appreciate hearing from any readers about their reactions/suggestions for this book. Please contact us at the addresses noted below.

Flint, Michigan
January, 2003

James P. Hanley, Jr. (emeritus faculty)
Paul A. Rozycki

To contact us:
(Mail)
Social Science Division
1401 E. Court St.
Flint, MI. 48503

(phone) (810) 762-0514
Mott Community College
(Fax) (810) 762-5670
(E-Mail)
prozycki@email.mcc.edu
jhanley@edtech.mcc.edu

TABLE OF CONTENTS

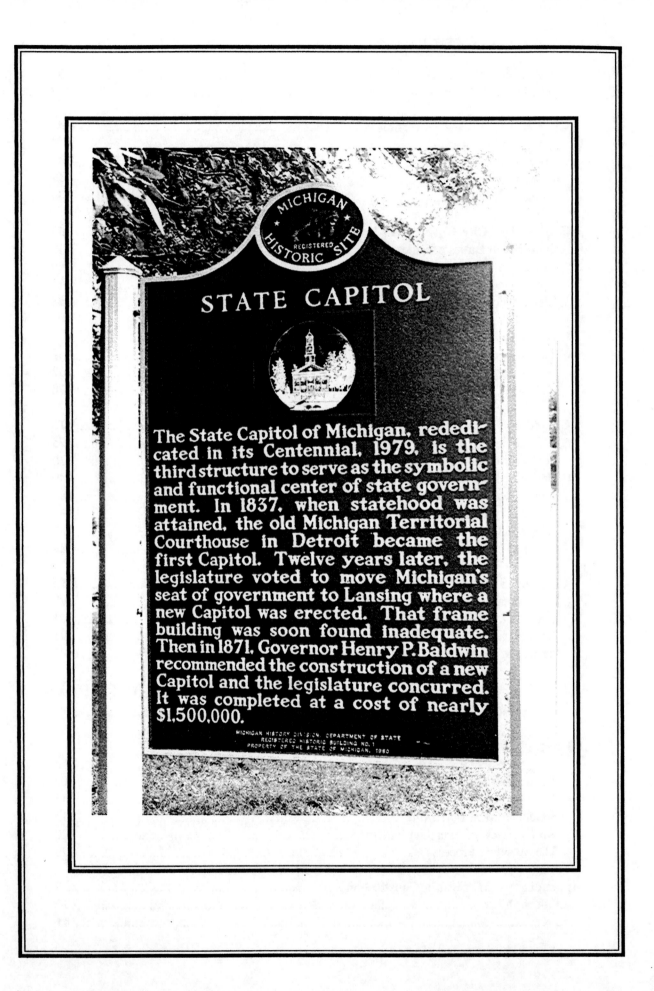

STATE CAPITOL

The State Capitol of Michigan, rededi-cated in its Centennial, 1979, is the third structure to serve as the symbolic and functional center of state govern-ment. In 1837, when statehood was attained, the old Michigan Territorial Courthouse in Detroit became the first Capitol. Twelve years later, the legislature voted to move Michigan's seat of government to Lansing where a new Capitol was erected. That frame building was soon found inadequate. Then in 1871, Governor Henry P. Baldwin recommended the construction of a new Capitol and the legislature concurred. It was completed at a cost of nearly $1,500,000.

MICHIGAN HISTORY DIVISION, DEPARTMENT OF STATE
REGISTERED HISTORIC BUILDING NO. 1
PROPERTY OF THE STATE OF MICHIGAN, 1960

Part 1

Michigan in the United States

Introduction

A Brief History of Michigan's Early Governments

Michigan in the Federal System

INTRODUCTION TO PART 1

In the hurried overview of American government that often takes place in the introductory survey course, state and local government is often relegated to a final chapter tacked onto a large "national" government textbook or is skipped altogether. The reason for this is obvious—it is impossible to cover the details of all fifty different states in a textbook meant for the national market.

This lack of coverage of state and local government is unfortunate. Students may leave an introductory course with a good understanding of the U.S. Congress yet find that their own day-to-day lives are more affected by the actions of their county commission or city council. State and local governments collectively are growing more rapidly than the national government and their impact on individual lives is likely to be more frequent.

If one looks beyond the obvious national roles in defense and Social Security and examines domestic policy the states play important roles. In education, transportation, welfare, criminal justice and commercial regulation the states play a major role. Approximately 80 percent of all governmental workers in the United States are employed by state and local governments.

States are often the source for new ideas in politics. Whether in the areas of environmental controls or tax revolts, the actions of state and local governments often come before those of the national government. States and localities often serve as policy laboratories.

Much of our politics has its roots on the state and local level. Our political parties are based in state and local organizations and many national office holders began their political careers on the state or local level.

This text surveys the politics and institutions of Michigan's state and local governments. The authors hope to provide a basic understanding of those factors that make Michigan's governments operate the way they do, a basic reference to the state's governments and perhaps some guides to political action for the citizen.

This book contains five major sections. The first briefly surveys the history of the state, describes how Michigan became a state and how Michigan fits into the sometimes very complex federal system.

The second section of the text deals with the most basic of all political motives—power seeking. What is power? How does one obtain it? How can it be used? These are the questions we attempt to answer in the second section dealing with parties, interest groups, elections and voting.

In all governments power is exercised through formal institutions. Part three of the text surveys the basic state level institutions in Michigan. How is power channeled through this governmental machinery? How did these state institutions develop? This section of the text reviews these questions as it looks at the executive, the legislative and the judicial branches of the state government.

Some of the most intricate and important kinds of governmental actions take place on the local level. Part four of the book looks at the local forms of government in Michigan. It is difficult to generalize about the many complex kinds of local government. Yet many of the most bitterly fought political struggles are on the local level—whether it be a leash law for pets or a zoning change to allow a bar into the neighborhood. The basic units of local government—the township, the village, the city, the county and local education are covered. This section concludes with a survey of some of the problems caused by the multitude of local governments that we have created.

Finally, all government must be paid for. Where does the money come from? Where does it go? The fifth section of the text surveys the major sources of revenue for the state and then examines the major expenditures.

The problems that Michigan faces and the resources it has to solve those problems are a reflection of the history of the state. We are like all states, and indeed all peoples, a product of our history. Before we look at today's institutions and politics, consider the the history of Michigan. Much of what we are today flows from what we have been. The following chapter reviews that history and the importance of the federal system in making Michigan what it is today.

Chapter 1

A Brief History of Michigan's Early Governments

Michigan's First Inhabitants

The French Era (1618-1760)

The English Period (1760-1796)

Michigan as an American Territory

Michigan Becomes a State

> *"There shall be formed in the said territory, not less than three nor more than five states..."*
> Northwest Ordinance, Article 5

Chapter 1

Learning Objectives

What were the three major prehistoric eras in Michigan?

What are some of the major Indian tribes in Michigan today?

When was the French period in Michigan history?

Identify some of the major events of the English era.

What was the Northwest Ordinance?

What was the importance of the Treaty of Greenville?

Summarize the Ohio-Michigan conflict over Toledo.

Key Terms to Know

Paleo-Indians	Archaic Period
Woodland Period	Northwest Ordinance
French Period	Etienne Brule'
English Period	District of Hesse
Treaty of Greenville	Stevens T. Mason
Toledo conflict	

This chapter will review the early history of Michigan covering the early settlement of the region and the events that formed the state. The discussion of Indian settlement is based on Richard Santer's *Michigan: Heart of the Great Lakes*. The summary of exploration in Michigan and its admission to the Union is developed from Ferris Lewis' *State and Local Government in Michigan*.

MICHIGAN'S FIRST INHABITANTS

Perhaps 11,000 years ago, before the last glacier left what is now the state of Michigan, the first inhabitants began moving into the area. Archeologists generally agree that there were three major periods of prehistoric cultural activity in the state: 1) the Paleo-Indian hunter period which existed from 11,000 to 4,500 years ago, 2) the Archaic period which existed 4,000 to 2,500 years ago and 3) the Woodland period which existed from 2,500 years ago until the first French contact in the seventeenth century.

Paleo-Indian Hunters

The very first inhabitants of the state were probably descendants of the first human beings to migrate across the Bering land bridge from Asia to North America. These hunters, like many around the world at the time, often moved frequently to follow the game animals. Thus, they were probably not truly permanent residents of the Michigan peninsulas. At a site just north of what is now Detroit, stone tools, caribou bones and other evidence of human inhabitation that date back 11,000 years have been found. As the glacier melted and retreated northward it is probable that these early hunters followed the shorelines and streams created by the melting ice and began populating the state.

Between 9,000 and 4,500 years ago, the waters in the Great Lakes rose to cover the surrounding shorelines and create swamplands where there had once been woods favorable to hunting. As this period of flooding decreased the supply of animals, the human population that depended on the animals decreased also.

Archaic Period

As the lakes receded about 4,000 years ago, conditions again changed to provide more favorable hunting and fishing activities in the area. As these conditions improved, Indians from southern regions began to migrate to the area. These migrants, called the Archaic Indians, brought many cultural customs with them. The most notable were the religious and ceremonial customs that focused on burials. Many of their artifacts are found today in and around areas used as burial grounds. Many of these relics are copper tools from the Lake Superior area, flint "turkey tail" points from Indiana, carved stone objects and shells from the coast of Florida. The evidence seems to suggest that these people lived in small villages and engaged in extensive trade with other Indian groups on the North American continent.

The Woodland Indians

The Woodland era began about 2500 years ago and continued until the time of the first French contact in 1618. The Indians of this period were different from the Archaic Indians because they produced pottery for the first time. The Woodland Indians were also different from the Indians of recent centuries. They constructed mounds and garden beds which were not a part of the customs followed by the Indians first encountered by the French. The Woodland period can be divided into three stages: early, middle and late.

The Early Woodland Indians introduced burial mounds, the earliest being located along the lower Muskegon River. This era may also have seen the introduction of agriculture.

The Middle Woodland stage began about 2100 years ago and is commonly known as the era of the "Mound Builders." These Indians built many mounds to their dead. More than one thousand mounds have been identified so far. In Michigan these mounds are found most commonly along the St. Joseph, Grand and Muskegon Rivers and in the Saginaw Valley. Perhaps the most significant and impressive of these mounds is the Norton Group near Grand Rapids. These mounds, excavated by the staff of the Grand Rapids Public Museum and the University of Michigan, contained examples of what may be some of the highest degree of artistry attained up to that time. Many pieces of decorated pottery, arrowheads, hammered copper, knives, drills, pipes and other examples of the craftsmanship of this time were uncovered.

The Late Woodland stage began about 700 A.D. when the Indians began to practice widespread agriculture. The life of the tribes adapted to the changing seasons so the planting and harvesting could be more productive. Evidence of the early use of corn as early as 1000 A.D. was found in Monroe county. During this time trade and cultural interchanges took place with tribes from Illinois, Indiana and Ohio.

Today's Indians: The Tribes of Michigan

Knowledge of the earliest Indians is based upon limited information and speculation about how the people lived. Since the beginnings of the French exploration the Indians have been studied in detail.

Though estimates vary, it has been calculated that at the time the French first arrived in Michigan (1618) that there were about 15,000 Indians in the area. Of these about 12,000 lived in the lower peninsula. There were three major tribal groupings: the Chippewa, the Ottawa and the Potawatomi. These three groups were all part of the larger Algonquin speaking group. Many of the present day place names in Michigan are derived from Indian language. Places such as Okemos, Osceola, Neguanee, Mecosta, Kalamazoo, Tahquamenon, Kichitikipi and Ontanogon all owe their origins to Indian words.

The *Chippewa-Ojibwa* were the "northerners" in the state. Originally their major concentrations were in the upper peninsula and the northern part of the lower peninsula. When Detroit was founded by Cadillac in 1701 many of the Chippewa began to migrate southward. Some moved as far south as the Saginaw area. Like their predecessors of the Late Woodland era the Chippewa engaged in hunting and fishing. It is the fishing activity and disputes over treaty provisions that has created conflict between the Indians of northern Michigan,

the sports interests, commercial fishing interests and the Department of Natural Resources in recent years.

The term *Ottawa* translates as traders. These Indians first came into contact with the French on Manitoulin Island (Ontario) in Lake Huron. Early in the seventeenth century the Ottawa began to move west from the Ottawa river area of Canada. Since that time they have lived in a number of settlements on the eastern shore of Lake Michigan and have lived as far south as the Benton Harbor area. The Ottawa also lived in several parts of the northern lower peninsula. Today, among other places, their influence is significant in the area around Harbor Springs on the Little Traverse Bay.

Though the Ottawa lived in the areas where agriculture was possible, they seem to have preferred trading. Much of their activity was devoted to exchanging furs for agricultural products. The Ottawa generally had large villages which were rarely fortified.

The third major group of Michigan Indians, the *Potawatami*, were originally located in Wisconsin. By the latter years of the seventeenth century many had moved to the St. Joseph River basin. This tribe resisted and avoided the attempt to remove them and place them on reservations in the 1830's and 1840's. As a result today there are many Potawatami around Dowagiac township in Cass county.

Though these groups are the largest in Michigan many other tribes and groups of Indians have played a role in the history of the state. Some of the other groups include the Miami, Wyandot (Huron), Menominee and Sauk Indians. Some of these groups only inhabited a part of the state and others only stayed for a short time, but they were part of the early and current Indian history of Michigan.

THE FRENCH PERIOD 1618-1760

The first Europeans to reach what is now Michigan were two Frenchmen. Etienne Brule', an interpreter and aide to explorer Samuel Champlain, wintered near what is now Sault Ste. Marie in 1618-

19. About two years later Brule' explored the St. Mary's River and was accompanied by the explorer Grenoble. They found copper nuggets and were the first to realize the economic wealth of the area.

After this initial exploration, other Frenchmen followed. Some came to explore for minerals, others came to hunt for and trade furs with the Indians. Yet others came to convert the Indians to Christianity. As the number of explorers, hunters and missionaries increased, the French founded several missions and trading posts. The first of these were located at St. Ignace (Fort Du Buade), at Niles (Fort St. Joseph) and at Detroit (Fort Pontchartrain). At this time there were only a few soldiers stationed at these frontier outposts, and probably no more than four thousand French within the current borders of Michigan. Today one sees many reminders of the days when the King of France was the Monarch of Michigan. Many state place names are French, such as St. Ignace, Detroit and Sault Ste. Marie. Some private land grants, often long narrow farms (called long lots), are still intact. The purpose of these was to insure that each farmer had access to the river. Some cities, like Dearborn, still reveal these long lot patterns centuries after the French left.

THE ENGLISH PERIOD 1760-1796

After the fall of New France in the French and Indian war, England gained control of what is now Michigan. After Quebec had fallen to the English in 1760, Major Robert Rogers was sent by the British to take control of the various Michigan forts held by the French. British troops remained in control of the forts for the duration of the French and Indian war.

The Michigan peninsulas saw a number of changes under British rule as the King and the Privy Council tried to manage the King's interests in the Great Lakes area. In the years between 1760 and 1814 Michigan saw the following under British rule:

1760-1763—With the end of the French and Indian war and the Fall of New France, the British gained control of Michigan.

1763-1774—As a result of a series of raids led by Pontiac, an Ottawa Chief, Michigan came under direct rule of King George III. He attempted to limit English settlement in the area until the Indian land claims could be resolved.

1774-1791—In 1774, to provide greater control over the area, the British parliament passed the Quebec Act which annexed all territory north of the Ohio River to the province of Quebec. The Quebec Act was a major grievance in the American Revolution.

1791-1796—Though the Treaty of Paris (1783) established American independence and included Michigan in the territory of the new nation, the British refused to leave the region because of the lucrative fur trade. In 1791 Michigan was incorporated into Ontario by the British parliament. In 1796 American troops occupied forts at Detroit and Mackinac and drove the British out.

1812-1814—During the War of 1812 the British occupied forts at Detroit and Mackinac.

MICHIGAN BECOMES AN AMERICAN TERRITORY

As the Revolutionary war ended, Michigan became American territory after being part of Canada for one hundred and fifty years. The treaties following the war provided that all the land as far west as the Mississippi river and north to the Great Lakes was American territory. In spite of the treaty the British refused to surrender the Northwest Territory until 1796. Though the British still had formal control of the area the Continental Congress began to develop plans for the territory. In 1785 the Congress passed a Land Ordinance that set up procedures for the survey and sale of land in the Northwest Territory.

Two years later the Continental Congress passed the Ordinance of 1787, the Northwest Ordinance. This provided for the creation of an American government in the territory. It consisted of an appointed governor, secretary and a three judge court. The Northwest Ordinance also created procedures for forming states out of the territory as the population grew. When there were five thousand people in the area the settlers would be able to elect a state assembly. When the population reached sixty thousand they could apply for statehood.

The Ordinance of 1787 (Northwest Ordinance) was one of the most significant acts of the Continental Congress and laid out principles that still have importance. In particular the Northwest Ordinance:

Permitted religious freedom.

Guaranteed the writ of Habeas Corpus, trial by jury, reasonable bail and freedom from unusual punishments.

Guaranteed that property would not be taken by the government without fair payment.

Stated that the government would encourage a sound educational program.

Stipulated that Indian lands were not to be taken without consent.

Provided that the area was to form at least three and not more than five states.

Prohibited slavery in the Territory.

Even today this document is used to resolve conflicts such as water rights and boundary disputes.

Even though the act was passed by the Continental Congress in 1787, Michigan was still under British control. There were to be more complications before the new nation would take possession of the Territory.

In 1791 the British Parliament passed the Canadian Constitutional Act which divided the province of Quebec (which then included Michigan) into two parts. Michigan was considered part of upper Canada and was placed in the District of Hesse. In 1792, under this act Detroit held its first popular election and chose representatives to the Parliament of Upper Canada. This was to be a brief arrangement. In 1795 the United States and Great Britain agreed, under the provisions of a new treaty, that the

United States would take control of the western lands (including Michigan) that had been agreed to at the end of the Revolutionary war.

On July 11, 1796 American military forces finally occupied Detroit. Up until 1800, Michigan was part of the single Northwest Territory. After 1800, however, the Northwest Territory was divided into two separate territories, the Northwest Territory and the Indiana Territory. (See the map on the following page.) At that time what was called the Northwest Territory included the present state of Ohio and the eastern half of Michigan's lower peninsula. The rest of Michigan was part of the Indiana Territory.

As people began to move into the area more changes were in store. Settlement increased in Ohio and rather quickly Ohio applied for admission as a state. In 1803 Ohio became a state and then all of what is now Michigan became part of a new Indiana Territory.

Michigan became a separate territory in 1805. Detroit was chosen as the seat of government, and the next year became the territory's first incorporated city. As a territory, Michigan was again ruled by appointed governors, secretaries and judges as had been the case under the Northwest Ordinance. General William Hull was the first territorial governor and he was followed by Lewis Cass in 1813.

As population increased there were demands for land treaties that would cede the Indian lands. The first of these was the Treaty of Greenville in 1795, where the Indians gave up a small area around the Detroit river and land near Mackinac. Later, in 1807, Governor Hull signed the Treaty of Detroit which opened more land in southeast Michigan for settlement. At this time however, no land was surveyed or offered for sale to the public. In 1818, after the first land surveys were made, it became easier for individuals to purchase land. More land in the eastern part of the lower peninsula was opened for settlement by the Treaty of Saginaw in 1819. Other treaties followed over the years and by 1842 the entire state had been given up by the Indians.

The first delegate was sent from the Michigan territory to the U.S. Congress in 1819. In the 1820's more and more settlers began entering the state. Soon the counties of Wayne, Monroe, Macomb,

Development of Michigan's Boundaries

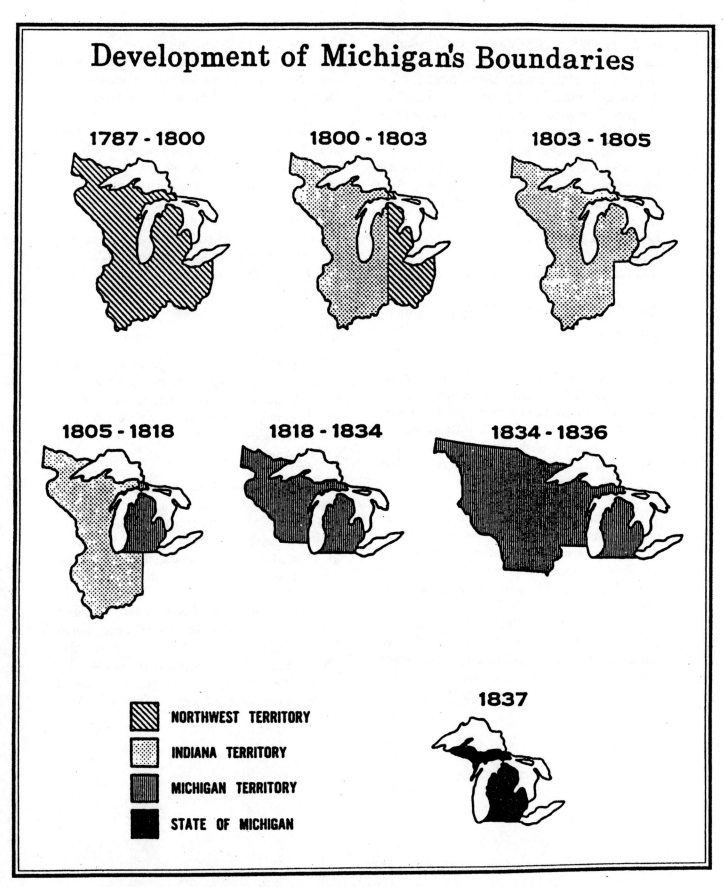

1787 - 1800

1800 - 1803

1803 - 1805

1805 - 1818

1818 - 1834

1834 - 1836

NORTHWEST TERRITORY

INDIANA TERRITORY

MICHIGAN TERRITORY

STATE OF MICHIGAN

1837

Source: Adapted with permission from Senninger, Earl J., *Atlas of Michigan,* 3rd ed. Flint Geographical Press, 1970.

9

Oakland and Mackinac were settled and incorporated. In 1825 the Erie Canal opened making it easier for settlers from New England and upstate New York to migrate to Michigan. Since many of the earliest settlers to the state were from New England, Michigan developed both county and township governments. Today only a few states have this dual system of local government. By 1823 the population had grown large enough for Michigan to have its own territorial legislature, composed of nine men chosen by the President. A little later Detroit was chosen as the territorial capital. In 1827, for the first time, a legislative council was chosen by a popular vote.

MICHIGAN BECOMES A STATE

By the mid-1830's the population had grown to such an extent that statehood became an immediate goal. A convention to draw up a state constitution met in Detroit in 1835. The Constitution of 1835 was ratified by the public and Stevens T. Mason was chosen as the first governor of the soon-to-be State of Michigan.

As statehood approached, a dispute arose over the Michigan-Ohio border. When the Northwest Ordinance was drawn up, it stated that Michigan's southern boundary should be a line drawn due east from the most southern point of Lake Michigan. This would place Toledo, Ohio within the Michigan boundaries. When Ohio had become a state some of the details of its northern border were not clearly defined. Since Ohio had just built a canal from Toledo to Cincinnati, it was in no mood to surrender Toledo to the new state of Michigan. The U.S. Congress settled the dispute by giving the Toledo area to Ohio and, in exchange, giving the Upper Peninsula to Michigan. The act which settled the dispute, the Enabling Act of 1836, also provided for the admission of Michigan into the Union.

After Congress passed this act, a convention to ratify the new proposal met in Ann Arbor in September of 1836. The proposal was initially rejected. A second convention met, also in Ann Arbor, in December and accepted the proposal. Later the U.S. Congress accepted the work of the December convention and admitted Michigan into the Union as the twenty sixth state. President Jackson formally signed the admission bill on January 26th, 1837.

The State Capital

Michigan's first state capital was located in Detroit in an area later called Capitol Park, at Griswold and State streets. Detroit was to be only the temporary state capital since the new state Constitution gave the legislature the power to choose a new location for the capital.

The chance to become the state capital set off a strong contest among many of the growing cities in the state. At one time or another Ann Arbor, Albion, Battle Creek, Charlotte, Dexter, Eaton Rapids, Flint, Marshall, Owosso and other cities vied for honor of becoming the state capital.

Finally, a section of the township of Lansing, in Ingham county, was chosen for the new capital. The new capital city, which was first to be called Michigan, was cleared from the woods in 1847. The name of the new city was changed to Lansing in 1848 when the legislature met there for the first time.

Chapter 2

Michigan in the Federal System

Types of Governmental Organization

The Articles of Confederation-The First National Government

The New Constitution-A Federal System

State Roles in the National Government

National Impact on the States: Money, Policy and Law

> *"Subject to provisions of the general law this state may enter into agreements with...other states, the United States..."*
>
> Article III, Sect. 5 Michigan Constitution

Chapter 2

Learning Objectives

Describe the distribution of government authority in unitary and confederal forms: What benefits and problems are found in each?

Basically, what is a federal system and what are its advantages and disadvantages?

Describe the weaknesses of the Articles of Confederation.

During the Civil War, the states attempting to leave the union were called the "confederacy." What principles of government and territory did they believe in?

Summarize the major elements of federalism in the United States.

Why are there often conflicts about which level of government has a particular power in the U.S.?

Identify 5 ways states have an important effect on the national government.

Summarize the process of amending the national Constitution.

Describe shifting patterns of government spending in the U.S. since 1930, and explain them.

Summarize ways in which the national government affects the states.

How can states cooperate with each other?

How do states compete with each other?

Key Terms To Know

unitary form	supremacy clause	rendition
confederal form	electoral college	federal form
ratification	articles of confederation	gnp
delegated powers	implied powers	reserved (residual)
concurrent powers	interstate compact	powers
	full faith and credit	

One of the most important questions about government is really about territory. What territory is under a particular government's rule? Plainly, there are many possibilities here—a government could exist on a neighborhood scale, or larger, or larger yet. Conceivably, a government could exist over the entire planet! Realistically, most questions about government and territory deal with nations. This chapter will explore issues about how governmental authority can be organized in one nation. These questions have been very important in the history of the United States. There have been at least three different kinds of organization proposed.

TYPES OF GOVERNMENTAL ORGANIZATION

In a *unitary* system one government exists and it has authority over all the people within the nation. There are no independent governments over any parts of the area. The central government could create area governments, but it would control their powers completely.

Some advantages of this approach are its simplicity, the standardization of rules and policy, and the fact that all citizens would receive equal services from the same government. A major disadvantage is that the unitary approach might prevent policies designed for the different needs of specific regions. Thus, nations with strong regional differences usually find the unitary approach unworkable. A unitary form has never been in effect at the national level in the United States.

In a *confederal* form there are many independent governments. Each has authority over a state and a central government has authority over the whole. This central government is created by agreement among the states and is usually rather weak. It has only those powers which are allowed by the states. It often lacks the authority to enforce its rules within the territory of any one of the states unless that state agrees. While a unitary form gives all power to one central government, a confederal form gives most authority to the smaller units. The United Nations organization can be viewed as a confederal government.

A major advantage of confederation is that it allows a great amount of local or regional control. A major disadvantage is that the central government might be too limited in authority and unable to meet the needs of the nation as a whole. The United States has had experience with a confederation and its problems, a point to be discussed later.

A *federal* system is the most complicated of the three types. In a federal system there are at least two levels of government, and they are considerably independent of each other. Neither level is created by the other. In the United States the Constitution creates each level and outlines the powers of each. It is possible to clearly assign powers, giving some to the nation and others to the states, with no uncertainty or conflict between them. This is not always the case in the United States. There have often been disputes as to the balance of powers between nation and states.

Some advantages of federalism are that it usually combines a strong national government to meet nation-wide needs along with strong governments with authority over the states to meet the different needs of the different regions. Federalism's disadvantages are that it can allow inequality of services from state to state, and can produce conflicts between the national and state levels concerning authority. The United States has a federal system, which will be studied in more detail.

THE ARTICLES OF CONFEDERATION: THE FIRST NATIONAL GOVERNMENT

To work more closely together in the war against England, the Continental Congress adopted the Article of Confederation in 1777. This document served as a constitution for the nation until 1789. In many ways the Articles of Confederation were a major step forward in forming a unified government but because of the feelings for strong states' rights at that time, the national government lacked power and organization in many respects.

There were major weaknesses in the Articles of Confederation. Each state, regardless of size or population, had one vote in the Continental Congress. There was no national executive department or judicial department. Congress had no power to tax but had to requisition the states for the money it needed to pay its debts and expenses. A unanimous vote of all thirteen states was required to amend the Articles. Congress had no real power to enforce the laws it passed.

There were other problems. There were state trade wars and fourteen kinds of money in circulation. There was no uniform system of bankruptcy. There was the question of what to do with the new western lands. Thus a convention was assembled to consider changes in the government of the United States.

THE NEW CONSTITUTION - A FEDERAL SYSTEM

When the U.S. Constitution was written in 1787, the framers chose to reject confederation and decided to organize a federal system. They kept the states as semi-independent governments, but also strengthened the national government in many important ways.

The following are some of the most important features of the U.S. federal system, taking into account the Constitution, amendments to it, and interpretations of it:

- *Some powers are denied both nation and the states.* (Examples may be found in Article I, sections 9 and 10 and the Bill of Rights.)

- *Some powers are granted to the nation and denied the states.* This very important category includes the national powers to set the value of money, regulate interstate commerce, enter into treaties with other nations, and wage war. (See Article I, section 8 and 10.)

- *The powers of the national government are of two types.* Some are <u>delegated</u> or <u>enumerated</u> - mentioned in the Constitution. In some cases, these powers are very specific, in others, they are rather vaguely stated. The other type of national power is *implied* - powers the national govern-

ment has because they can be interpreted as "necessary and proper" to fully carry out the delegated powers. Thus, the Constitution gives some flexibility to national powers, and what the national government can do depends partly on how one "implies" its powers. (See Article I, section 8.)

- *The states are given some very important roles in the operation of the national government, and some important guarantees.* The states are used as the basis for electing the President and the Congress, have a role in amending the Constitution, must consent to any change in their boundaries, can expect to have their valid laws honored by other states, and can enter into agreements with each other if Congress approves. (See Article IV and Article I, section 10 for examples.)

- *The powers of states are hardly mentioned in the U.S. Constitution.* It was assumed that, except where specifically prohibited, states would continue to have the powers usually associated with government. Among these residual or reserved powers would be those of setting up local governments within their boundaries, passing laws governing marriage and divorce, creating school systems, protecting public health and safety, and so forth.

- *Some powers are held by both nation and states.* These are called concurrent powers. An example is the power to tax: it is delegated to the nation, and not prohibited to the states. Thus both levels can tax.

- Since both levels can often claim the right to exercise the same power, *conflicts often arise as to where the authority of each begins and ends.* Such conflicts are often the result of different interpretations of the language and intentions of the Constitution. The Constitution does offer some guidance in settling these disputes. The *supremacy clause* (Article VI) makes it clear that the U.S. Constitution, and all valid national laws (including treaties), are "the supreme law of the land" and state constitutions and state laws must always be compatible with the national Constitution and national laws. While this principle seems clear, we still witness many disputes as to which level should do what.

- *This framework can be altered by a process of amendment.* Historically this has involved the national legislature and the states. Thus, both levels must agree to any change in the language of the constitution.

STATE ROLES IN THE NATIONAL GOVERNMENT

One can view the national government as a collection of state and local interests. Consider the following points as they apply to the three branches of the national government.

The National Legislature

Every member of the U.S. Congress (Senate and House of Representatives) is elected to speak for a state or a part of a state. None are elected nationally. The Senate has 100 members, two from each state. Each is elected for a term of 6 years. The House of Representatives has 435 members. A state's share of these seats is determined by its share of the nation's population. The smallest states have only one member. The largest state (California) has over fifty. Each of these members is elected from a district of between 625,000-647,000 people, and serves a 2 year term of office.

Several U.S. Supreme Court rulings of the early 1960s require each state to redraw its election districts after each census. Every ten years new districts of equal population size are created in each state. In Michigan, the state Constitution places the responsibility for redrawing U.S. House districts in the hands of the legislature and governor. As a result of the 2000 census Michigan will lose one seat and thus 15 new districts have been created. Michigan's population is increasing, but its share of the national population is decreasing.

The Presidency

A presidential nomination depends a great deal on state politics. Any presidential candidate will first campaign in a series of state primaries, party caucuses or party conventions in order to try to secure delegate votes at the party's national convention. The key to the nomination is the ability to assemble a string of victories in important states. More information on these matters will be presented in chapter 3.

In the presidential election itself, the states play a decisive role. In the *Electoral College,* each state has the same number of electoral votes as it has members of Congress. Michigan, with 2 Senators and 15 House members, now has 17 electoral votes. (We had 18 electoral votes in the 1990s, 20 in the 1980s and 21 in the 1970s.) On election day, the candidate with the most popular votes in a state receives all of that state's electoral votes. The candidate who receives a majority (270) of the nation's electoral votes (538 in total) is officially elected when the members of the Electoral College meet at their respective state capitols in December.

The Judiciary

United States judges are nominated by the president, and approved by the U.S. Senate. Before a president nominates a person to be a U.S. District Court judge it is common practice (often called "senatorial courtesy") to check with the U.S. Senators from the state in which the judge is to serve to gain their acceptance of the nominee.

Amending the National Constitution (See U.S. Constitution, Article V)

The states are partners in the national constitutional framework of federalism. It is no surprise, then, that the states have a role in changing the basic national law. The usual approach to amending the U.S. Constitution is for both the U.S. House and Senate to *propose* an amendment with a 2/3 vote in each and submit the proposal to the states for *ratification* (approval) by their legislatures. The approval of 3/4 of the states is necessary before an amendment becomes valid. The *repeal* of any amendment requires another amendment, using the same procedure.

State Lobbying in Washington

States are often directly affected by the policies of the national government. To advance their interests, or protect them, the states try to influence national decisions. This is done in many ways. The members of Congress from a state are expected to

Figure 2.1

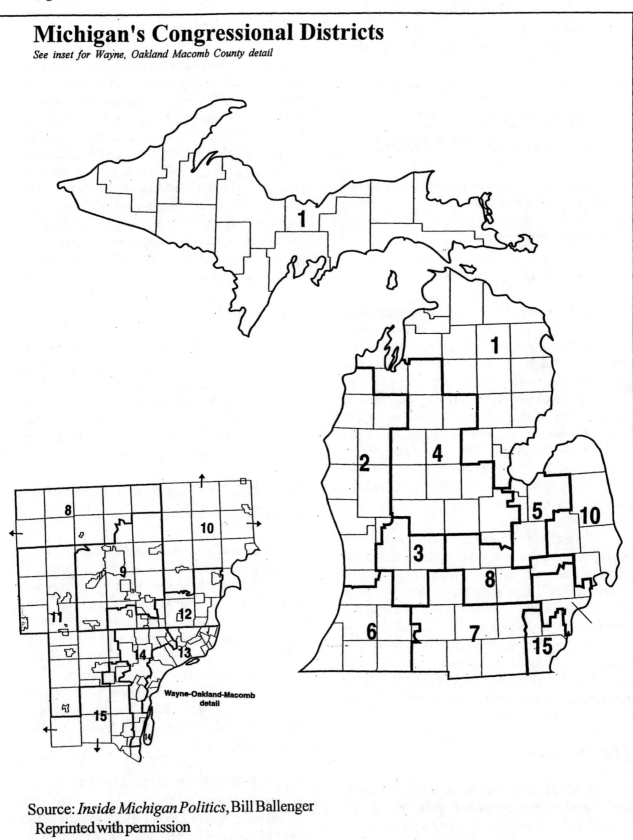

Michigan's Congressional Districts

See inset for Wayne, Oakland Macomb County detail

Wayne-Oakland-Macomb
detail

Source: *Inside Michigan Politics*, Bill Ballenger
Reprinted with permission

rally to its cause. Sometimes, a prominent official of the president's administration can be relied upon to push for the state's goal. Some states, including Michigan, maintain an office in Washington to keep up on developments which could affect the state. It is not unusual for states with common interests to join together from time to time. Michigan has allied itself with other Great Lakes states on some issues, and all "Frostbelt" states on others.

Even the local governments within a state have developed techniques for lobbying the national government. Mayors, school officials and others often work personally, and through associations of local officials with similar problems, to advance the cause of local units of government.

NATIONAL IMPACT ON THE STATES

In 1930 government played a much smaller role in society than today. Only 10% of Gross National Product (GNP) was accounted for by government spending. Of this, three-fourths was spent by state and local governments. By the late 1990s, government spending accounted for about 33% of GNP, and the balance between nation and states had shifted. The national government spent about 23% of GNP. The states and localities spent only 10% of GNP, or only one-third of government spending. Why this growth? Why this shift?

Consider the summary of differences between 1930 and 2000 in the United States shown in Table 2.1. That table helps to explain the changes in government activity since 1930. How the national government can affect the states is one important aspect of these changes.

Money and Budgets

The national government distributes money to the states and localities. Currently about 10 percent of the national budget is aid to state and local governments. On a nation-wide basis this money is about one-fourth of all the revenues of those governments.

States vary greatly in the amount of money they receive per capita from the national government. Some states do better than others in receiving national aid, relative to national taxes paid by their citizens. In the mid-90s, New Mexico received $1.83 for every dollar paid; New Jersey only 69 cents. Michigan receives about 76 cents back for each tax dollar sent to Washington. Recently the top five recipient states averaged about $7,000 per person. The bottom five, which included Michigan, received about $4,100 per capita. The national average is about $5,000.

Policy and Programs

National programs often have large impacts on state and local governments. Some of these actions are specifically aimed at a particular state problem and are often the result of successful lobbying by state or local government officials. A few recent Michigan examples include the federal loan guarantee to Chrysler, attempts to limit auto imports, the law that established Sleeping Bear National Lakeshore and the decision to close Wurtsmith Air Force Base in Oscoda.

Table 2.1

In 1930	KEY FACTORS	In 2000
rural areas	population lived in	urban areas
lower	need for public services	higher
lower	political organization of groups	higher
lower	government spending on social programs	higher
no	permanent military establishment	yes
little	U.S. role in world	extensive

The decisions of the national government are not always desired by a state or its people. When the government closes a military base it may cause economic problems for the surrounding area, as occurred when the Kincheloe Air Force Base in Michigan was closed. When the national government proposed installing a large underground submarine communication system in the Upper Peninsula many voices in the area rose in opposition. In spite of this and in spite of substantial lobbying from many state leaders, the project, known as the ELF/Seafarer, proceeded. Recently states have been concerned about "unfunded mandates" where the national government requires some action on the part of the states but does not assist in paying for it.

Law and the Constitution

The programs of the President and the Congress are not the only ways in which the national government affects the actions of state and local governments. The federal courts, in particular the U.S. Supreme Court, often make rulings that greatly alter state and local actions.

Though police protection and criminal prosecution are primarily a state and local function, the actions of police have been signficantly modified by U.S. Supreme Court rulings. For example the case of *Miranda v. U.S.,* 1966, established guidelines for the questioning of criminal suspects. This changed the actions of every Michigan official in the criminal justice system, from the attorney general of the state to the law enforcement official in the most rural township in the state. U.S. Supreme Court decisions (*Baker v. Carr,* 1962) in the 1960s required all states to reapportion election districts every ten years.

Traditionally the operation of the public schools has been a local matter. Nonetheless, the U.S. Constitution applies to local schools, and when the U.S. Supreme Court ruled that legally imposed segregation in public schools was unconstitutional (*Brown v. Board of Education,* 1954) the federal courts became involved in local school policy. The attempt to integrate the schools often prompted a bitter storm of protest from those who either opposed the goal or the method of the federal courts. Nowhere was this protest greater than when the courts ordered busing to integrate the schools.

Michigan found itself in the center of the busing controversy when federal district Judge Stephen Roth ordered "cross district" busing between Detroit and many of the surrounding suburban school districts. Though the Supreme Court later reversed the Roth plan (*Milliken v. Bradley,* 1974) the national government's impact was clear. The issue was to be decided by the federal courts, not the states.

INTERSTATE RELATIONS: COOPERATION AND COMPETITION

States do not exist as independent units in the federal system. They interact with other states. They form agreements with other states and they come into conflict with other states and regions of the nation.

Cooperation

The shape and location of the states is largely a matter of historical and geographical accident. State boundaries are not drawn with an eye towards solving area-wide problems. Typically, states are shaped by the fortunes of history (treaties, wars, boundary disputes) and geography (lakes, rivers, mountains.) Yet many concerns and problems cross state lines. Air and water pollution may cross state lines, bridges may connect two states, or in Michigan's case, two nations, the U.S. and Canada.

States may, with the approval of Congress, form *interstate compacts* for the purpose of solving area wide problems. Obviously the fate of the Great Lakes is of importance to the state of Michigan. In 1982 the states of Michigan, Minnesota, Illinois, Indiana and Wisconsin as well as the Canadian province of Ontario began to form a Great Lakes Water Policy Compact that would allow the area states to keep control of the water in the Great Lakes. This proposed compact is one of several that involves Michigan in a cooperative manner with other states.

Interstate compacts are an optional form of cooperation that many states have chosen to pursue.

Another kind of cooperation, called *full faith and credit,* is not a matter of choice. The U.S. Constitution requires that "Full faith and credit shall be given in each state to the public acts, records, and judicial proceedings of every other state." (Article 4, section 1.) Though there are a few rare exceptions, this means that any civil matter such as a contract, will, deed, or marriage certificate legally made in one state must be recognized by all other states as valid. This applies only to civil matters. States are not expected to enforce the criminal law of another state.

According to the U.S. Constitution, Article 4, section 2, an individual who commits a crime in one state and then escapes to another must be returned to the first state for trial. This return of defendants is called *interstate rendition.* If a person commits a crime in Michigan, then drives to Ohio, he must be returned to Michigan by the Ohio authorities to face trial in Michigan. Occasionally a governor will refuse to return a prisoner.

Competition

Though states cooperate in many ways, they are separate political units and they do have different interests that can bring them into conflict with one another. These conflicting interests emerge as the states compete with one another both within the region and outside it. Within the midwestern region competition exists when the State of Michigan runs ads in Indiana encouraging Indiana residents to "Say Yes to Michigan" and spend their vacation (and dollars) in Michigan. Similarly, the State of Illinois may urge citizens to "Go Chicagoing" and spend their vacation dollars in the Windy City. When a major industrial concern is giving thought to building a new plant, states often compete with each other offering advice, assistance, tax breaks and other incentives to encourage the company to locate in their state.

Different regions of the nation also compete for new business. Recently this contest has pitted the older industrialized states of the midwest and east (the Frostbelt) against the newer and more rapidly growing states of the south and southwest (the Sunbelt). Though there are many factors in the Frostbelt versus the Sunbelt contest, much of the conflict revolves around economics to a prospective employer. The Sunbelt offers lower wage rates (often nonunion) and lower energy rates (at least in the winter). The Frostbelt has tried to counter those arguments by reminding employers that the northeast does have a skilled labor force (though unionized) and also has the infrastructure (roads, railroads, shipping, communication, etc.) needed to conduct business. During the 1980's the result of this competition was a substantial economic shift towards the Sunbelt.

In 1999, the federal courts were called upon to settle an environmental dispute between states with older coal-fired power plants, (like Michigan) and states with cleaner, newer and more expensive electical power, such as those in the Northeast. Michigan felt that its cheaper power gave it a competitive advantage over the more expensive power in several Northeastern states and wished to retain the advantage.

Clearly, the politics and government of Michigan are not isolated from its neighbors, or the nation as a whole. Nevertheless, in many ways Michigan should be considered separate from the whole. Michigan's population of nearly ten million is larger than that of over one-half of the world's 190-plus nations. The state would be among the worlds richest nations and would rank in the top 50 among Fortune 500 corporations. In a federal system, states have much independence, and many important issues are decided by the state and its localities. These governments provide many significant services. The rest of this book will deal with the ways Michigan—a large, resourceful and quite independent state—makes its decisions.

Tribal Government in Michigan

One additional level of government in Michigan involves the tribal powers of the state's Indians who live on reservations. Currently, there are twelve federally recognized reservations in Michigan and several more groups seeking recognition. Almost 70,000 people live on Michigan reservations.

In general the governing powers of Indian tribes has reflected changing federal policy towards the Indians. Since the early 1960's the federal government has followed a policy of self-determination with regard to Native Americans, which has led to a greater degree of self-government on tribal lands. While some of the Indians' power of self-government is based on the idea of "national sovereignty," in practice the Indian tribes are not sovereign in the same sense that a foreign nation is sovereign.

The federal government, through treaties and court rulings, has defined and limited tribal jurisdiction. Nonetheless, the power of tribes to govern themselves remains substantial in both the civil and criminal areas.

Tribes have exclusive jurisdiction over minor crimes, on Indian territory, where both the victim and the accused are Indians. Congress has given the federal courts authority over a number of major crimes and requires tribes to provide most of the major rights guaranteed in the Bill of Rights. The criminal law is complex and who has jurisdiction depends on where a crime was comitted, the nature of the crime and the nature of the parties involved. In some cases, the tribe has exclusive jurisdiction, in some cases the federal courts do, in some cases there is concurrent (shared) jurisdiction and in a few cases the state has power.

In the area of civil law tribes have a much greater power within their own territory. In contrast to the criminal area, Congress has imposed few limitations in this area. Tribes have power to regulate marriages, divorces, child custody, control taxation, hunting and fishing and zoning in their own territory.

Most tribes elect a board of directors, an executive chairperson and maintain tribal courts to apply tribal laws.

Part 2

Power-Seeking in Michigan

Introduction

Political Parties in Michigan

Interest Groups in Michigan

Elections in Michigan

Voting and Activism in Michigan

Introduction to Part 2

Learning Objectives

What does "power" mean in politics?

What kinds of behavior make up political activity?

Identify some major figures in Michigan's political history. For what are they each noted?

Summarize Michigan's political history in terms of party strength.

Key Terms To Know

power
politics

INTRODUCTION TO PART 2

The term "power" has many definitions, depending on the field of study. It means one thing in physics, another in athletics, another in electronics, and another in politics. In politics, *power* usually means the capacity of one (a person, group or nation) to convince another to do something according to one's own preferences. Or, power refers to A's ability to get B to do something B would not have done without A's efforts. It should be obvious from these brief definitions that power is a very common aspect of everyday life. It exists in clubs, families, friendships—everywhere.

Government and Power

To govern something is to control it. Thus government has power. But government is people who decide (perhaps within limits set by a constitution) what controls will exist, on whom, for how long and so forth. Not all government does is in the form of control. Government distributes goods and services, opportunities and protection. Once again, there are decisions—what services? for whom? at what cost? to whom?

Government, then, usually involves choice. Whenever there is a choice--a decision—to be made, we can expect people (individually or acting through groups) to seek to influence that choice. People will seek to have choices made in their favor. *When people seek to have choices made in their favor, they are playing politics. When people play politics, they are seeking power.*

So much for theory. How does this occur in the real world? That is what these chapters are about. There are many avenues to power. Some seek power through political party organizations, trying to control government offices by winning elections or getting appointed to office. We also see power-seeking interest groups. Their main concern is to influence policy—they are less concerned with who is in office than with what policies become law. Power-seeking can also be seen at the individual level—citizens seek power at the ballot box, by gaining personal influence or by holding office.

In beginning, it is helpful to review the history of power seeking in Michigan. In the summary which follows note how individuals, interests and parties have tried to influence the choices (decisions) of governments in Michigan.

A Brief History of Michigan Politics

The story of power-seeking in Michigan is the history of the parties, issues and people of the last one hundred and seventy years of government and politics in Michigan.

Since 1813, when Michigan was a territory, there have been 47 governors. Twenty-seven of these were Republicans, seventeen have been Democrats, two were Whigs and one was a Fusion Candidate. From 1813 until the mid-1850s, Michigan was heavily Democratic. Because of his support for Michigan statehood many state voters remained loyal to Andrew Jackson's Democratic party. The dominant figure of state politics during this period was Lewis Cass, who fought in the Indian wars, was a hero of the War of 1812, served as a territorial governor, ran for president and served in the U.S. Senate.

In its early years Michigan's politics showed a strong preference for the Yankee/Puritans who moved from upstate New York. This ethic made Michigan the first state to prohibit capital punishment. The support for abolition of slavery led to the formation of the Republican party.

With the birth of the Republican party at Jackson in 1854, and the events of the Civil War, Michigan took a sharp and long-lasting turn into the Republican camp. From 1854 until 1928, the state delivered its votes to the Republican party. Until 1948 the Republicans were the major power in Michigan politics, holding the governorship for 80 of 94 years and keeping the majority of both chambers of the state legislature for 44 of 47 sessions. Republican domination was so strong in the early years of the 20th century that from 1918 until 1928 no Democrats served in the state Senate and only nine served in the state House. The Michigan Republicans tended to be of the progressive Teddy Roosevelt variety, who carried the state in 1912. As part of the progressive agenda of the day Michigan Republicans supported women's suffrage, initiative and referendum.

One dominant figure of the era was Hazen S. Pingree. Once a mayor of Detroit, he served as governor from 1897 to 1901. He was an active progressive reformer who argued for taxes on railroads, the popular election of U.S. Senators, "home rule" for cities and limits on graft and corruption. In his own time, Pingree was rather unsuccessful, but many of his ideas were enacted in the 1908 state constitution. Alexander Groesbeck was perhaps the second major figure of this era. As governor from 1921-1926 he directed the building of many of the state's highways and reorganized much of the state's governmental structure.

With Franklin D. Roosevelt's victory in 1932, Michigan swung into the Democratic column. During the 1930's and 1940's the Democrats were generally successful, although the Republicans did show strength on several occasions. In 1940, Republican Wendell Wilkie took Michigan over FDR and in 1944, Thomas Dewey, a Michigan native, nearly topped President Roosevelt in the state. In 1948, Dewey outpolled President Truman in Michigan. Today's Democratic and Republican parties in Michigan were shaped by the events of this era.

During the middle and late 1930's the labor movement began to develop. Conflicts arose between auto workers and the management of auto companies over the right to organize a union. Democratic governor Frank Murphy (1937-38) played a major role in labor's drive to unionize the industry. This brought many union supporters into the Democratic party and began the close working relationship between organized labor and the Michigan Democratic party.

This merger was completed in 1948 when Democrat G. Mennen "Soapy" Williams was elected governor. Before the 1948 election the Democratic party had been known as a "patronage" organization—seeking government jobs and other financial rewards for its members. In 1948, in a booming post-war auto economy, political jobs were less significant and the Michigan Democratic party evolved into an "issues oriented" organization. This occurred as the forces of labor were joined by other liberal voices in the state, especially many professors and activists centered in the universities. This "liberal—labor alliance," though it has seen some change and internal conflict, is still the mainstay of the Michigan Democratic party organization.

During this same period, the Republican party in Michigan was also forging a coalition which was to have frequent election success. Beginning in the 1940s the Republicans brought together the traditional conservative outstate Republicans from rural and small town Michigan and the moderate progressive Republicans, often drawn from the urban area management groups. This modern Republican coalition had some success in appealing to independent voters and some Democrats with moderate candidates such as former governors George Romney (1963-69) and William Milliken (1969-82).

In the 1980's Democrat Jim Blanchard held the governorship (1982-90) only to lose it narrowly to conservative Republican John Engler in 1990. In 1992, while Bill Clinton carried the state for the Democrats, Republicans were able to gain seats in the state House and even the party balance 55-55. In 1994 Republicans re-elected Governor Engler in a landslide garnering over 60% of the vote. They also captured one open U.S. Senate seat and took control of both the state House and state Senate. In 1996 Clinton carried the state for the Democrats, Carl Levin retained his U.S. Senate seat and the Democrats regained a majority in the state House. In 1998 John Engler won a third term as governor, easily beating Democrat Geoffrey Fieger. Al Gore carried the state for the Democrats in 2000. In 2002 Jennifer Granholm was elected Michigan's first woman governor and Carl Levin was elected to a fifth term in the U.S. Senate. Both were Democrats.

With the 2000 reapportionment, the state lost one seat in the U.S. House, giving Michigan 15 members. The Republican state legislature redrew the new districts to shift the balance of power in the U.S. House delgation to favor Republicans. Prior to the 2002 election there were 9 Democarats and 7 Republicans in the U.S. House. After the 2002 election, the 2002-2004 U.S. House delegation now has nine Republicans and six Democrats from Michigan.

Chapter 3

Political Parties in Michigan

Michigan—A Competitive State

General Features Of Michigan's Major Parties

Party Structure

Nominations In Michigan's Major Parties

Michigan Parties And Presidential Elections

Minor Parties In A Two-Party System

Strong And Weak Parties

"It really is a thankless job, a labor of love" he said of the party chief post.
-Gary Corbin, Democratic Party Chair, *Flint Journal,* 2/12/95

Chapter 3

Learning Objectives

Why can Michigan be described as a competitive, two-party state?

Describe the party office of precinct delegate.

What are the ways a party nominates candidates for office?

How do Michigan parties select delegates to the national party conventions?

How are presidential electors nominated and elected? What do they do?

Why are minor parties disadvantaged by the typical election rules?

What are the geographic patterns of party support in Michigan?

Summarize the factors which cause a party organization to be strong.
Which factors make parties weak?

Key Terms To Know

two-party system
one-party region
precinct delegate
crossover voting
presidential preference primary
statewide primary
party caucus

presidential elector
electoral college
single-member district
winner take all rule
industrial corridor
third (minor) party
"strong party" system

Michigan's Political Parties

Political parties are organizations that exist mainly for the purpose of winning elections. All of their activities are aimed at influencing policy by holding office.

MICHIGAN--A COMPETITIVE STATE

Michigan's party system, like that of nearly all the other states, revolves around the competition between Democrats and Republicans. Michigan is usually considered a competitive two-party state. The two major parties are considered fairly evenly balanced and in any given state-wide election either one has a reasonable chance of winning.

Recent state election results illustrate this. For the last three decades we have had a Republican governor about twenty years and a Democratic governor about ten. We now have a Democratic governor again. Presidential voting has been Republican since 1972 until the Clinton and Gore victories in 1992, 1996 and 2000 but the state legislature has been mixed over the decades.

Not all parts of Michigan are as competitive as the whole. The strength of the parties is often concentrated. In some counties in Michigan, one of the parties is dominant—the other hardly ever wins. As examples, consider Wayne county, which has voted Democratic in every Presidential election since 1928, and Sanilac county, which has not voted Democratic in a Presidential election since 1852! Thus, there are some *one-party regions* in Michigan. The chances are very good that nearly all the officials elected county-wide in your home county are of the same party.

GENERAL FEATURES OF MICHIGAN'S PARTIES

American political parties are very loosely organized or decentralized. Though we often speak of a two-party system, the nation could be said to have 100 major parties—a Republican and Democratic organization in each of the 50 states. Likewise, within Michigan, perhaps there are not two major state parties but one hundred sixty-six—one for each of the major parties in each of the state's 83 counties. The national parties are really combinations of the different state parties, and those are, in turn, combinations of party organizations in parts of the states.

Our ways of electing officials cause this fragmentation of parties. Every election in the United States (even that for president and vice- president) is held at the state level, or in a district within a state. Since parties exist to win elections, their organization reflects the manner in which we choose elected officials. As we will see, this structure places a great deal of power at the lower levels of party organizations.

The second key characteristic of major American political parties is their internal disagreement on policy. In many other nations, if one is a member of a political party, one is expected to accept the ideas and programs of that party. This is not always true in the United States, or in Michigan. This is due to our political parties' loose organization and their desire to win elections in many different places. In order to win, they will use different ideas to appeal to many different groups. Thus, Democrats and Republicans in Michigan may be liberal (left), moderate (center), or conservative (right).

Thirdly, the parties tend to have a low level of internal party discipline. This means that party organizations have little direct control over their own officeholders, and little ability to punish them for being disloyal. A state representative, for example, might oppose her own party leadership because of the interests of her home-district voters. While the party leaders might criticize her, she might well be reelected by the voters back home.

PARTY STRUCTURE

There is an old political statement which says: "All politics is local politics." Nowhere is this more obvious than in the structure of the parties in the United States. Take a look at Figure 3-1. Clearly, influence flows from the bottom levels of the parties, towards the top levels. Top levels reflect the

Figure 3.1

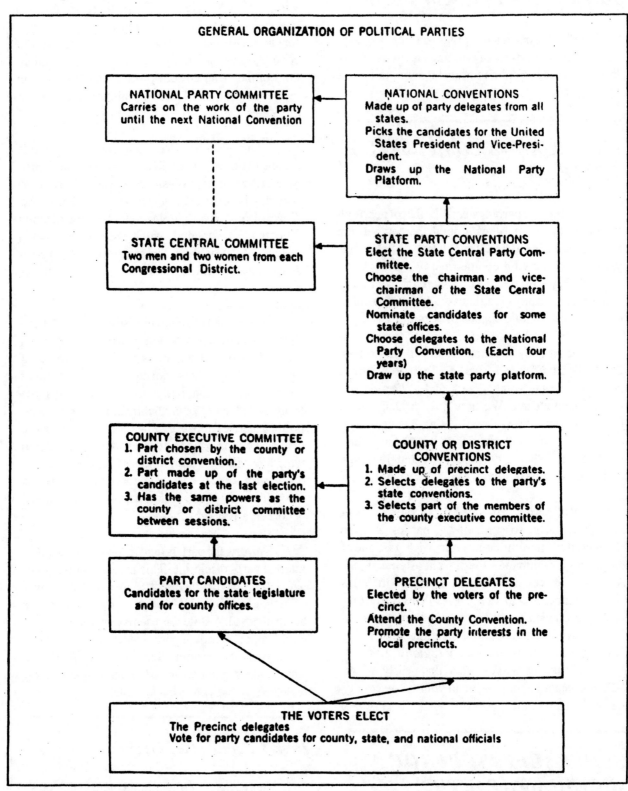

GENERAL ORGANIZATION OF POLITICAL PARTIES

NATIONAL PARTY COMMITTEE
Carries on the work of the party until the next National Convention

NATIONAL CONVENTIONS
Made up of party delegates from all states.
Picks the candidates for the United States President and Vice-President.
Draws up the National Party Platform.

STATE CENTRAL COMMITTEE
Two men and two women from each Congressional District.

STATE PARTY CONVENTIONS
Elect the State Central Party Committee.
Choose the chairman and vice-chairman of the State Central Committee.
Nominate candidates for some state offices.
Choose delegates to the National Party Convention. (Each four years)
Draw up the state party platform.

COUNTY EXECUTIVE COMMITTEE
1. Part chosen by the county or district convention.
2. Part made up of the party's candidates at the last election.
3. Has the same powers as the county or district committee between sessions.

COUNTY OR DISTRICT CONVENTIONS
1. Made up of precinct delegates.
2. Selects delegates to the party's state conventions.
3. Selects part of the members of the county executive committee.

PARTY CANDIDATES
Candidates for the state legislature and for county offices.

PRECINCT DELEGATES
Elected by the voters of the precinct.
Attend the County Convention.
Promote the party interests in the local precincts.

THE VOTERS ELECT
The Precinct delegates
Vote for party candidates for county, state, and national officials

Source: Lewis, Ferris E., *State and Local Government in Michigan,* Hillsdale Educational Publishers, Hillsdale Mi. (1979) p.123. Reprinted with permisson.

pressures and influences from lower levels. At the grass roots level, *precinct delegates* are elected within their voting precinct at the August primary in even-numbered years. The number of delegates varies from precinct to precinct according to party rules and formulas. These delegates attend a county or district convention and select delegates to the state convention, who in turn select delegates to the national convention.

Any registered voter may seek this party office. As a practical matter, those who run are usually elected. One may run for precinct delegate by filing an "affidavit of identity" with the county, city or township clerk's office about twelve weeks before the August primary. Since there is often little competition, one may run a write-in campaign by filing an affidavit before the election. Only one vote is required to win. Vacancies in precinct delegate positions caused by death or resignation can be filled by the county convention.

Precinct delegates serve two-year terms, without pay. In addition to attending party conventions, they often distribute literature for the party's nominees, identify party supporters and help get out the vote. Since these positions are filled frequently, and are often open for the taking, this aspect of the major parties is often called the "soft underbelly of American politics." Understanding this vulnerable part of the parties helped Republican Barry Goldwater (1964) and Democrat George McGovern (1972) win presidential nominations by having their supporters elected to precinct delegate positions. In 1988, the supporters of TV evangelist Pat Robertson nearly prevented George Bush from getting the Republican presidential nomination from the state. Interest groups which hope to influence party decisions often encourage their members to seek precinct delegate slots.

NOMINATIONS IN MICHIGAN'S MAJOR PARTIES

The major decisions made by political parties involve deciding whom to nominate for office and developing the platform—the party's positions on issues. When major parties decide who they will nominate for a public office they use one of the following methods: 1) the primary election, 2) the party convention or 3) the party caucus. Which method is used is determined by state laws.

The primary election is perhaps the most visible of these methods. The primary allows the voters to choose party nominees directly. For non-presidential primaries Michigan uses the "open primary" which does not require a voter to disclose his or her party. This type of primary is used in only a few states and allows "crossover" voting. This means supporters of one party can vote in another party's primary. This may result in weaker parties.

In all even-numbered years, the *statewide primary* is held on the Tuesday after the first Monday in August. During the appropriate years, the party nominees for the following offices are chosen: governor, U.S. senator, U.S. representatives, state senators, state representatives, county officers, county commissioners, and township officers.

The second method of choosing party nominees is the *state party convention*. These are held every year, and the purposes of each are somewhat different. During the fall of "off-year" elections (even-numbered non-presidential years—1994, 1998, 2002, 2006 and so forth) the state convention nominates candidates for lieutenant governor, secretary of state, attorney general, some Michigan Supreme Court positions and some seats on various education boards. In the fall of those years, party conventions also nominate people to serve as presidential electors from Michigan, and nominate candidates for some positions on Michigan's Supreme Court and the state education boards. In the spring of odd-numbered years, the party conventions elect the party's state central committee and other party officials.

A third method of nomination is a *party caucus,* certainly the least important of the three. A caucus is a small group of party officials and supporters, usually at the local level. This group may nominate candidates for certain offices if there is an opening because a nominee decides to pull out of the race before the election, or dies between the primary and the election.

MICHIGAN PARTIES AND PRESIDENTIAL ELECTIONS

As a result national political parties' regulations, state laws and the U.S. Constitution, Michigan voters can affect both the nomination and the election of the president of the United States.

Delegate Selection

In presidential election years, candidates for president are usually very busy seeking delegates to their party's national convention. These delegates will officially nominate the party's candidate. Each state has its own rules to determine how these delegates are chosen.

Between 1972 and 1980 the selection of the party's national convention delegates was based on the results of a *presidential preference primary.* The election was held in May and candidates were given delegates in proportion to the share of the popular vote they received.

In 1984 and 1988 each party held a series of party *caucuses*. A caucus is a gathering of party officials, faithful followers and office-holders. At these caucuses, (usually held at the congressional district level) votes were cast for presidential candidates and delegates were awarded to candidates roughly in proportion to the votes they received. Finally, the state party chose additional delegates to the national convention.

The presidential primary approach was used by both major parties in 1972 and 1976, but only the Republicans used it in 1980. In that year, the Democrats used the caucus approach. In 1984 and 1988 both parties used the caucus system to choose their delegates to their national conventions. Those caucuses were open to any registered voter who signed a statement indicating that they were a member of the appropriate party. In earlier years the caucus was open only to formal party members. The Republicans began their caucus selection in January and the Democrats began with their county caucuses in March.

In 1992 Michigan switched to a "closed primary" which required voters to register ahead of time with either of the major parties or "no party preference." However, because of public reaction, both parties modified their plans. Democrats allowed any voters to register as a party member on the day of the primary, except those who were registered Republicans. Republicans allowed any registered voter to cast a ballot in their primary. In 1996 and 2000 Republicans used an open primary and Democrats used a type of caucus for presidential delegate selection. These often complex procedures apply *only* to the presidential primary. All of Michigan's other primaries are "open."

Selection of Presidential Electors

After the national conventions are held and the candidates for president and vice-president are known, the parties perform another important task, the nomination of *presidential electors.* At the fall convention (usually held in late August or September), the state parties each nominate a list of people to serve as electors. The group is equal in number to the number of electoral votes of the state.

Each state's electoral vote is equal to its number of members in the U.S. Congress. All states have 2 U.S. Senators, and the number of members of the U.S. House of Representatives varies from 1 to 55 (California), roughly according to population. So, the electoral votes of states vary from 3 to 57. Michigan, beginning with the 2004 presidential election, will have 17 electoral votes, a loss of one from the 1990s and three less than the 1980s.

Picking a Winner

On election day, voters indicate their choice for president and vice president, but each person is really voting for the list of electors nominated by that ticket's party. The entire group of electors nominated by the party whose candidate receives the most popular votes in Michigan is elected. All other slates of electors are defeated. Clearly, this is a "winner take all" system. Thus, citizens select a group of people, chosen by and loyal to a party, to cast Michigan's electoral votes for president and vice-president. This is done in Lansing, in December. All other states except Maine and Nebraska use a procedure essentially similar to this. The result of the presidential election is determined by adding up the number of state electoral votes won by each. The electors of all the states and the District of Columbia make up the *Electoral College*, totalling 538 electoral votes. The candidate receiving a majority of electoral college votes (270) is elected.

MINOR PARTIES IN A TWO-PARTY SYSTEM

Third parties or minor parties seek office for a number of reasons. Some feel that one day they will be strong enough to win offices, and possibly displace one of the major parties. Others see the campaign as an opportunity to tell the voters about their particular ideas. Some of these, such as the Libertarian party or Ross Perot's Reform party run many candidates in many states. Others, such as Michigan's Tisch Independent Citizens party, are based in only one state. The Libertarian, Socialist Workers, Communist and Green parties advocate a full range of programs and a large-scale change in American society. Others, such as the Prohibition party (eliminate alcohol) or the Tisch Independent Citizens party (reduce taxes) focus their attention on just one or a few issues. Whatever their reasons for raising their issues for discussion, these parties almost never win elections at any level of government. This failure may reflect the lack of appeal of their ideas, but there are other reasons for their lack of electoral success.

In the United States, most offices are filled by elections in what are called *single member districts*. Only one person per district is elected. Those parties without the most votes in an election receive no representation at all. In some European nations a party that has 10 percent of the vote will receive 10 percent of the seats in the legislature or parliament. In another approach, used in some nations, a district can send 2 or 3 or more people to the legislature, improving the chances that a minor party will win some seats. In the United States, the *winner take all,* single member district system offers little reward to a minor party unless it receives the most votes in an election.

Furthermore, it is not always easy for a minor party to be on the ballot. A minor party must usually have a record of some electoral success or go through the process of gathering many names on petitions from around the state. This process can be expensive and time-consuming.

Each state has its own rules governing access to the ballot. In Michigan's August primary any party whose major candidate received 5% or more of the votes cast for the office of Michigan secretary of state in the last general election may nominate candidates for statewide office.

If a minor party does not meet this requirement it will be unable to nominate candidates at the August primary. Its candidates in the general election will be selected by convention. Usually, a state convention of the minor party nominates its complete slate of candidates—those for both state and local offices.

To appear on the November general election ballot, a party must either have received 1% or more of the votes cast for the winning candidate for Michigan's secretary of state at the last election, or file petitions with the secretary of state's office which contain the signatures of one percent of the registered voters in Michigan. The signatures must come from different parts of the state.

WHO SUPPORTS DEMOCRATS AND REPUBLICANS?

Democratic Party Patterns

Organized labor and the Michigan Demorcratic party have long been political allies. The close working ties between the two has given the Democratic party great strength in the industrial corridor of the state. Driving up I-75 from Monroe, through Detroit, Pontiac, Flint, Saginaw and Bay City, one moves through one of the greatest concentrations of industry in the world and also one of the greatest collections of unionized workers. These areas represent the backbone of the Michigan Democratic party. A strong pro-union climate also tends to keep much of Upper Peninsula, with its historically low income level in the Democratic party.

County-by-County Vote for President -- 1992

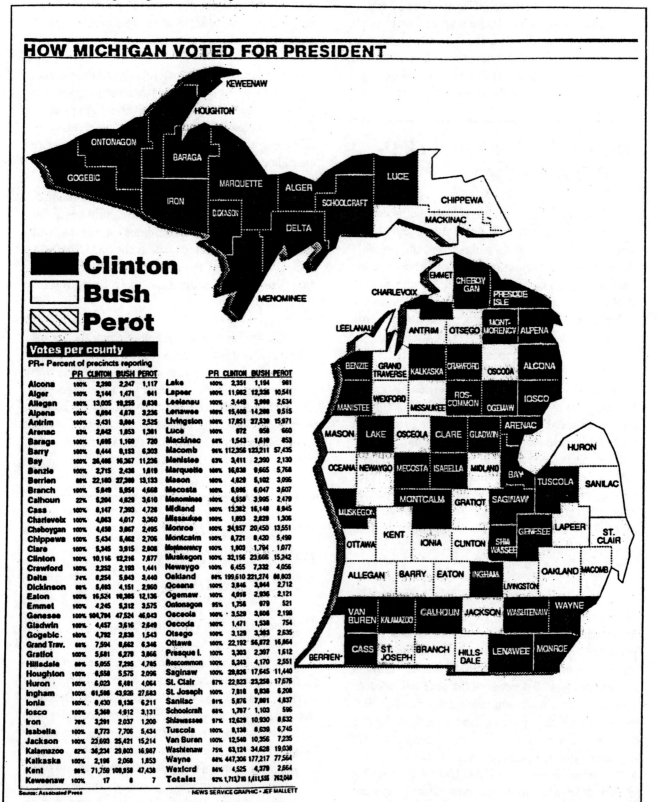

HOW MICHIGAN VOTED FOR PRESIDENT

Clinton
Bush
Perot

Votes per county

PR= Percent of precincts reporting

	PR	CLINTON	BUSH	PEROT
Alcona	100%	2,398	2,247	1,117
Alger	100%	2,144	1,471	941
Allegan	100%	13,005	19,255	8,838
Alpena	100%	6,894	4,870	3,236
Antrim	100%	3,431	3,864	2,525
Arenac	83%	2,842	1,853	1,381
Baraga	100%	1,695	1,160	720
Barry	100%	8,444	8,153	6,303
Bay	100%	26,486	16,367	11,236
Benzie	100%	2,715	2,436	1,619
Berrien	88%	22,180	27,380	13,133
Branch	100%	5,849	5,954	4,668
Calhoun	22%	5,204	4,829	3,610
Cass	100%	8,147	7,393	4,728
Charlevoix	100%	4,063	4,017	3,360
Cheboygan	100%	4,450	3,867	2,495
Chippewa	100%	5,434	5,462	2,706
Clare	100%	5,345	3,915	2,808
Clinton	100%	10,116	12,216	7,877
Crawford	100%	2,252	2,193	1,441
Delta	74%	8,254	5,643	3,440
Dickinson	88%	5,483	4,151	2,960
Eaton	100%	16,524	16,365	12,135
Emmet	100%	4,245	5,312	3,575
Genesee	100%	104,794	47,524	46,043
Gladwin	100%	4,457	3,616	2,649
Gogebic	100%	4,782	2,830	1,543
Grand Trav.	88%	7,594	8,662	6,346
Gratiot	100%	5,681	6,279	3,866
Hillsdale	88%	5,055	7,295	4,785
Houghton	100%	6,558	5,575	2,096
Huron	100%	6,023	6,481	4,064
Ingham	100%	61,596	43,926	27,583
Ionia	100%	8,430	8,135	6,211
Iosco	100%	5,360	4,912	3,131
Iron	78%	3,291	2,037	1,200
Isabella	100%	8,773	7,706	5,434
Jackson	100%	23,690	25,421	15,214
Kalamazoo	62%	36,234	29,800	16,987
Kalkaska	100%	2,198	2,068	1,853
Kent	88%	71,759	108,950	47,438
Keweenaw	100%	17	8	7

	PR	CLINTON	BUSH	PEROT
Lake	100%	2,351	1,194	981
Lapeer	100%	11,982	12,336	10,541
Leelanau	100%	3,449	3,960	2,634
Lenawee	100%	15,400	14,280	9,515
Livingston	100%	17,851	27,530	15,971
Luce	100%	872	958	660
Mackinac	100%	1,543	1,619	853
Macomb	96%	112,356	123,211	57,435
Manistee	83%	3,411	2,390	2,130
Marquette	100%	16,838	9,665	5,768
Mason	100%	4,829	5,102	3,096
Mecosta	100%	6,096	6,047	3,607
Menominee	100%	4,550	3,995	2,479
Midland	100%	13,382	16,148	8,945
Missaukee	100%	1,893	2,829	1,306
Monroe	100%	24,057	20,450	13,551
Montcalm	100%	8,721	8,420	5,499
Montmorency	100%	1,903	1,794	1,077
Muskegon	100%	32,156	23,666	15,242
Newaygo	100%	6,455	7,332	4,056
Oakland	88%	199,610	221,274	86,803
Oceana	100%	3,846	3,944	2,712
Ogemaw	100%	4,016	2,936	2,121
Ontonagon	95%	1,756	979	521
Osceola	100%	3,529	3,606	2,199
Oscoda	100%	1,471	1,530	754
Otsego	100%	3,129	3,393	2,635
Ottawa	100%	22,192	56,872	16,864
Presque I.	100%	3,303	2,397	1,612
Roscommon	100%	5,243	4,170	2,551
Saginaw	100%	28,026	17,645	11,440
St. Clair	87%	22,823	23,258	17,676
St. Joseph	100%	7,818	8,836	6,208
Sanilac	81%	5,876	7,861	4,837
Schoolcraft	68%	1,787	1,103	596
Shiawassee	97%	12,629	10,930	8,632
Tuscola	100%	8,138	8,639	6,745
Van Buren	100%	12,540	10,356	7,235
Washtenaw	75%	63,124	34,628	19,038
Wayne	88%	447,306	177,217	77,564
Wexford	86%	4,525	4,370	2,664
Totals:	92%	1,713,798	1,411,555	762,048

Source: Associated Press

NEWS SERVICE GRAPHIC • JEF MALLETT

Reprinted with permission
The Detroit News

Table 3.1

WHICH PARTY DOMINATES MICHIGAN?

Party winning the Michigan election for: Party with a majority in the following years in the:

	President	Governor	U.S. Senator	State Senate	State House
64	D	R	D	D	D
66		R*	R	R**	R
68	D				D
1970		R	D	TIE***	D
72	R		R		D
74		R		D	D
76	R		D		D
78		R	D	D	D
1980	R				D
82		D	D	D	D
84	R		D	R****	D
86		D		R	D
88	R		D		D
1990		R	D	R	D
92	D				TIE*****
94		R	R	R	R
96	D		D		D
98		R		R	R
2000	D		D	R	R
02		D	D	R	R

* Prior to the 1966 election, Governors were elected to a 2-year term.

** Prior to 1966, State Senators were elected to a two year term.

*** The Lieutenant Governor presides over the State Senate and may vote in the case of a tie. During this time the Lieutenant Governor was a Republican.

**** In late 1983, two Democratic state senators were recalled from office because of their vote for an increase in the state income tax. In early 1984, Republicans were elected in each district.

***** Tied. Speaker and committee chairs alternated monthly.

Nationally the black vote has been heavily Democratic. The same is generally true of Michigan's black voters. Those cities with large black populations (Detroit, Pontiac, Flint, Muskegon, Saginaw, and Lansing) usually turn out large Democratic majorities. As you can see, many of those cities are also part of the industrial corridor. Sometimes, conflict within the Democratic party has divided union and black voters. In recent elections, white working class Macomb county has voted Republican, and was often called the home of the "Reagan Democrats" in the 1980s.

Republican Party Patterns

Republicans draw their major support from many groups--business, religious and social conservatives, farmers, disaffected Democrats and higher income groups. The party finds its strength in the suburbs, small town and rural Michigan and western Michigan. As a result of the 1994 election, the western lower peninsula is now a dominant force in the party. The upper management of the auto industry, living in fashionable Detroit suburbs such as Bloomfield Hills, Birmingham, Farmington, and the Grosse Pointes often speak for the moderate wing of the Michigan Republican party, supporting candidates such as William Milliken. This moderate approach has on occasion split the party along moderate-conservative lines. The Republican party of rural and small town Michigan can trace its roots back to the Civil War when parts of the state were settled by New England Yankees and upstate New Yorkers.

STRONG AND WEAK POLITICAL PARTIES

Politics, like nearly everything else, is always in the process of change. Political parties have changed a good deal over the years. Perhaps the most significant change has been the gradual shift towards a weak party system in the states. A weak party system is one where candidates often run on their own and only share a few ideas in common with their party. They receive their support directly from the public rather than from party members and officials. In short, a weak party system is one in which the parties are decentralized, lacking in common ideas, and low in party discipline. This may not be completely bad. Many innovations of recent years are valuable (ideas such as the use of primaries, and strong group organization) but they do tend to weaken the parties.

A system of strong parties also has its advantages. Here, the parties would each have a consistent set of beliefs, would be united, and there would be meaningful party discipline. In such a system, one knows who to blame and whom to praise.

Table 3.2 summarizes factors which strengthen or weaken parties. How does Michigan stack up? What about its parties? Its party system? Is it "strong" or "weak"? If this were 1950, or 1960, the answer would almost certainly be that Michigan's parties were strong. But as we enter the 21st centry the balance may have shifted. Michigan parties may be weakening. Some clues to this question have been discussed in this chapter, and others can be found in those which follow.

Table 3.2

Factors that strengthen or weaken political parties

PRIMARY ELECTIONS TO NOMINATE CANDIDATES	weaken
PARTY CONVENTIONS TO NOMINATE CANDIDATES	strengthen
MEDIA ADVERTISING IN CAMPAIGNS	weaken
USE OF PARTY ORGANIZATION IN CAMPAIGNS	strengthen
PUBLIC OR LOBBYIST PAC FINANCING OF CAMPAIGNS	weaken
MOST CITIZENS IDENTIFY WITH A PARTY	strengthen
PARTY ORGANIZATIONS THE SOURCE OF GOVERNMENT JOBS	strengthen
DO PARTIES HAVE CLEAR AND DIFFERENT IDEAS?	strengthen
ELECTIONS AT SAME TIME	strengthen
PARTY LABELS USED IN MOST ELECTIONS	strengthen
STRONG INTEREST GROUPS	weaken

Chapter 4

Interest Groups in Michigan

Types of Interests

The Media: Communications Link? Interest Group?

Sources of Interest Group Strength

Techniques of Interest Groups

Limits on Interest Groups

"The people have the right peaceably to assemble, to consult for the common good, to instruct their representatives and to petition the government for redress of grievances."

Article 1, Sec. 3 Michigan Constitution

Chapter 4

Learning Objectives

What is an interest group?

What are some of the major types of interest groups?

Why can the media be considered an interest group?

What are eight major sources of interest group strength?

What are five major techniques of interest groups? Give detailed examples of each technique.

What are four major techniques that a lobbyist might use with a legislature?

How do groups influence elections?

Key Terms To Know

interest group
public interest group
lobbying
electioneering
multi-client lobby firm
litigation
Michigan Campaign Finance Law
PAC
coalition
group ratings

An *interest group* is a power seeking organization which attempts to obtain or keep benefits from government. The principal focus of interest groups is on public policy. Such groups are a natural outgrowth of an open, democratic society, especially in Michigan, for governmental decisions have a great deal to do with determining the "quality of life" or "who gets what" in society.

The right of individuals to form and join such groups, and use them to influence governmental decisions, is well protected. Section 3 Article 1, of Michigan's Constitution states: "the people have the right peaceably to assemble, to consult for the common good, to instruct their representatives and to petition the government for redress of grievances." Similar language has been included in each of Michigan's past Constitutions and can also be found in the U.S. Constitution's First Amendment. Any effort to regulate the activities of such groups must be careful not to infringe upon their rights.

Most political interest groups are not exclusively political. Groups often serve as sources of business or professional information. Some groups are primarily social organizations, sponsoring educational, professional or recreational activities. In other words, political activity—power seeking in governmental decisions—is often only one of the functions of such groups. This should not cause us to underestimate the importance of such activity.

There are two types of lobbyists-those who work for only one interest and those who are part of a multi-client lobbying firm. As the term indicates, a single client lobbyist will work for only one firm, while the multi-client lobbyist will take on a number of clients, similar to a law firm.

TYPES OF INTERESTS

The various businesses within the state are plainly affected by its governments. The right to do business, the location of one's business, the tax costs of business, the obligations of the business to its employees, and many other matters are all related to public policy. People representing economic interests tend to predominate among interest groups.

A survey of business interest groups in Michigan would illustrate the extent of their organization. The *financial sector* (banks, credit unions, savings and loans, insurance companies, stock brokers and foundations) is well represented. As examples, consider the following organizations:

> Michigan Savings and Loan League
> Household Finance Corporation
> Michigan Credit Union League
> Michigan National Corporation
> Michigan Bankers Association
> Michigan Association of Community
>   Bankers
> Automobile Club of Michigan
> Alliance of American Insurers

The *manufacturing sector,* (producers of electricity, dies, tools, military tanks, spare parts, chemicals, forest products, cereals, and above all, automobiles and trucks) is very visible. As examples, consider the following:

> Michigan Petroleum Association
> Michigan Manufacturers Association
> Consumers Energy
> Distilled Spirits Council of the United States
> Michigan Forest Products Council
> Dow Corning Corporation
> Michigan Iron Mining Association
> Ford Motor Company
> Detroit Edison Company
> Michigan Road Builders Association
> Gerber Products Company
> The Wine Institute

The *commercial sector* (wholesalers and retailers who distribute finished goods to Michigan consumers) is also organized. As examples we have:

> Montgomery Ward
> Burger King Corporation
> Michigan Cable TV Association
> Michigan Automobile Dealers Association
> Michigan State Chamber of Commerce
> Service Station Dealers Association of
> Michigan Association of Theatre Owners
> Michigan Retailers Association
> Meijer, Inc.
> Pizza Hut
> The Detroit Lions, Inc.

The *professional and service sectors* (doctors, dentists, accountants, attorneys, teachers) are very well organized. Among the interest groups representing those who provide personal and professional services to Michigan residents are:

State Barbers Association
Michigan Association of Realtors
Michigan State Chiropractic Association
Michigan Society of Professional Engineers
National Male Nurse Association
Dental PAC of Michigan
Michigan Well Drillers Association
Michigan Funeral Directors Association
Michigan Nurses Association
Michigan Watchmakers Guild
State Bar of Michigan
Michigan Trial Lawyers
Michigan Education Association

The *agricultural sector* would include some examples from the manufacturing sector (finished food products) and the commercial sector (grocery stores), but consider the following as examples of those who raise and grow farm products in Michigan:

Michigan Farm Bureau
Michigan Agriculture Coalition PAC
Cattlemens PAC
Michigan Dairy Foods PAC
Michigan Association of Timbermen
Michigan United Thoroughbred Breeders and
    Owners Association

Employees, Private and Public. Those who work for businesses and governments constitute a major category of interest groups in Michigan. As noted in chapter 3, Michigan's business-labor relations have been and continue to be a very important feature of its politics. The earliest Michigan employee organizations with an interest in politics represented people employed by private business. Beginning in the 1960's the employees of governments in Michigan were allowed to bargain contracts concerning their working conditions and compensation. Consider the following examples of organizations which are politically active in the interest of public and private employees:

Michigan Council #25, AFSCME
International Union, UAW

Michigan Union, AFL-CIO
Michigan State Police Troopers Association
Fraternal Order of Police
Brotherhood of Railway, Airline and
    Steamship Clerks, Freight Handlers,
    Express and Station Employees
Michigan Education Association

Governments. Governments? Do governments attempt to influence decisions of other governments? Yes. Chapter 2 illustrated how state and local governments attempt to influence national policies. It is also true that many local governments, and groups of governmental officials, attempt to influence the policies of the state. This is because the state has tremendous impact on the organization, duties and finances of local governments. It is no surprise that those governments are organized to express their preferences in Lansing. Consider the following examples:

Michigan Association of Counties
Michigan Community College Association
City of Livonia
Flint Community Schools
Michigan Municipal League
Michigan Probate and Juvenile Judges
    Association
Michigan Townships Association
Michigan Association of School Boards
Michigan Sheriffs Association

Most of the organizations mentioned thus far seek benefits which go to their own members. In seeking these benefits, these groups will usually claim that what they want is also good for others. They may say, "What's good for realtors is good for home buyers and sellers" or "What's good for teachers is good for taxpayers and students". In fact, the main beneficiaries are usually those in the group itself.

There are some groups which seek policies of a different kind. Some groups seek programs which, if adopted, would bring the same benefit to non-members as to members. These groups are commonly known as *public interest groups*. We would think of a public interest group as one which everyone would join if they knew about the group and had a few extra dollars to contribute. A true public interest group is one which all could support. There are few such groups in reality, but many which present themselves as such. Examples of groups which make a claim to being a public interest group are:

American Civil Liberties Union
Common Cause in Michigan
Michigan Citizens Lobby
West Michigan Environmental Action
    Council
Public Interest Research Group in
    Michigan (PIRGIM)
Sierra Club

You will notice that some of the groups mentioned above do have opponents. For example, while the goals of environmental and conservation groups are generally viewed as in the public interest, other groups quarrel with the means to the goal, with the timing the group seeks, or with its definitions. While "clean air" might be everyone's desire, some wonder about how much we should pay for it: expensive equipment or no new factories? How fast should we bring it about? Could it mean job losses? What is "clean air"? How "clean" is "clean"?

Ethnic, Racial and Religious groups. Some groups organize themselves along ethnic, racial, or religious lines. These groups may exist to share common cultural values and traditions, but many enter the political fray to fight discrimination their group might face. Some examples of this kind of interest group are:

Black Grocers Association
Christian Science Committee on Publication for
    Michigan
Political Association of Spanish Speaking
    Organizations
American Polish Action Council
Italians for Pomaville
National Conference of Black Lawyers PAC

"Cause" groups. This last category is a very complex one. There are some groups which organize around a single issue (a cause) and a great many of these groups are temporary. Many such groups are at the local level, organized to pass the school millage or fight against the zoning for a new bar in the neighborhood. Occasionally, groups of this kind are formed to press a single issue at the state level, for

example, to permit capital punishment or to support the nuclear arms freeze. These groups often combine people who take different sides on almost all other matters. Yet, they come together on one particular issue and cooperate. Naturally, these groups are unstable. Once they have won or lost, they tend to break up and the members go their separate ways. Some examples of such groups are:

Michigan Abortion Rights Action League
Right to Life of Michigan
Ingham County Tenants Union
National Organization of Women
Michigan Paralyzed Veterans of America
Government Alert for Fundamentalists
Citizens for a One House Legislature
Michigan Family Forum

This brief survey of interest groups indicates that the people of Michigan are intensely organized. Perhaps you noticed a tendency for those who are somewhat "better off" to be somewhat better organized. There are not many examples of young people or poor people on the lists.

"Think Tanks." There are a number of groups such as The Mackinac Center for Public Policy, Public Sector Consultants, The Michigan Land Use Institute, The Michigan Prospect or the Citizens Research Council of Michigan that study, research and publish facts and opinions about major issues in Michigan politics. Some of these groups have a clear ideological bent, others are more middle of the road and non-partisan. These groups can often play a major role in setting the agenda for government officials and suggesting solutions to problems.

THE MEDIA - COMMUNICATIONS LINK? INTEREST GROUP? AGENDA SETTER?

In addition to a multitude of cable outlets, Michigan is served by over 40 television stations, most of which broadcast from major population centers. There are nearly 330 radio stations throughout the state. Michigan has over 200 newspapers published on a weekly or semi-weekly basis and over 50 daily newspapers, 20 of which publish a Sunday edition! Students at almost 50 colleges and universities publish campus newspapers. In addition, there are numerous publications of ethnic groups, religious groups, business groups, labor unions and the like.

In this maze of afternoon soaps, talkshows, prayers, music, commercials, store coupons, sports, comics, advice columns, vital statistics, web sites and weather reports, we can identify the ways in which the media is important in politics. The various media provide *news, analysis, and opinion.* In other words, much of what is known about what government is doing, why those actions are taking place, and whether or not they should occur, comes from the media.

Naturally, not all media provide the same coverage of government and politics. Weekly and semi-weekly newspapers usually are community-oriented and examine only local issues. With some exceptions, such as "talk radio," radio stations provide limited news and even less analysis. Television coverage is somewhat more elaborate—more time is devoted to news and "specials" that provide some in- depth analysis of public issues. Yet television takes editorial positions less frequently than newspapers.

It is the major daily and Sunday newspapers that provide the most visible and consistent coverage of politics and government. They tie together important information about the activities of power seekers and power holders, inside and outside of government. They bring state and local issues into the limelight or keep them out. They explore the motives and goals of individuals, interest groups and parties. They provide analysis of issues and, very importantly, they editorialize and provide *endorsements* of candidates and issues. They report, analyze and judge. In short, they play an important role in setting the governmental agenda in Michigan.

In one sense, the media, especially major newspapers, can be viewed as neutral observers of the political process, but we can also view them as participants. They shape the public's view of issues, and are an important force in shaping assessments of what should or should not be done. Furthermore, many studies indicate that citizens who are most involved in politics as regular voters, group leaders and office holders are the most attentive to the media. Thus, the media has extra influence over those who are the most influential.

THE SOURCES OF INTEREST GROUP STRENGTH

Brown and Ringquist describe Michigan's interest groups as heavily involved in the policy making process, sharing long-term professional relationships with the lawmakers and bureaucrats. They see lobbyists as professionals who have had to adapt to a professional legislature and bureaucracy.

Some pressure groups find that they achieve their goals quickly and completely. Others find that despite much hard work and effort, little is accomplished. Like any organization, pressure groups can be either strong or weak, successful or unsuccessful. The relative strength of interest groups flows from many sources. Some of the following causes of group strength reinforce each other. Others tend to counteract one another.

Size is a crucial factor in pressure group power. The more members a group has, the more dues it can collect and the more people it can mobilize for voting and other group action. Size however, can raise some problems. As the size of the group increases the more difficult it may be to satisfy and unite all the different members.

The second source of power for pressure groups is **cohesion.** How well does the group stick together? Some small groups that work well together may often be more successful than larger, diverse groups. If it is known that a group is very divided it will be difficult for a lobbyist for that group to speak with any real authority.

The **geographic distribution** of a group may be important. A group that has many members in Detroit might have a great deal of clout with the Detroit city council, but it may find that in Lansing it is treated simply as one of many local interests. A group that can claim large membership and support in many legislative districts around that state will find a more willing ear when it tries to speak to the legislature.

Prestige can play a large role in the type of reception a group receives. Doctors, lawyers and other professionals will usually find the doors of the legislature open and available to them. Those groups without social status (small hobby groups, religious cults, groups of the far right or the far left, for example) may find that the lawmakers are less attentive to their pleas. The status of a group may vary with the state of the times.

The **organization** of pressure groups is the fifth source of group strength. The organization of groups will vary. Some small temporary groups have practically no organization. At the other extreme, the organization of some of the largest pressure groups may resemble huge corporations or governments in complexity. A strong centralized organization may allow a group to react quickly to changing conditions and speak with a single unified voice. Sometimes, however, a strong centralized group may be created at the cost of local diversity and support. To counter this, many large state organizations are in a "federal" arrangement, where there is a strong state organization, and significant local organizations that do have some independence.

The success of an interest group may depend on the size, skills and expertise of its **staff.** An organization needs to have the staff to take care of the phone calls and paperwork that go along with any organization.

The **leadership** of a group may also be an important resource. A strong leader who has a positive image beyond the bounds of the group may be able to unify the group and appeal to the public with success. As leadership changes the organization and success of the group may change as well.

The **political environment** of a pressure group is a final factor which might affect its success of a group. A program introduced at a time when its ideas are popular and in vogue will find its goals easier to reach.

THE TECHNIQUES OF INTEREST GROUPS

To achieve their goals interest groups use five major techniques: lobbying, electioneering, public relations, litigation and direct action. Not all groups use all of these tools or combine them in the same way. Sometimes groups work together and combine their skills and efforts. Thus, groups often form coalitions with others when they share similar goals.

Lobbying is the activity most commonly associated with interest groups. In the early days of Congress, those who wished to influence its members would do so in the lobby of the capitol. Thus, the term "lobbyist." Today most of the business of the lobbyist takes place elsewhere but the term is still frequently used. Other terms used to refer to lobbyists are "government relations officer" and "government liaison officer."

When a lobbyist approaches a state or local legislator he or she has several tools to use. One of the most significant of these is information. State lawmakers must deal with a huge variety of issues which are often very complex. Time is short and the typical state lawmaker cannot possibly become fully informed on the many technical issues with which he or she must deal. Term limits allow lawmakers only two (in the Senate) or three (in the House) terms to learn their job. Enter the lobbyist. The lawmaker must deal with many issues but the lobbyist can specialize. Thus, the lobbyist is often the source of reliable information on a particular legislative topic. Quickly, the lawmaker begins to rely on the lobbyist for dependable information. In some cases where the lawmaker already supports the goals of the lobby group the lobbyist may almost become an additional staff member to the legislator. The lobbyist may help with counting probable votes or organizing support for a bill.

Lobbyists may have several kinds of information important to a lawmaker. First, of course, the lobbyist will have significant information on the contents of a bill, and be able to explain the details to the legislator. Second, a good lobbyist will know the impact of a law on the member's home district. A lobbyist trying to gather support for a bill will be more successful if he can tell the lawmaker: "This will mean 500 more jobs for your district," or "This will affect two thousand voters in your area." "Knowledge is power" the old saying goes. It is very true for lobbyists.

Persuasion is the second major technique for lobbying. A successful lobbyist should be able to walk into a lawmaker's office and say: "Here are five reasons why you should support this piece of legislation." The arguments should convince the legislator that there are indeed five good reasons to support the bill.

Not all groups do their own lobbying. Some organizations hire lobbying expertise from firms in a rapidly growing industry—that of the multi-client lobby business. These firms, often formed by former legislators, bureaucrats or top staff personnel, offer governmental contacts for a price. In Michigan, the dominant firms are Public Affairs Associates, James H. Karoub Associates and Governmental Consultant Services. Representatives of these firms are considered the most influential in Michigan.

The discussion so far has dealt with lobbying techniques as they apply to the legislature. Though the legislature is often the most common place to find lobbying groups it is not the only one. Lobbyists also attempt to influence members of the executive branch. Administrative lobbying has become more and more important, because the executive branch of government has become more involved in rule making and regulation that affects important interests. Many administrative departments see lobbyists as frequently as the legislature.

Electioneering is the second major area of operation for a lobby group. Obviously, a lobbyist's job would be much easier if he could count on having a number of state legislators or city council members or county commissioners who already supported his ideas. Interest groups enter the election process in several ways. If there is a vacant position to be filled they may recruit probable supporters to run for office. Groups may also endorse candidates. The right endorsement from the right group will go a long way to assure election. Some groups can provide workers to make phone calls, put up posters and stuff envelopes.

Interest groups often issue evaluations of candidates based on their votes on issues or their responses to questions. For example, Governor Engler, a conservative Republican, usually receives a high rating from conservative pro-business groups and a low rating from liberal union groups.

Last but not least is money. Money is essential in politics and lobby groups are in a position to provide financing for candidates and ballot proposals. Most commonly this financial aid is channeled through a Political Action Committee. A political action committee (PAC) is an arm of an interest group that is allowed to raise funds for particular candidates or causes. As a result of recent campaign finance laws the use of PACs has grown tremendously. Most interest groups of any size makes some use of PACs.

> *"Money is the name of the game: legislators need it and PAC's have it. But what role is left for individual citizens?"* Karen Holcomb-Merril, Executive Director, Common Cause in Michigan. (Flint Journal, 10/15/89)

In 1992 more than 65% of Michigan state house members contributions came from PACS. The state's 38 senators accepted an average of $89,000 from PACs. The typical Michigan House member accepted about $31,000 from PACs. According to Common Cause, a public interest lobby group, more than $6.6 million was contributed to Michigan lawmakers during the 1990 campaign. Because of the increased importance of PACs, many political analysts feel that individuals are playing less significant roles in campaigns today. Others feel that, in spite of the concerns about PACs, the current system is better than the previous arrangement where a few wealthy individuals could fund campaigns, for their own benefit.

Pressure groups sometimes use "direct democracy" to reach their goals. Through the use of initiative or referendum drives, groups try to get their ideas adopted into law or incorporated in the Michigan Constitution. This will be examined in more detail in chapter 5.

The electioneering activities of PACs are of increasing concern to political analysts. Have big spenders pushed out other interests, reducing the "pluralism" of U.S. politics? Are individual legislators too closely tied to a particular group or groups? In Michigan about 70 cents of every campaign dollar spent on lawmakers campaigns comes from special interests groups.

Lobby groups also engage in *public relations* or advertising campaigns to influence the public on issues or ballot proposals. In 1994 the Michigan A.A.A. and other insurance interests joined together to attempt to pass a proposal that would limit lawsuits against insurance companies. In spite of their efforts the proposal lost. In 2002 a number of health organizations, such as the American Cancer Society and the American Heart Association attempted to amend the state constitution to shift the "tobacco settlement money" to fund their activities. Many lobby groups use traditional advertising to put their message across.

Litigation (legal action) is another tactic of lobby groups that has been growing rapidly in recent years. As the courts play a larger and larger role in public life one can expect lobbyists to make greater efforts to influence them. Though many groups use the courts only occasionally, some interest groups specialize in litigation. The NAACP (National Association for the Advancement of Colored People) has initiated many lawsuits trying to achieve greater racial equality. The American Civil Liberties Union (ACLU) commonly brings cases to court when it feels that constitutional rights have been violated. Environmental groups have gone to court to block projects that they felt would harm the natural ecology.

Finally, some groups use *direct action and protest* as a tactic. These activities range from strikes, sit-ins, and verbal protests to the illegal tactics of terrorism and bombing. The success of these tactics may depend upon the situation. The sit-ins of the early civil rights marchers generally did produce some success. It is less clear whether similar and stronger tactics of pro-and anti-abortion groups will produce success.

LIMITS ON INTEREST GROUPS

As lobbying has become more and more significant, the need to regulate lobbyists has grown. Michigan law requires that a lobbyist spending over $1675 per year register with the Michigan secretary of state and pay a small fee. Lobbyists are required to file regular reports detailing the money they spend trying to influence the legislative or executive branch of the government. There are more than 400 lobbyists registered with the secretary of state.

When groups enter the election arena they must abide by a number of laws, rules and regulations that apply to the election process. Since the mid-1970's, and the Watergate scandal, both the national government and many states have developed laws that regulate election campaigns and the money that flows into them. In 1976 Michigan enacted the Michigan Campaign Finance Law which requires candidates to make campaign contributions public and limits the amount of money any person or group may give to a candidate. The law is very complex and detailed. The most significant parts of this law are summarized in chapter 6.

In the past, society did not show the same amount and intensity of group organization as it does now. Some observers of interest groups argue that we would be better off without the organization and activities just reviewed. These critics maintain that such groups focus too closely on single issues, causing us to "miss the forest for the trees," and that these groups are too self-interested.

Others argue that interest groups contribute to democracy. They allow voters a role in day-to-day decisions of government, not just in elections, and provide voters important information. Thus, they help voters hold officials accountable for their actions.

Whatever the case, groups seem to be here to stay. Americans are noted for being joiners. The topic of interest groups will return frequently in later discussions because it is impossible to separate interest groups from most other aspects of politics in Michigan.

Lobbying Power in Lansing

The following are lists of several cagetories lobbying firms as ranked by *Inside Michigan Politics*, a newsletter that covers the politics and personalities of the state political scene.

**Lobbying Organizations:
The Top Ten**

1. Michigan Chamber of Commerce
2. Public Affairs Associates
3. James Karoub Associates
4. Governmental Consultant Services Inc.
5. Muchmore, Harrington
6. Michigan Legislative Consultants
7. Cawthorne, McCollough & Cavanagh
8. Right to Life of Michigan
9. Dykema Gosset
10. Capitol Services, Inc.

**Multi-Client Lobbying Firms:
The Top Ten**

1. Public Affairs Associates
2. James Karoub Associates
3. Governmental Consultant Services Inc.
4. Muchmore, Harrington
5. Michigan Legislative Consultants
6. Cawthorne, McCollough & Cavanagh
7. Dykema Gossett
8. Capitol Services, Inc.
9. Governmental Policy Consultants, Inc.
10. McKinney & Associates

**Single Interest Lobbying
Organizations: The Top Ten**

1. Michigan Chamber of Commerce
2. Right to Life of Michigan
3. Michigan Insurance Federation
4. Michigan Farm Bureau
5. NFIB/Michigan
6. Michigan Trucking Association
7. Ameritech
8. Michigan Realtors Association
9. Michigan Bankers Association
10. Michigan State Medical Society

Source: *Inside Michigan Politics*,
Nov. 13, 1995

Chapter 5

Elections In Michigan

National Laws And Michigan Elections

Types Of Elections

The Organization And Administration Of Elections

Direct Democracy In Michigan

> *"The legislature shall enact laws to preserve the purity of elections, to preserve the secrecy of the ballot, to guard against abuses of the elective franchise, and to provide for a system of voter registration and absentee voting."*
>
> Article II, Sect. 4 Michigan Constitution

Chapter 5

Learning Objectives

What are the different ways in which the national government affects elections in Michigan?

What is the difference between indirect democracy and direct democracy?

Why are elections without party labels not always truly non-partisan?

Summarize the steps in the different types of partisan elections in Michigan and the different types of non-partisan elections.

What are the different nomination processes in Michigan?

Most elections are in even-numbered years. Which are not?

What is "gerrymandering"?

What are the basic steps in preparing for and conducting elections? Which officials are responsible for what elections?

How can citizen initiative change state laws and the state Constitution?

How do the two kinds of initiative differ?

Distinguish between constitutional amendment and constitutional revision.

Identify the roles of the state legislature in referendum, initiative and constitutional amendment and revision.

What is the next year in which the question of revising the state's Constitution will automatically be on the ballot?

Key Terms To Know

indirect democracy	nomination	election commissioners
direct democracy	majority	election scheduling committee
partisan election	plurality	election inspectors
non-partisan election	ward	board of canvassers
primary election	recount	gerrymandering
general election	clerk	referendum
initiative	amendment	revision

Elections are a basic ingredient of democracy. Officeholders seeking to be reelected are held accountable for their actions. Election results may be an indication of the kinds of policies citizens want government to pursue. In some cases, the elections themselves determine the policies. Directly or indirectly, power-seekers and the choices of governments are influenced by elections.

NATIONAL STANDARDS AND MICHIGAN ELECTIONS

In view of the importance of elections, it is not surprising that the U.S. Constitution, laws and court rulings deal with the topic.

The earliest national rules were minimal, and election matters were largely left to the states. As time went by, the U.S. Constitution became more precise on some election matters. The 14th amendment (1868) required each state to give its citizens "equal protection of the laws" and "due process." The 15th amendment (1870) guaranteed the right of freed slaves to vote. The 17th amendment (1917) required the popular election of U.S. senators from each state. The 19th amendment (1920) required states to allow women to vote. The 23rd amendment (1961) allowed the District of Columbia the right to vote for president in the electoral college. The 24th amendment (1964) eliminated the poll tax, a requirement that one pay a special fee in order to vote. The 26th amendment (1971) requires states to allow those 18 and older to vote. (A state may lower the voting age below 18, if it desires.)

National laws relating to elections also became more common. In 1965 Congress passed the Voting Rights Act, designed to assure that all eligible voters had an equal right to register and vote. This act was of great importance to black voters of the deep south. Congress has also required foreign-language ballots in some parts of the nation where there are many non-English speaking people.

U.S. Supreme Court rulings have also affected the election process. Voting districts with equal populations have been required. Requirements that only people who own property in a community be allowed to vote in its elections on tax matters have been declared unconstitutional. State laws setting residency requirements for voting are also subject to review by the U.S. courts. If a state required people to live there for, say, two years before allowing them to vote, a court would strike this down.

One important effect of this national government involvement has been to standardize and democratize elections in the United States much more than in the past. While the national government does set some basic ground rules, states may make important choices on election procedures.

TYPES OF ELECTIONS

Voters in Michigan, and in most states, face a complicated variety of elections. By keeping a few key factors in mind, it is possible to sort out this confusion.

Direct or Indirect Democracy?

In *indirect democracy* the voters select a person to hold a particular office. The link between the election and policy is indirect. The people choose an office holder, who makes policy. In *direct democracy,* citizens make policy at the election. A law is the result of the election. Later in this chapter, we will devote a complete section to direct democracy. Let us look first at the important factors in indirect democracy elections, those in which voters choose officeholders.

Partisan and Non-partisan Elections

In partisan elections, the candidates are identified on the ballot by party label. All national elections are partisan. Except for judges, all state level offices in Michigan are partisan. All county offices are filled in partisan elections, as are all township offices. Some cities and all villages use party labels in their elections.

In other elections, the candidates are listed on the ballot without party labels. This is a non-partisan election. All school elections are non-partisan. Most Michigan cities use non-partisan elections. All judicial elections are non-partisan.

Simply because an election is non-partisan does not mean that party influence is absent. Many non-partisan officials have been active in a political party. Interest groups which tend to support the philosophy of one of the parties may play a role in helping a person of similar philosophy win a non-partisan office. While non-partisan elections do remove the party label, they do not necessarily remove the differences of philosophy or policy between candidates. One of the best examples of this is found in the way Michigan chooses its Supreme Court justices, and this will be discussed later.

Primary and General Elections

In a primary election, the "field" of candidates for an office is narrowed down to the final contestants. Thus, a primary is a nomination process. A general election is the final election, selecting the winner(s) of the office. Combining this category with the preceding one, there can be partisan or non-partisan primary elections and partisan or non-partisan general elections. In Michigan the following election combinations are used:

```
PRIMARY                              GENERAL
partisan _____ A _____ partisan

non-partisan _____ B _____ non-partisan
```

In (A) the nominating is according to party. Voters are free to select which party's primary they will vote in, but may only vote in the primary of one of the parties. Michigan law thus creates the possibility that voters who normally support one party will decide to vote in the primary of the other party—"raiding" it, or spoiling its nomination process. For example, if you were a Democrat and there were no significant contests in the Democratic primary, you could "cross over" and vote in the Republican primary. Since you want Democrats to win, you could vote for the Republicans whom you thought would be easiest to defeat. This temptation would be greatest when a primary is being held for only one office. This is rare. Because many of Michigan's election districts are dominated by one party, due to gerrymandering (p.54) or other factors, often the primary election is the most important. (See Chapter 3 for a description of Michigan's presidential primary.)

Candidates seeking an office in which there is a partisan primary must first file *petitions* to get their name on the primary ballot. A certain number of registered voters must sign these petitions to qualify the person for the ballot. This figure is usually the number of voters equal to between one and four percent of those in the election district who voted in the last election for the office of secretary of state.

The candidate who gets the most votes in the party's primary is nominated. In the general election, they will face those nominated by any other party. In the general election, voters may "split" their ticket— voting for one party's candidate for one office, another party's candidate for a different office, and so forth. This sequence (partisan primary and partisan general election) is very common in Michigan. The governor, U.S. senators, U.S. representatives, state senators and representatives, county officials, township officials and some city and village officials are all selected in this fashion.

In (B), candidates for an office who have secured the required number of nominating signatures are all listed on the non-partisan primary ballot. No party labels are used. A number of candidates equal to twice the number of offices to be filled are nominated. This is again determined by the "most votes" or plurality rule—the top vote-getters are nominated. In the non-partisan general election, the top vote-getter wins the office. Many cities use this sequence to fill the city's offices. All judges in Michigan are chosen in this fashion, except those of the state's Supreme Court.

Other Means of Nomination

While the primary election is the most common means of nomination in Michigan, it is not the only possibility. For some offices, other means of nomination are used.

One of these is nomination by *party convention*. Here, the respective party officials select nominees for an office, and voters determine the winner in a general election. In Michigan this approach is used for some important state-level offices. Candidates for secretary of state, attorney general, the state Supreme Court, the state Board of Education, the governing bodies of the three major state universities (Michigan, Michigan State and

Figure 5.1

MICHIGAN ELECTION METHODS

METHOD OF NOMINATION	ELECTION	EXAMPLES
File petitions and win a partisan primary.	partisan	Governor, U.S. Senators, members of the U.S. House of Representatives and the Michigan legislature, all county and township elected officials, and elected officials in some cities and villages.
File petitions and win a non-partisan primary.	non-partisan	All judges except those of the state Supreme Court, officials in many cities.
Party convention	partisan	Lieutenant governor, secretary of state, attorney general, members of the state Board of Education, presidential electors and U-M, MSU and WSU boards. Minor parties often nominate by convention for various offices.
Party convention	non-partisan	Supreme Court justices.
File petitions	partisan	Some villages.
File petitions	non-partisan	Members of local school and community college boards.
File affidavit declaring own candidacy.	non-partisan	Any judge seeking reelection.

NOTE: Candidates for county offices or state representative may file a $100 fee instead of petitions.

Wayne State) and presidential electors are all nominated by party convention. For all these offices except the Supreme Court, the final selection is by a partisan general election. (As noted earlier, the members of the Supreme Court, although nominated by party conventions, are chosen for office in a "non-partisan" general election, in which parties usually help their nominee campaign.)

Although it rarely happens, a party convention, or a group of party officials called a party caucus, may also nominate a candidate for an office if the candidate nominated in the party's primary becomes ineligible to run in the general election. Thus, if a nominated candidate dies before the election, seeks some other office, or decides to pull out, party officials may replace that person with someone else.

Another kind of nomination is quite common. This is called *nomination by petition.* Here, depending on the office, a person wishing to become a candidate simply files nominating petitions containing the names of a legally required number of registered voters. Again, the requirement is usually one percent of the number of votes cast in that particular election district for the office of secretary of state in the last election. In the case of school districts, one must obtain signatures equal to one percent of the votes received by the top candidate in the last board election.

Those nominated make up the general election field. No primary election is held. The person (or two, or three, depending on the number of offices to be filled) with the most votes is elected. This kind of procedure is used in school board elections. A special method of nomination is available only to judges, except those of the Supreme Court. If a judge plans to seek reelection, he may nominate himself by filing an affidavit declaring his candidacy.

One final note at this point: the rule determining who wins is the *plurality* (most votes) rule. The top vote-getter wins. A majority vote (50 percent plus 1 or more) is not a requirement. Figure 5-1 summarizes the kinds of nomination and election approaches used in Michigan.

The "election schedule" (Figure 5.2) shows a series of elections which could confront a voter over

a period of time. Exceptions to this schedule do exist. If a vacancy exists in a office, and it is not filled by appointment, a *special election* might be called. School millage elections are often held on a schedule of their own.

THE ORGANIZATION AND ADMINISTRATION OF ELECTIONS

Holding an election requires the participation and cooperation of a great number of officials and citizens. In this section, we will review the basics of election management.

Creating Election Districts

Every election is held within a specific boundary. In some cases, the boundary stays the same from election to election, and never needs to be redrawn. For example, elections for president, U.S. senator, governor and others are held on a state-wide basis. The state's boundaries are fixed. Likewise, the boundaries of counties, townships, cities, villages and school districts seldom change.

In many cases, members of a particular decision-making body are chosen from districts which are redrawn from time to time. Rulings of the U.S. Supreme Court in the 1960's and 1970's required election districts to be roughly equal in population size. This is intended to make each citizen's vote equal in weight, or provide "one person, one vote." The court rulings, and the state laws which implement them, require that districts be redrawn soon after the results of the regular U.S. census are published. Thus, every ten years, new population figures become the basis for adjusting election district boundaries.

Many governmental bodies in Michigan are made up of officials elected from districts. Many city and village legislatures consist of members elected from districts which are often called "wards." All state legislators are elected from districts, as are all county commissioners. So are all members of Michigan's delegation to the U.S. House of Representatives.

Figure 5-2

MICHIGAN ELECTION CALENDAR

OFFICE	YEAR								
	1998	99	2000	01	2002	03	2004	05	2006
NATIONAL									
PRESIDENT			X				X		
US SENATOR (6 year term, 2 per state, 1 elected each time)			X		X				X
US REPRESENTATIVE (all 15)	X		X		X		X		X
STATE									
GOVERNOR/LT. GOV.	X				X				X
SECRETARY OF STATE	X				X				X
ATTORNEY GENERAL	X				X				X
MEMBERS, STATE EDUCATION BOARDS	X		X		X		X		X
STATE SENATORS (all 38)	X				X				X
STATE REPRESENTATIVES (all 110)	X		X		X		X		X
JUDICIAL POSITIONS (6 or 8 year terms)	X		X		X		X		X
LOCAL									
COUNTY BOARDS OF COMMISSIONERS (all members in each county)	X		X		X		X		X
COUNTY OFFICERS (Prosecutor, Clerk, Treasurer, Reg. of Deeds, Drain Comm., Sheriff.)			X				X		
TOWNSHIPS			X				X		

CITIES, VILLAGES, K-12
and COMMUNITY COLLEGE BOARDS-Generally, cities, villages and school boards hold elections in odd-numbered years. There are some exceptions to this, however. Also, terms of office vary quite a lot between the various governmental bodies.

NOTE: In the case of state education boards, judicial positions and K-12 and community college boards, only some members of the governing body are elected at any one time, for terms are staggered. This is common practice in cities and villages also.

Figure 5.3

REDISTRICTING PROCEDURES IN MICHIGAN

Office (Number of Districts)	Responsibility of:	If no plan by a certain date?
U. S. House of Representatives (15)	State Legislature and Governor (state law is passed)	U. S. Courts may intervene
Michigan State Senate (38) Michigan House of Representatives (110)	State Legislature and Governor (state law is passed)*	State or U. S. Courts
County Commissioner (In all 83 counties, the County Board varies in size from 5 to 35 depending on the county's population.)	County Apportionment Commission (County Clerk, Prosecutor and Treasurer and chairpersons of the two main parties in each county- usually the Democrats and Republicans. They determine the number of districts, and draw them.	State Court of Appeals may intervene, if asked
Member of City or Village Legislature (Number of districts varies from place to place. Some don't use districts but elect at large.)	Varies. Can be the Election Commission of the community (see page 53 for membership) or another body set by charter.	Seek action in Circuit Court

GENERAL GUIDELINES IN ALL CASES: Districts should be close to equal in population, compact, cross over government boundaries as little as possible, and be convenient for election administration. The voting strength of minorities should not be diluted by any new district plan.

* Before 1983, the state legislature election districts were created by a Legislative Apportionment Commission. It contained 4 members from each political party receiving more than 25% of the votes for governor in the last election - always the Democratic and Republican parties. If this group failed to come up with a plan, the state Supreme Court created the districts. In 1983, the state Supreme Court declared this method unconstitutional, and allowed the current method to occur.

There are different approaches used to draw the districts for different offices. Figure 5-3 provides a summary of the various procedures. Unless overturned in court, the election district maps developed through these procedures remain in effect for the next ten years. Redistricting has great impact on the election process, and on the fortunes of parties and candidates. Figure 5.4 illustrates this.

Preparing For and Conducting Elections

The major election official in Michigan is the secretary of state. The secretary's Election Bureau is responsible for carrying out the state's election laws. This division provides local clerks with advice, information, and training about elections. The forms used in elections are prepared by the division, and it administers campaign laws.

All counties, townships, villages, and cities have *Clerks* and *Boards of Election Commissioners*. City election commissions include the clerk, attorney and assessor unless its charter provides otherwise. In villages the commission is the village president, clerk and treasurer, unless its charter provides otherwise. Township commissions consist of the clerk, supervisor and treasurer of the township. The county election commission is made up of the clerk, the senior Probate judge and treasurer. These commissions are responsible for most of the detailed procedures described below. In the case of school district elections, many of these procedures are handled by the school board. The secretary of the school board is the chief elections official of the district, and an administrator is designated to carry out election responsibilities.

Ballots are prepared in a timely fashion. Most elections are held according to a schedule set in advance, and ballot preparation can be planned in advance. In the event of special elections, the *County Elections Scheduling Committee* has a role. It consists of the county clerk, a city clerk, a township clerk and a member of a local school board. (The last three are appointed by the county Board of Commissioners.) This committee schedules the special election taking into account factors like other scheduled election dates and whether voters can be adequately notified and registered.

Next, clerks organize the polling places. Each city, village, and township clerk is responsible for establishing voting locations for neighborhoods in the community. These are called *precincts*. According to law, depending on the kind of voting device used, only a certain number of voters may vote in any one location. Each registered voter must be assigned a location in advance of the election. These laws are aimed at avoiding congestion and fraud at the polls. The next step is the preparation and delivering of equipment. Election equipment must be in working order, be accurate and sufficient supplies must be available for use at each location.

Proper staffing at election locations is very important. Clerks must assure that each precinct has a well-trained *Board of Inspectors*. These precinct workers operate the polls, and see that election laws and procedures are followed. They are responsible for arranging election equipment and materials, opening the polling place at 7a.m., verifying *registrations*, instructing voters, issuing *ballots*, protecting the ballots from abuse, and enforcing laws about campaigning too close to the polls. One hundred feet is the limit. They may also assist a person who is blind, illiterate, or unable to operate the voting device. They are responsible for closing the polls at 8 p.m., and gathering and verifying the validity of the ballots. Political parties are also allowed to have *challengers* at the polls to make sure their interest are protected.

If the precinct uses paper ballots, the inspectors count them at the precinct, report the totals to the clerk, and seal the ballot boxes. In places where voting machines are used, the counters at the back of the machines are read by the inspectors, reported to the clerk, and the machines (with the results still showing) are closed, sealed and locked. More and more Michigan communities are using computer punch card voting devices or optical scanners. This process usually yields quick results. In light of the confusion surrounding the 2000 presidential election in Florida, many states are now considering standardizing voting methods.

The final stages involve an official counting of votes. This is done by a *Board of Canvassers*. There are separate boards at the various levels of government, each with responsibility for particular offices. These four-person boards are appointed by

Figure 5.4

GERRYMANDERING

The term "gerrymandering" means to draw election districts so one party or group has an election advantage over another. A simple example will illustrate the process.

Suppose you lived in a state where half the people supported the X party, the other half the O party, and the people were to elect four representatives. One way to draw the election districts might be as follows: (Assume each X or O represents the same number of citizens)

District 1	X	X	X	X WINS
District 2	O	O	O	O WINS
District 3	X	X	X	X WINS
District 4	O	O	O	O WINS

This district plan might seem to be fair since there would be two Xs and two Os elected, which reflects the state's party balance.

However, one doesn't have to be "fair" in the districting process. Consider what could happen if the X party had the chance to draw the election district lines. Remember, court rulings require that district populations be equal but do not dictate the shape of the districts. Look at what party X could do:

Districts	1	2	3
	X	X	X
	O	O	O
	X	X	X
District 4	O	O	O

The X party wins districts 1, 2 and 3. Only 4 is won by the Os. Thus, in a state where votes are evenly balanced it is possible for one party to win a large legislative majority through gerrymandering.

Gerrymandering is commonly done to favor one party over another. A different type of gerrymandering is group gerrymandering, done either to prevent or assure the election of a person representing a particular group.

the appropriate governmental level, members serve 4 year terms, and no more than two members can be of the same political party. Their major function is to review the conduct of the election, validate the votes cast, and certify a set of final, official results. In addition, these boards may be involved in reviewing petitions for valid signatures, and language of ballot proposals.

In cities and townships of fewer than 5 voting precincts, canvassing is performed by the county Board of Canvassers. Larger cities and townships perform their own canvassing. The state Board of Canvassers is involved in all state-wide elections, all elections for national officials, and those for many state legislators and judges.

Occasionally, an election result is very close, or even more rarely a concern about fraud or election mismanagement exists. In such cases, an affected citizen (usually a defeated candidate) may petition for a recount. If the contest was an election to the state House or Senate, a recount is conducted by that body. Otherwise, the appropriate board of canvassers conducts the recount. State law provides guidelines and strict deadlines for the procedure, which might or might not involve all precincts and ballots. The election results as determined by the recount become the official results.

What if there is a tie? If the election is one which the state Board of Canvassers has certified as tied, the state legislature decides the matter. If the election is one canvassed by a county or other local board of canvassers, the question is settled by drawing lots at the county clerk's office.

This concludes the discussion of indirect democracy—where voters choose officeholders. The next section reviews elections in which voters determine policy at the polls—direct democracy.

DIRECT DEMOCRACY IN MICHIGAN

Direct Democracy involves the citizens in the making of policy. A law is the direct result of a vote. This kind of election is only seen at the state and local levels in the United States. Citizens have no direct role in national policy-making—national law is made by elected representatives of the people (the president and Congress) or by appointed officials (courts or department officials.)

In approximately half of the states, the citizens have the right to participate directly in the making of laws or state constitutions. Michigan, compared to other states, provides its citizens with many such opportunities, through language in the state Constitution (Article 2, section 9) and laws.

There are a number of forms of direct democracy. One is called *referendum,* of which there can be some variations. The other is called *initiative,* of which there can also be variations.

Referendum Provisions In Michigan

Suppose the legislature passes a law (a statute) which some people strongly object to. Unless the law is one which appropriates money to state institutions, or one which meets deficiencies in state funds, a public vote on the law can be forced. A *referendum* will be held if a number of registered voters equal to at least 5% of the number of votes cast in the last election for all candidates for governor sign petitions requesting it. These signatures must be secured within 90 days of the end of legislative session in which the law was passed. Once the signatures have been certified by the secretary of state, the law in question is suspended until the referendum vote. This vote is held at the next general election. A simple majority rule is used to determine whether the law takes effect.

Another form of referendum occurs in Michigan if the legislature refers a law to the voters before it takes effect. (This can be done with any law except one appropriating money.) If the vote on the law is favorable, the law takes effect 10 days later.

Later we will also see that any change in Michigan's Constitution also requires a favorable vote of the people, another form of referendum.

Initiative and Laws in Michigan

The term "initiative" means the people have the power to propose and enact laws. If the legislature, for some reason, has not passed a law which some people strongly want, those people have the right to place the issue directly before the voters. This power extends to any law which the legislature is allowed to pass under the state's Constitution.

First, petitions must be circulated. These must contain the full text of the proposed law. They must be signed by registered voters equal in number to at least 8% of the number of votes cast for all candidates for the office of governor in the last election. Once these petitions are certified as accurate by the secretary of state, they are presented to the legislature, which has 40 days to consider the proposed legislation. It may not amend the proposal in any way, but decides whether to pass or reject the law as presented. If passed, the law would be subject to referendum as discussed above. If the legislature rejects the proposed law, the initiated law is placed on the ballot at the next general election.

If the law is passed by a majority vote, it takes effect 10 days after official certification. Such an initiated law may not be vetoed by the governor. The state legislature may not amend or repeal it except by a 3/4 vote in both the House of Representatives and the Senate.

During the time in which the legislature is considering the initiated law, it might decide to propose a different law on the same subject. If so, both proposals would go on the ballot at the same time. If both were approved, the one with the greatest number of votes would take effect. If the legislature's proposed law won, it could not be vetoed by the governor, but could be amended or repealed by the legislature at a later date by simple majority votes—as in the case of referendum.

Direct Democracy and Michigan's Constitution

An *amendment* to the state's Constitution may be proposed by citizens. (An amendment is a change in a particular part of the document.) Petitions bearing the text of the amendment must be signed by registered voters equal in number to at least 10% of the total vote cast for all candidates for governor in the last election. At least 120 days prior to the election, the petitions must be filed with the secretary of state, and that office must certify those petitions as valid at least 60 days prior to the election.

An amendment may also be proposed by the legislature. A 2/3 vote in both the House and Senate is required, and a vote on the proposal is held at the next general election or at a special election.

Any amendment, whether initiated by voters or referred by the legislature, must be approved by a majority of those voting on the question at the election. If approved, an amendment takes effect 45 days after the election.

Another way of changing the Constitution is by *revision*. While an amendment changes only a part of the document, a revision involves a complete rewriting or changes in many parts of the Constitution. A revision is proposed by a state constitutional convention and approved by voters. The process operates in the following way.

The 1963 state Constitution provides that every 16 years (beginning in 1978), the question of whether to call a convention must be placed on the fall general election ballot. Within these periods of 16 years the question could also be placed on the ballot by initiative petition or by the legislature. If the calling of a convention is approved by a simple majority voting on that question, a convention must be formed within 6 months. Delegates to the convention would be chosen at partisan elections in each of the 110 House and 38 Senate districts. They would meet at the state capitol the following October. Any changes which the convention proposes are submitted to the voters at least 90 days after it adjourns. The specific date of the election is determined by the convention, and any proposed changes approved by a majority of voters would take effect according to a schedule set by the convention.

There is one final point in this study of direct democracy in Michigan. Procedures such as initiative and referendum do not exist only at the state level. State law provides that these practices shall also exist in many local communities. Voters in counties, cities, villages, and townships have powers of referendum with reference to acts of their legislatures. They also have the power of initiative for statutes (ordinances) they might wish to pass. Also, voters in cities and villages may act to amend or revise their government's charter. More detail about direct democracy at the local level will be provided in part 4 of this book.

Chapter 6

Voting and Activism in Michigan

Becoming and Remaining a Voter

Patterns of Voter Participation

The Voting Decision and the Voting Act

Beyond Voting: Activism

"All political power is inherent in the people. Government is instituted for their benefit, security and protection."
Article 1, Sec. 1 Michigan Constitution

Chapter 6

Learning Objectives

What are the qualifications for registering to vote in Michigan?

What steps would you take to register?

How can a person's registration go out of effect?

How is voter participation related to different types of elections?

Which groups tend to have the highest/lowest participation levels?

Identify various ways by which a citizen can become better informed.

Under what conditions may a voter vote "absentee"?

Briefly, what activities are involved in party and interest group activism?

What are some factors which cause people to run for office?

What are the most important steps in organizing a campaign for office?

What guidelines might an officeholder follow in order to stay in office?

Key Terms To Know

registration
voter turnout
straight ticket
split ticket
independent
absentee voting
candidate
candidate committee
campaign manager
recall

So far, much of the focus in this part of the book has been on groups, laws, and organizations. The discussion which follows will examine the election process from the point of individuals— voters, activists, and candidates.

BECOMING AND REMAINING A VOTER

Non-voting, and not registering to vote, are very common. Many Americans do not register, and many of those who register fail to vote. These acts, or inactions, might be considered as "statements." Perhaps these individuals reject the "system" and wish it were radically different. Perhaps they simply are not informed about procedures involved in registration and voting.

The basic requirement for voting is that one be a *registered voter*. It is through the registration process that society attempts to prevent fraud in elections. To register to vote in Michigan, one must be a citizen of the United States, and be eighteen years of age at the time of the next regularly scheduled election. The person must have lived in the local community for at least thirty days by the time of the election. They must register at least thirty days prior to the election. Registration may take place at any office of the secretary of state any Family Independence Agency Office, or at the office of the clerk in the township or city in which the person resides. Village residents must register twice—at the village clerk's office in order to vote in village elections, and at the township clerk's office in order to vote in township elections. (This is so because villages remain a part of a township.) Mail in applications are also available on the <Michigan.gov> website.

State laws require clerks, or their deputies, to be available at certain times in order to receive registrations. Many clerks provide services beyond what is required. Registration drives in shopping centers, schools and on a door-to-door basis are not unusual. When registered, the person will be provided a card which is proof of registration. This card will also show the place at which they are required to go to vote—the voting location for their precinct.

If a registered voter moves to a different community in Michigan within 60 days before an election, he or she may vote, in that election only, at the place of earlier registration. If a voter moves *within* the same community, they may vote at their old precinct and their registration will be updated. If a person moves within Michigan in a presidential year and cannot meet the thirty day residence requirement, he or she is permitted to vote for president and vice-president by absentee ballot in Michigan.

Compared to other states, Michigan has a high rate of second-home ownership. Questions often arise as to voting rights if a person owns two homes. Basically, the test established by law is the test of principal residence. A person may register in only one community, the one in which he or she spends a majority of time during the year. This same test applies to a person who owns a home in Michigan and in another state. College students are free to choose either their "home town" or their "college town" as their place of residence for voting purposes.

One of the most important aspects of registration in Michigan is that a voter does not have to indicate a party preference in order to register, or to vote, even in a partisan primary. In this respect, Michigan is unlike most other states. In over twenty states, using a closed primary, registrants must identify a party preference, or call themselves "independent" or "unaffiliated." A person not indicating a party preference, is not allowed to vote in any partisan primary election held in those states.

In Michigan, an open primary state, voters have more choice and more privacy. A person may register without indicating a party preference and may vote in the primary election of *any* party, but in the primary of *only one* party. The choice is made privately.

Staying Registered

When registered voters move to a new community, they must re-register. Notice of the new registration will be provided to their old community and their name will be removed from its voter list. Names are also removed when the local clerk receives notice of deaths in the community, provided monthly by the county clerk.

Some voters names are placed in an inactive file. This will not prevent the person from voting, but might cause a delay while the registration is checked. One could be placed in the "inactive" file by not performing at least one of the following for four consecutive years: voting, registering, recording changes of address, signing a petition, applying for an absentee ballot or declaring a party preference. People in jail awaiting trial are entitled to vote by absentee ballot, but those serving a criminal sentence may not vote while confined in jail or prison. Their voting right is reinstated upon release from confinement.

PATTERNS OF VOTER PARTICIPATION

It is estimated that between 80 and 90 percent of those eligible to vote are actually registered. Not all those registered will vote. Voter participation [voter turnout] varies from election to election. In any given election turnout will also vary from group to group.

Election Factors and Voter Turnout

The following are some general statements about election factors and voter turnout. Partisan elections tend to attract more voters than non-partisan. General elections have considerably higher turnout than primary elections; often triple that of a primary election. Voter turnout is highest in presidential years, about one third lower in gubernatorial years, and lowest (sometimes as low as 5-10%) in odd-numbered years. Turnout is usually highest in elections for highly visible state and national offices, lowest in school and other local elections. Contests at the top of the ballot tend to receive more votes than those lower on the ballot. Of all these factors, those which seem to matter most are those related to election timing. As an illustration of this consider table 6.1.

Clearly, elections vary in their turnout. Most of the time it is considered a good idea to have a high turnout for elections. Isn't it ideal if as many people as possible vote? Perhaps—but, depending on your goals, you might prefer a lower turnout.

Table 6.1

VOTER TURNOUT-FLINT, MICHIGAN

Typical Turnout in Different Types of Elections

TYPE OF ELECTION		PERCENT TURNOUT
November General Election	—Presidential years	65%
	—Gubernatorial years	50%
	—Odd-numbered years in which City Mayor chosen (non-partisan)	40%
	—Odd numbered years in which only City Council seats were filled	20%
August Primary Elections		25%
June Local School Elections (non-partisan)		15%
October 1998—Mott Community College Millage/Bond election		2%

Source: Tabulated from records maintained by the Flint City Clerk. (1990-2000)

Let's say that in a certain area there were 1000 voters and 900 of them were very opposed to any tax increase. Also, assume 100 people are well organized and active and would like to pass a millage for a new school. How can they win if they are outnumbered 9-1? They can, if the opposition fails to turn out to vote. What could they do if their goal were to reduce turnout?

Consider all the possibilities:
—An election at an odd time (other than November).
—An election with only one item on the ballot.
—An election with little publicity.

For example, an election in January (odd time and bad weather) with little publicity, on only a millage (no presidential or senatorial election to draw voters) would almost certainly have a very low turnout—5 or 10 percent or less would not be unusual. Now if the group made sure that all of its 100 supporters of the millage voted, and hoped that most of the opposition stayed home, it might have a good chance of winning, even though heavily outnumbered.

The surest way to increase voter participation would be to schedule more elections together. A possibility might be to shift all elections into a "fall of even-year" framework. Critics of this would argue that voters would be confused by such "long ballots" and that congestion at the polls might increase. They would also maintain that local communities should have the right to separate their issues from state and national issues by using separate elections. They would say that low voter turnout is best corrected by a responsible public, and that low turnout is acceptable because it only shows that those who care most are voting. What do you think?

Group Factors and Voter Turnout

Precinct analyses and surveys (polls) of voters indicate that turnout varies from group to group. Young voters vote much less than older voters. Voter turnout increases with education—those with higher levels of education vote more than those with less. The same kind of relationship exists between income and voting. Blacks, Hispanics, and native Americans vote less than whites—a result of the comparatively lower levels of education and income

of these groups. Likewise, suburban voters usually turn out in greater proportion than central-city residents. There is hardly any difference in turnout between men and women. Membership in community organizations seems associated with high voter participation. Curiously, people who call themselves "independents" vote less frequently than those who are supporters of one of the major political parties.

These patterns of participation are important in an election from the point of view of parties and candidates. If the voters who would normally support them are low-turnout voters, the party or candidates will have to work harder than if their followers were very likely to vote. Generally, Democratic party oriented voter groups turn out at lower levels. Republican identifiers tend to have a higher turnout rate. Thus in an evenly contested race the Republicans would have the advantage.

THE VOTING DECISION AND THE VOTING ACT

Many conditions must be met before people will vote. They must be eligible and registered. They must know there is an election scheduled. This is easy in the case of "big" elections, but the existence of "less important" or special elections may not be realized by all.

The Voting Decision

Many individuals feel a duty to vote, and such a sentiment will surely contribute to voting. Many others view voting as a chance to indicate their preferences and influence policy and thus are motivated by self-interest and power-seeking.

Let us view the decision as a combination of information and judgement. Then, we can approach the problem by discovering ways of becoming informed and ways of making judgements. Keep in mind that no one is perfectly, fully informed and that perfect, certain judgement is unlikely to exist. People are no more likely to be perfect voters than perfect home-buyers. The task is to be better—and as competent as is reasonably possible.

Becoming Informed

There are some ground rules for being better informed. It goes without saying, perhaps, that a grasp of the organization and powers of government is helpful. Classes in government, and the reading of books like this one, will help. Reading newspapers and news magazines on a regular basis provides information about governments and issues.

Making Judgements

Once citizens cross a threshold of basic information, staying well informed is probably not all that difficult. Improving the ability to make judgements presents a more challenging problem. Voting requires choice, and choice requires preference. How can a person discover his/her own preferences without having public issues consume every waking moment of their lives?

Some people make use of an imperfect but (to them) fairly satisfactory shortcut. They "buy brand names." They vote straight tickets. Somehow they have become so strongly identified with one of the major parties that they will always support its candidates.

Are there drawbacks to this approach? Of course. Chapter 3 pointed out that candidates of the same party often disagree with each other. Straight party voters might be supporting inconsistent views. Is there some sense in such a straight party vote? Of course. It simplifies the voting act and is often associated with high voting turnout. It may well mean the voter votes for most of the candidates whom they would have supported anyway, after they had invested a lot of time and effort in researching the issues. Straight ticket voting was more popular in years past than it is today. In 1960 almost two-thirds of the American public voted a straight ticket. Today about two-thirds of the voters voted split tickets. In the 2002 election Michigan voters were given the option of ending "straight ticket" voting but chose to retain it.

Some people claim to be "independent." They "vote the person, not the party." Studies have shown that such "independent" behavior is really not all it appears to be. Most independents are ticket-splitters at the top of the ballot, but either do not vote the whole ballot or drift into a party pattern in more obscure contests. Studies also indicate that independents actually turn out less than people who identify with a party, and are, as a group, less informed than party indentifiers.

The above kinds of voting styles—straight party or ticket splitting independent—will not help a voter in all cases. In a non-partisan election, all voters are forced into "independent" behavior. They must focus on the candidate without a party label guide. This is also the case on ballot proposals. What guides are available to the voter?

Of course, strong feelings on an issue can, as in party elections, serve as a guide. In non-party elections how voters see the candidate's personality may be important. Also, a person desiring to vote and to influence policy has a number of other readily available short-cuts to judgement. There are sources of information which can make up a kind of "consumer guide" for voters.

Many interest groups carefully monitor issues and make public their judgements about how to vote on ballot proposals and candidates. They follow the votes of officeholders on issues that concern them and report the results (scores or ratings) to their members and the public. A member of the group, or a regular newspaper reader, could use these interest group endorsements as important factors in their decisions.

Likewise, a reasonably well-informed person desiring to influence policy through voting might survey newspaper endorsements. Different newspapers often have different political positions reflected in their editorials. If voters are aware of this, they can utilize the pattern of endorsements as a guide to voting. For example, the Detroit News is generally more conservative than the Detroit Free Press. If you think of yourself as a liberal, and/or tend to vote Democratic, you might survey both papers' endorsements and give more weight to those of the Free Press. If the reverse is true, go with the News. (If they agree, someone, or some issue, has impressed differing people quite a bit and probably deserves serious consideration.)

Newspapers in Michigan also regularly publish a "Voters' Guide" before every major election. The guide usually prepared by the League of Women

Voters, lists and briefly describes all the candidates running for office and the proposals on the ballot. State officeholders also print a basic summary of ballot proposals for the voters. Many websites also provide good information about officeholders, candidates and elections.

To summarize, this complicated task of deciding how to vote can be simplified somewhat. One can decide based on slogans, emotions, or candidate styles. One can use party label as a guide, or rely on newspaper or interest group endorsements. The most difficult task of all is to be so knowledgeable as to be truly independent. Only a few can possibly do this. Such a few would not include these authors. For most people, the voting decision depends on being fairly well informed, open-minded, and deciding whose knowledge and judgements to trust.

The Act of Voting

Once the decision has been made on how to vote, the rest is easy. Know where the voting location is. Experience will teach a voter when to go to the polls to avoid crowds. (This depends on the average age, work patterns and turnout levels of the precinct.) Election workers will clearly instruct a voter as to how to utilize the equipment. The legal limit of time one has at the voting stand or booth is two minutes, but it is seldom enforced. Taking notes, or a list, is helpful and legal.

Ballots are clearly organized. The first part of the ballot is the partisan section. In a general election, the ballot allows one to vote a straight ticket for any party by so indicating. One may also vote a straight ticket except for a few offices by indicating one's straight ticket preference and then indicating any exceptions. Or, a person may vote separately for each office. If a voter is allowed more than one vote for an office, this is clearly indicated on a ballot.

In a partisan primary, care is taken to arrange the candidates' names according to the office and according to party. All seeking nominations in the same party are grouped together. This helps discourage voters from illegally voting in the primary of more than one party. If there is a contest for nomination, the names of the candidates are rotated from precinct to precinct. This helps give fair treatment in ballot position. The same person's

name is not always the first to be seen at the top of the ballot.

Following the partisan part of the ballot is the non-partisan section. Only offices, candidates and an indication of how many votes one can cast are listed. Party labels do not appear. On all non-partisan ballots, names of candidates are rotated from precinct to precinct.

The next section of the ballot contains state and local ballot proposals. Each proposal is indicated by a number (state) or letter (local). A brief summary of each is printed on the ballot. The full content of each is officially filed with either the secretary of state or local clerk and is available to voters at election precincts as well as at those offices. A place is provided on the ballot for a "yes" or "no" vote.

Absentee Voting

Michigan law allows a voter to vote absentee. One may do so if one is: physically disabled, unable to vote on election day because of the tenets of one's religion, an election inspector away from his or her own precinct, 60 years of age or more, confined in jail awaiting trial, absent from the community on election day, a Michigan resident living in the District of Columbia, or a Michigan resident currently serving in the U.S. armed forces outside of Michigan.

Persons seeking to vote absentee in a primary election, general election or both must provide a written request to their local clerk, indicating their reason for voting absentee. This must be done by 2:00 p.m. on the Saturday before the election. Voting can occur at the clerk's office up to 4:00 p.m. on the day before the election. Voting can also be done at home, and the ballot must be returned to the clerk's office in time to be counted according to the normal schedule. To be safe, absentee voters should vote early. More and more Michigan residents take this opportunity. In a typical even-year election, 5-10% of the ballots will be absentee.

Whether voting at the polls or absentee, well-prepared voters will find the task of indicating their preference quite easy. The real work in voting---- becoming informed and making judgements—takes place between elections.

BEYOND VOTING: ACTIVISM

Many people are not satisfied with limiting their political activities to voting. For a variety of reasons, they seek a more continuous and direct influence on decision-making. There are many ways of doing this, short of running for office.

Party Activism

Political parties offer obvious opportunities for direct influence. The earlier discussion of party structure and decision-making reviewed how an individual can become involved. A basic step (beyond contributing money) is to become a precinct delegate. From that position a person can conceivably influence elections and platforms from the local to the national level. Details about this office were presented in chapter 3. Since parties deal with a wide range of issues, and seek to win in a wide variety of places and districts, party involvement provides a clear opportunity to focus on problems, conflicts, compromises and election strategy.

Interest Group Activism

This second activist style can be combined with the first, but need not be. In fact, it seems that more people are being attracted to interest group activism than party activity.

From the review of interest group activity in chapter 4 it should be clear that groups can be an attractive avenue for power-seeking. Groups usually focus on a few key issues, and a citizen may find group activism to be a way to target their own resources and concerns. The basic avenue to group activism is to join and contribute money to the group(s) of one's choice. Participation in meetings, grassroots activities, and "get out the vote" drives are open to supporters. Larger, better-established interest group organizations employ people as lobbyists and researchers, and many other groups hire such help on a temporary basis. Many groups encourage their members to become active in a party, hoping to influence its platform. For a person whose concerns are focused on a few issues, and more on policy than on holding office or influencing elections, interest group activity can be rewarding and effective.

Personal Activism

Some people seek to influence politics without becoming officeholders or affiliating with parties or groups. They might be found working on election campaigns of friends —the motivator is friendship, not party or policy. They write letters to officeholders and newspapers on a broad range of topics. Rather than devote all their available time to one group's goals, they contribute money to many groups. They can frequently be seen attending meetings of governmental bodies, which are nearly always open to the public.

WIDE-OPEN ACTIVISM: SEEKING OFFICE

In the United States there are over 450,000 elected officials. In Michigan alone, there are nearly 20,000. In every election year, thousands of Michiganians try to be elected to some public office, and countless others tried to be appointed to zoning boards, planning commissions, and the like.

Why Do People Run For Office?

People seek office for many reasons. Some run with a sense of civic duty. They view their candidacy as an obligation to the community. Others seek name recognition, hoping that a candidacy will help their business or professional career. Others are motivated by issue concerns—they seek office to have a chance to affect a particular policy. Still others may be more program or philosophy-oriented. They have ideas about many issues and what government should (or shouldn't) do about them. There is one thing they all have in common, whether they will admit it or not—they are power-seeking.

To some extent, seeking office may run in families. Many candidates will say their motivations are based in their childhood and upbringing. Nationally, we can see many examples: Roosevelts, Tafts, Kennedys, Browns, Goldwaters, and Bushs. In Michigan, we have the Fitzgeralds, Levins, Romneys, McColloughs, Dingells, and Hertels. For others, motivation may be rooted in schooling and profession. A background in the social sciences, law and business seems associated with the candidacies of many people. For yet others, some event or issue may be the important trigger, as may an attraction to a role model.

In most cases, identifying the basic motivation and its source is difficult. They are probably interwoven—most candidates would likely mention a combination of factors.

Deciding to Run

Being motivated is one thing. Actually seeking office is another. "To run or not to run, that is the question." It is not easy to answer. Many factors should be considered. Am I eligible for the office? Am I a citizen, the right age and a resident of the disttrict? How much time will be involved? How much money will it take and can that amount be raised? Can I finance myself? Is there an incumbent running for reelection? Do I need to be an active party member to run? Will there be a primary contest or can I be assured of at least being nominated? Is the district so "safe" for my party that I can be assured of winning if nominated? If not, is the district so competitive that I will at least have a chance of winning? If I have no chance of winning, is it worth it anyway, for my party or principles, sense of duty or name recognition? On whom can I count for help? If I win, is there a chance of moving up? Am I able to take losing? If I win, can I perform well in the office I seek? Finally, and perhaps most importantly for many candidates, what will this decision and its consequences mean for the family? Are we ready for all this?

Some of these questions can be easily answered. Election rules are known. Most people have a sense of how well-known and liked they are, and how much time, help, and money they have available to them. An election district's voting patterns can be carefully analyzed, based on its past voting behavior. As noted in chapter 3, the rise of independents and strong interest groups means that one can run in a party's primary without having been an active member—just circulate petitions. Other factors vary in importance for each individual.

Running

The person who has decided to run needs to get organized. The amount of organization needed will depend on the office sought. Small-scale local office seeking will not require as many specialized activities and people as large campaigns.

The differences in campaign organizations are usually differences in degree. Regardless of the office sought, nearly all campaigns require the same kinds of tasks. Any candidate must answer the following questions:

Based on analysis of the voters, what parts of the district are most and least likely to support me? Which are "on the fence"?

What issues am I prepared to emphasize? Am I going to run against someone else's record? Make pledges of my own? Use some combination of these?

Which individuals and groups are likely to play a role in this campaign? Whose endorsement can I get, and how?

Should I plan a single campaign approach (mailings, door-to-door work, TV and radio ads, name recognition), or must I combine these? If so, how should I mix them?

Depending on what I've decided to do, how am I going to finance it? Can I cover the cost? How and from whom will I raise money?

How will I organize the basic operation of preparing literature and commercials, putting up yard signs, passing cards at the polls, paying the bills, finding a headquarters, and a place (and refreshments) for my "victory party"?

Thus any campaign must organize many specialized activities. It is important that these not be kept entirely separate from each other. Care must be taken to keep the campaign parts together. This responsibility falls upon the candidate and, in large-scale campaigns, the *campaign manager*.

The decisions about campaign approaches are not left entirely to the candidate. There are some basic legal requirements which must be followed. There is an obvious public effect of campaigns, and it is natural that there are laws governing the process. Some of the most important laws affecting campaigns are those setting standards of fair campaign practices and those governing campaign finance. These are summarized on the following pages. Full details on such matters are available from the secretary of state and county clerks.

Suppose one wins. What happens next? In the case of some offices there are important decisions to be made right away. In November 2002, Jennifer Granholm was elected Governor of Michigan, the first Democrat to be elected to the office since 1990 and the first woman. The day after the election, almost without doubt, Ms. Granholm had to begin to plan her transition. How could she be prepared for the office on January 1, 2003? Would the former governor help her? On whom could she depend? Which persons would she appoint to key executive positions? What programs would she propose or change in the State of the State Message early next year? How could she possibly thank those who helped elect her? What would the current legislature and governor do in November and December? How could she arrange the details of the inauguration ceremony and festivities?

For most officials, taking office involves fewer worries. There is an oath to take, usually at the county clerk's office. There are people to thank, and others, with whom one will serve, to meet. There may be decisions to make about who should be chairperson of the county board or president of the city council or school board. Most officials don't have to relocate, or ponder scores or hundreds of appointments. They just settle in to begin making the decisions their office requires.

And, more often than not, they begin to think about the next campaign.

Staying in Office

Most elected officials seek reelection, or run next for a higher office. Studies show that most incumbents (those who hold an office) are successful in being reelected. Being in office provides a person with a number of important resources which can be skillfully used to help the person be elected

again. In this section, we hope to identify some of these.

Officeholders can stay in the public eye. Depending on the level of office, this can be done in different ways. More prominent offices provide help for those who hold the position. With staff help, press releases and newsletters can be used to keep one's name and actions before the voters. With or without staff help, an officeholder can make it a point to stay visible by making appearances before groups, and doing door-to-door work between campaigns. A few officeholders, such as the governor, are in the public eye automatically.

Another important part of staying in office is providing help to constituents—helping solve their problems with government. This is sometimes referred to as "cutting the red tape." As governments provide more and more services, individuals are often frustrated in having problems with government straightened out. Officeholders can often intervene to speed up solutions.

Listening to key groups in the district or community is very important. Voting against organized home district voter opinion is very risky. Being informed about group opinions, and trying to anticipate future opinions, is critical. A string of wrong votes, or even one or two on important issues, will invite competition at the next election. Such behavior might even cause an officeholder to be removed from office during his term.

All officials elected in Michigan, except judges, are subject to *recall* by the voters in the district in which they were elected. This procedure requires that a petition be signed by registered voters who live in the election district. The petition must contain signatures equal to at least 25% of the number of votes cast in the community or district for all candidates for the office of governor at the last general election. The reasons for recall must be clearly stated on the petitions, and will be reviewed for clarity by the county election commission. If the petition is certified as clear, a special election is promptly scheduled, usually within 30 to 90 days. Fewer than twenty states have a recall provision.

At that election, the people vote "yes" or "no" on the question of whether the official should lose his office. If an official is recalled, the vacancy is filled either by appointment or through another special election. State law determines the method used, and it depends mainly on how much time is left in the term of the vacant position. In any event, the person recalled may not be appointed or elected to the position created by their recall. While judges are not subject to recall by voters, they can be removed in other ways. These rare cases will be discussed in detail in chapter 9.

Of course, officials who hold an appointed office are also subject to removal. Some officials serve "at the pleasure of" a chief executive—the mayor, or governor for example. Also, many top officials in a government are often subject to impeachment and removal by the legislative branch of government. In rare instances, individuals lose their office by virtue of being convicted of a criminal offense. In such cases, many resign rather than face legal removal. Of course, they may still face criminal penalties.

Moving Up, Or Out

As noted earlier, most elected officials seek reelection. Most who do are reelected. Those who are not reelected have usually failed to do the kinds of things mentioned above—careful voting and service to people. In 1990 Gov. James Blanchard was defeated by State Senator John Engler in a surprising upset. Another reason for not being reelected is redistricting. Every 10 years election districts are redrawn and many officials find themselves having to fight for renomination or reelection in new territory, perhaps against another incumbent. In 2002 several Democratic members of the U.S. House were forced out of their positions as a result of redistricting. The new boundaries may mean a new political balance, and candidates might not survive the reelection effort. The effects of redistricting and gerrymandering on elections were summarized in chapter 5.

Some people desire higher office. One of the key factors involved in their choice is timing. Some incumbents can seek election to a higher office without losing their current position. In 1982, for example, Oakland County Prosecutor Brooks Patterson first sought the Republican nomination for governor. He was defeated by Richard Headlee in the Republican primary. Then he was nominated by the Republican state convention as the party's candidate for attorney general. He lost in the general election. He remained Oakland county prosecutor through all this. He had been elected to that position's four year term in 1980, and could safely run for the other offices in 1982. Others may not be in the same situation. In 2002 Representative David Bonoir sought the Democratic nomination for governor and lost. Due to redistricting he chose not to seek reelection to the U.S. House. Attorney General Jennifer Granholm ran for governor and was successful. Had she lost, she would have also lost her position as Attorney General. Timing and the scheduling of elections are important.

People often leave office voluntarily. Life's circumstances change, and some officials resign during their term—to take a new job, or move, for example. Others simply decide not to seek reelection. Obviously, many factors might account for this—health, redistricting, career, strain on family life, relocation, or loss of interest. Most of the turnover in office is related to this "voluntary quitting" phenomenon.

Term Limits:Michigan's Response

In the 1992 election, Michigan voters approved a proposal (Proposal B) that limited the terms of a number of elected officals. The amendment to the Michigan Constitution attempted to limit the number of terms that Michigan officeholders could serve either in Lansing or in Washington.

However, in 1995 the U.S. Supreme Court found that a state's attempt to limit the terms of the U.S. Congress was unconstitutional would require an amendment to the U.S. Constitution.

The new amendment restricts the Michigan governor, lieutenant governor, secretary of state and attorney general to two four-year terms. It also limits members of the state House to three two-year terms and the state senators to two four-year terms. The state term limits began on Jan 1, 1993 and do not apply to terms served prior to that date.

CAMPAIGN FINANCE LAW

The Michigan Campaign Finance Law of 1976 provides a means by which the public can be aware of the contributions a candidate receives. The law requires a candidate to file financial reports indicating the source of campaign contributions. It requires that reports on campaign funding be available before election day so that voters will be aware of a candidate's financial backers, and that final reports be filed after the election. Limits are set on individual and group contributions, and a variety of other regulations indicate the kind of records that must be kept, how campaign committees must be formed and what kind of financial reports must be made.

There are a great many details to the Michigan Campaign Finance Law— too many for a complete discussion in this book. However, the following chart might help to indicate the basic nature of the law. For example, the maximum contributions for a given election cycle are as follows:

	Political Commitees and Individuals	Independent Committees District and County Political Party Committees	State Central Party Committees
Governor	$3,400	$34,000	$68,000
Lt. Governor	$3,400	$34,000	$68,000
State Senator	$1,000	$10,000	$10,000
State Rep	$500	$ 5,000	$ 5,000
Many other state elective offices (varies with size of the district)	$3,400	$34,000	$68,000

The same campaign law also provides for the public financing of gubernatorial elections. Candidates for governor are eligible for public financing if they raise $75,000 in contributions of $100 or less. They may then receive $2 for every $1 they collect in amounts of $100 or less. The state campaign fund will pay up to 75 percent of that amount. In a contested primary election a major party candidate may receive up to $990,000 of state funding. For the general election each major candidate receives $1,125,000. No candidate may spend over $2 million total for a single election. This public funding program is financed by a $3 "check off" provision on the state income campaign ($6 for joint returns). The campaign fund is similar to the presidential check-off on the federal income tax form.

In 1996, amendments to the Campaign Finance Law set contribution limits for campaigns for all local offices in Michigan. These limits vary by the office and by the population of the district (county, school district, city) in which the election is held. The law sets dollar limits on contributions by individuals, political committees, independent committees and county, congressional district and state party committees.

The administration of the law is the responsibility of county clerks, the secretary of state, county prosecutors and the state attorney general. Reports are filed with either the clerks or secretary of state and violations of the law are prosecuted by either the prosecutors or attorney general. Which officials are involved depends on the office sought by a candidate.

Source: League of Women Voters of Michigan, *The State We're In,* Lansing, 1998

Part 3

State Government in Michigan

Introduction

Michigan's Executive Branch

Michigan's Legislature

Michigan's Judiciary

Introduction to Part 3

Learning Objectives

What is meant by "separation of powers"? What are the branches into which the powers are separated? Why is this done?

What are "checks and balances"? Give examples of how this is achieved in Michigan.

Why is "separate institutions sharing governmental power" a good description of the organization of Michigan's state government?

Key Terms To Know

separation of powers
checks and balances

This part of the book will examine Michigan's state-level decision makers. These offices exercise the major powers of state government.

The U.S. Constitution makes references to the executive, legislative and judicial branches of state government. The people who wrote that document were speaking from experience because the 13 states in existence at the time were usually organized along these lines. The national Constitution does not, however, provide much detail on state government. The specifics of the organization of state governments are found in state constitutions and state laws.

Generally, the states use the national government as a model. All states divide governmental decision-making between executive, legislative and judicial offices. This division into three branches is commonly known as separation of powers. Each branch has authority over one aspect of government's decision making. The legislative branch legislates—it makes the laws. The judicial branch adjudicates—it resolves disputes about these laws, and interprets their meaning. The executive branch executes—it carries out or administers the laws. These branches may only take those actions which are allowed by the state's Constitution and those acts may not violate the Constitution or laws of the United States.

What is the purpose of dividing the authority to make, adjudicate and enforce laws? Why not just elect a person or a few people and give this person or committee full use of government's authority? In a few words, the purpose is this: dividing government's authority prevents that authority from being controlled by a few.

To fully accomplish this goal, one must do more than separate the three functions. The offices must be arranged so that no branch can use its share of authority without having to answer to one or both of the others, or to the people. This will not only prevent the executive from legislating or adjudicating, but also prevent the executive from executing without controls by the legislature, the courts, or the people.

This idea, closely related to separation of powers, is called checks and balances. Each branch of government has a say in the work of the others. Each can check the work of the others. Sometimes the check allows one branch to stop an action of another. In other cases, one branch may be able to influence the decision of another.

In Michigan, this is achieved in a number of ways. Some of the checks are established in the state Constitution. For example, the governor may veto any bill passed by the legislature. If the governor vetoes a measure, a two-thirds majority in each house of the legislature is required to make the bill a law. This is a higher majority than the simple majority (fifty percent plus one) normally required for passage.

Other checks are less formal. For example, the governor is required to submit a proposed budget to the legislature each year. The legislature does not have to approve this proposal. It can make many changes. However, the governor's proposal usually sets the tone of the budget debate and serves as a practical limit on the options of the legislature.

As another illustration, consider the following chart:

Figure I.3.1

OFFICE	NUMBER	TERM (YRS)	METHOD OF SELECTION
Governor	1	4	statewide-partisan
Legislature			
Senate	38	4	districts-partisan
House	110	2	districts-partisan
Supreme Court	7	8 (overlapping)	statewide non-partisan

Since the branches differ in size, term of office and method of selection, it is possible that those in control of the different offices will have different points of view on issues, especially if they are of different parties. Even if the same party has majority control of all the offices, the internal conflicts and differences within the major parties (mentioned in chapter 3) will probably result in conflicts between the branches.

The chart below summarizes Michigan's version of "separation of powers, checks and balances." (The text will examine many of these details in later chapters.) The chart shows how state government is made up of "separate institutions sharing powers." Each branch has ways of checking the others. The powers of one are overlapped by one or more powers of each of the others! This overlapping, or sharing, is what allows the checking to occur.

Thus Michigan, like other states and the national government, blends separate institutions into one government. This "oneness" is reflected in the fact that all officers take the same oath (Michigan Constitution, Article 11, section 1.) It reads:

"I do solemnly swear (or affirm) that I will support the Constitution of the United States and the Constitution of this state, and that I will faithfully discharge the duties of the office of (_____), according to the best of my ability."

Figure I.3.2.

CHECKS AND BALANCES: HOW BRANCHES OF STATE GOVERNMENT AFFECT EACH OTHER			
	EXECUTIVE	**LEGISLATIVE**	**JUDICIAL**
EXECUTIVE POWER OF:	ENFORCE the laws	Creates departments and agencies Senate may reject people nominated to head departments Approves budget Reviews department rules May impeach and remove executive officials May ask Supreme Court to rule on governor's ability to serve	May declare acts of executive unconstitutional May rule on ability of governor to serve, if asked
LEGISLATIVE POWERS OF:	Special messages to legislature Call special sessions Appeals to public on issues Prepares and administers budget Veto of bills Item veto of money bills	MAKE the laws	May declare acts of the legislature unconstitutional Interprets the laws of the state as cases arise
JUDICIAL POWERS OF:	May grant reprieves, pardons, commutations Request rendition of persons from other states Appoint judges in case of vacancy May initiate court proceedings	May create new courts Defines powers of courts to hear certain kinds of cases (jurisdiction) for law violations	INTERPRET Constitution and laws

Chapter 7

Michigan's Executive Branch

Origins Of The State Executive

Becoming And Remaining Governor

Being Governor: The Roles Of The Governor

The Governor As Executive

Chapter Appendix: Michigan—Some Bureaucratic Basics

> *"The executive power is vested in the governor."*
> Article V, Sect. 1, Michigan Constitution

Chapter 7

Learning Objectives

Were early governors "strong" or "weak"? Why were the offices made that way?

How does one become governor of Michigan? What kinds of backgrounds have recent Michigan governors had?

How can a vacancy exist in the governorship? What happens when the office is vacant?

How does one become Lieutenant Governor? What are the principal duties of the office?

Identify the various roles of the governor. What actions are taken in each role?

Describe the veto powers of the governor.

How can the governor affect the sentences of people convicted of a crime in Michigan?

How is the governor helped by staff in the executive office?

What are the departments of Michigan state government? How do the departments differ from each other?

Can it be said that the governor has complete control over the executive branch? Why not?

How are the departments of state government established? How can this organization be changed?

Key Terms To Know

governor	pardon	lieutenant governor
reprieve	succession	commutation
roles	chief executive	veto
bureaucracy	line item veto	advise and consent
staff - Executive Office	executive order	party leader

In the 1963 Constitution, Article 4 deals with the legislature and Article 5 deals with the executive. Here, the executive branch is presented first. Why? Has the legislature slipped in importance? Not necessarily. Has the executive branch increased in importance? Absolutely! The executive branch can be viewed as the engine of government. On issue after issue, the governor and other executives play the leading role. This chapter explores the reasons for this.

The Constitution of 1963 strengthened the executive in a number of important ways. The governor is a widely-recognized person, a symbol of state government to many citizens. People often relate to state government through the actions of this single person—whole periods of time are understood by reference to the governor (the "Williams era"). Frequently, the governor is a leader — a person who (with some help) identifies problems, develops his own preferred solutions, and influences public opinion, group leaders, and legislators in order to make those preferences law. Governors are power-seekers. Governors are well situated to respond to crisis, whether "payless paydays" (Williams), urban problems, including riots (Romney) or economic stagnation (Blanchard and Engler). Many rules and regulations are made by government agencies, not legislatures. As the person who (in most cases) has the most influence over these agencies, the governor is in a position to shape these rules.

For these and other reasons, the governor can be considered to be at the center of political conflict and decision-making in Michigan. While governors share power with legislators and judges, the executive is usually the most active in attempts to find and use it.

ORIGINS OF THE STATE EX-ECUTIVE BRANCH

Every state has a governor. These offices first developed with the colonial governors, who were usually agents of the king. In carrying out the king's wishes, colonial governors often upset the colonists, and the office began to be looked upon with disfavor. Because of this dislike, the earliest state constitutions limited the governorship. While the office was kept as the top executive office, it was held on a short rein by a number of devices. Terms of office were usually short—2 years was common, as in Michigan from statehood until 1966. In some states, governors were prohibited from holding office for more than one or two terms. Often, they were not allowed to veto the acts of the legislature, or to appoint many people to other executive positions. Sometimes, the governor would have to share executive authority with other elected or appointed officials. In many cases, the governor was appointed by the legislature! Of all of Michigan's constitutions, that of 1850 best reflects the philosophy of weakening the governor.

Recent thinking about the office of governor is different. Lately, in Michigan and many other states, the office has been made stronger. In Michigan's 1963 Constitution, for example, the term of office was lengthened to 4 years. The number of other elected officials was reduced and the power of the governor to reorganize the executive branch was strengthened.

Michigan's governor is among the most powerful in the nation. One student of governorships compared state executives by taking into account the length of term, the ability to get re-elected, the type of veto power, and appointments and budget powers. Based on this study Michigan's governor ranked as the 13th strongest in the nation. In the midwest Michigan's governor is considered stronger than those of Indiana and Wisconsin and weaker than those of Illinois and Ohio. Several New England states and much of the deep south have weaker governors. West Virginia, Maryland and New Jersey are considered to have the strongest.

BECOMING AND REMAINING GOVERNOR

The formal requirements for becoming governor are minimal. Any candidate for governor must be at least 30 years of age. He or she must have been a registered elector in Michigan for the four years preceding the election, and be nominated for the office by a political party. Major party nominations are in the August primary. (See discussion in chapter 5).

These formal requirements for becoming governor will probably not be the only ones considered by the voters. Many are eligible to be governor. Many wish to be governor. Many run for the office. But few are nominated, and fewer still are chosen. What kinds of backgrounds do these people have? The summary of the backgrounds of Michigan's last seven governors, which appears in this chapter, sheds some light on these informal or unwritten qualifications. If elected, one's term begins at noon on January 1 following the election. Unlike the legislature, the governor's office is always in session.

Remaining Governor

As a result of a successful term limit drive in 1992, Michigan's governor is limited to two four-year terms. There are also a number of ways one can lose the office during a term. A vacancy in the office can be caused by death (this happened once), by resignation (4 times) or by impeachment and removal by the legislature (this never has happened). The office also becomes vacant if the governor is convicted of an "infamous" crime, or an offense violating the oath of office. The office is vacated if there is a finding that the election was void, or if the governor-elect refused to take the oath of office. A vacancy would occur if the governor ceased to be a legal resident of the state, or is recalled. If a governor were recalled, most legal experts argue that the lieutenant governor would take over, though there is some debate on the point.

The governorship can be temporarily vacant. This occurs when the governor is travelling outside the state. The Constitution provides (Article V, section 26) that a majority of the state Supreme Court shall determine the inability of the governor to serve, if asked by the president pro tem of the state Senate and the Speaker of the House. The court can also decide, at its own initiative, if and when the inability ceases. This provision is intended to deal with circumstances such as extended illness, and has never been used since first established in the 1963 Constitution. When there is a vacancy in the office of governor the lieutenant governor assumes responsibility. If the vacancy is permanent, the lieutenant governor becomes governor. If the vacancy is temporary, the lieutenant governor becomes acting governor.

The Lieutenant Governor

The lieutenant governor is next in line for the office of governor and must meet the same legal qualifications as a candidate for governor. The term of office is 4 years.

Candidates for the office of lieutenant governor are nominated at party conventions after the August primaries. The convention usually nominates a person selected by the party's candidate for governor as a running-mate. In the general election, voters vote for the pair as a "ticket." Thus, the elected governor and lieutenant governor are always of the same party and usually compatible with each other. This was not always the case. Prior to the 1963 Constitution, lieutenant governor nominees were chosen in party primaries and separately elected. The lieutenant governor and governor might have been of the same party but different philosophies, or even of different parties! The latter never happened.

The Constitution establishes some duties for the lieutenant governor. In addition to possibly becoming governor, the lieutenant governor presides over the state Senate, may vote if there is a tie in that body and performs such duties as may be requested by the governor. The Constitution does not permit any power of the governor to be delegated (permanently given) to the lieutenant governor, but governors often assign important responsibilities to the lieutenant governor.

There are two ways in which the office of lieutenant governor can become vacant. A vacancy would exist if the lieutenant governor becomes governor, which has happened five times. The office of lieutenant governor could also become vacant through the death or resignation of the lieutenant governor, each of which has happened two times, or removal by the legislature. See p. 83 for details on succession.

BEING GOVERNOR: THE ROLES OF THE GOVERNOR

A governor wears many hats at the same time. This section will identify most of these roles and show how they overlap. In order to perform all these roles effectively, a governor must be an individual of many talents and will need a lot of help in performing his complex job. Some of the roles are defined by the state Constitution or laws, sometimes quite precisely. Many of them have grown by custom and have developed as the political system and technology have changed.

Executive Roles

The governor is the head of the executive branch of the state. It is the duty of this branch to enforce (carry out) the laws of the state. Of all the roles, this one is surely the most important and complex. There are hundreds of state agencies grouped into 20 departments. The range of state laws and programs is vast, and the control of administration of laws requires constant, painstaking effort. The entire next section of this chapter will be devoted to this role.

Symbol of the State

The governor is known to nearly all people of the state. Advanced media coverage has encouraged this. The executive branch is a fairly unified branch and most executive authority is vested in a single person. The prominence of the governor as the head of a branch seems to cause many citizens to view the governor as the government! While obviously incorrect, this tendency underscores the symbolic importance of the office. The office becomes identified with the state, its people, and their hopes and frustrations.

Ceremonial and Diplomatic Roles

The governor can frequently be seen leading ceremonies in the state. Speaking at graduation exercises, receiving out-of-state dignitaries, leading hikers across the Mackinac Bridge, and representing Michigan at various national conferences are all examples of these ceremonial roles. These activities attest to the symbolic importance of the office.

The governor is often a chief diplomat when he meets with other governors to discuss relationships between states. Sometimes a governor will meet with foreign leaders to discuss matters of mutual concern. Michigan's close proximity to Canada makes this role especially important.

Party Leader

The governor is the highest ranking state official elected under a party's label. While U.S. senators also get elected state-wide, their national office does not translate into the kind of state party leadership shown by governors. As pointed out earlier the parties are based more on state organization than national.

Immediately after nomination in the party primary, a candidate for governor can begin to enhance his own appeal and strengthen the party by influencing the party convention's choice of nominees for lieutenant governor, secretary of state, attorney general, and state education boards. A governor (or candidate) can help others in the party in their campaigns for various offices.

Governors are in a position to make many appointments to state executive positions during their term of office. Most of these appointments are subject to rejection by the Senate but this happens rarely, even when the Senate is controlled by the other party. Furthermore, a governor may fill any judicial vacancy by direct appointment and may also fill any vacancy in the office of secretary of state, attorney general or U.S. senator by direct appointment. These appointive powers give a governor the opportunity to consolidate power by appointing his party and personal supporters to various positions. In those cases where law requires appointees to be of a different party (some examples of this are presented below) the governor may seek to appoint people with a philosophy as close as possible to his own.

Legislative Roles

While governors can't make laws, they can, and usually do, have great influence on the legislative process. Much proposed legislation originates in the governor's office. With staff help, the governor develops ideas which eventually take shape in the form of bills for consideration by the legislature. The most visible example of this is in the budget process. The governor's office develops a comprehensive executive budget document for consideration by the legislature. This document eventually takes the form of bills. These bills set the legislative agenda.

Many laws are actually in the form of rules, definitions, and regulations made by executive departments. These departments and their agencies are under the influence of the governor, and the rules the departments propose will likely reflect the governor's wishes. These rules are subject to veto by the legislature as discussed in chapter 8.

The governor's legislative roles include efforts to shape the opinion of the public and legislators. A governor can influence the legislative process through state-wide television appeals to citizens for their support, by conferences with media representatives, speeches to interest group conventions and special messages to the legislature. If a problem is viewed as urgent the legislature may be called into special session by the governor, to deal with that question only.

The Veto

The governor has the power to veto any bill passed by both houses of the legislature. He or she has 14 days, measured in hours and minutes, to act. If the governor approves of a bill, it must be signed within 14 days to become law. If the governor disapproves of the bill, and the legislature has adjourned within those 14 days, the bill will not become law. This is known as a "pocket veto." If the governor disapproves of the bill, but does not want to veto it and if the legislature is still in session, the bill will become law without the governor's signature.

If the governor disapproves, and the legislature is still in session, the bill may be sent back to the house in which it originated, along with the governor's objections. That chamber must reconsider the bill. If the bill is passed by that chamber with a vote of two-thirds or more, the bill is to be sent to the other chamber for its consideration. If passed in the second chamber with a two-thirds vote or more, the bill will become law despite the governor's objection. The veto power is summarized in the following chart:

Figure 7.2

EXECUTIVE VETO PROCEDURE

Governor may within 14 days:

Sign Bill	Becomes law.
Veto Bill	Return to legislature. Becomes law only if overridden by two-thirds vote in each chamber.
Do Nothing	Becomes law without his signature if the legislature is in session.
	Does not become law if legislature has adjourned.

The governor's veto power is even stronger in the case of appropriation bills. These are bills requiring that a certain amount of money be spent for particular state programs. The governor may veto any distinct item or items in such a bill. This is a line-item veto. Parts approved become law. Any part rejected is not law, unless the item veto is overridden by the legislature as outlined above.

These veto powers certainly put the governor right in the middle of the legislative process. Even if the legislature is in the control of another party, governors can use the veto as a "bargaining chip." It is a power rarely used, but even its threat can help a governor influence legislation. When used, the veto is rarely overridden.

During legislative deliberations on bills the governor's office is organized to keep up with the status of important bills and influence decisions. The governor's staff and other executive branch officials can often be seen in legislative committee meetings and legislators' offices. They will be seeking to get votes lined up for bills the governor wants. This lobbying can be very effective, because the executive officials are usually well armed with a combination of statistics, evidence, appeals to party loyalty and other debating points.

Judicial Roles

A governor can have considerable impact on the judicial system of Michigan. As noted earlier, the governor may fill any judicial vacancy by direct appointment. The state Senate may not reject the governor's choice. Thus a governor has the chance to shape the philosophy and quality of justice in Michigan.

Subject to guidelines established in laws, the governor may grant reprieves, commutations and pardons for all offenses, except in cases of impeachment. (Unlike the power of the U.S. president in these matters, the governor may not grant a pardon for an offense until a person has been convicted of it.) A reprieve is the delaying of punishment. A commutation is a change in penalty to one of less severity. A pardon is the forgiving and releasing of a person from punishment for an offense they committed. Some pardons are complete. Others are conditional, requiring certain behavior from the person. These are known as parole. (See chapter 9 for more detail.)

The governor may also request governors of other states to return to Michigan a person who has fled its justice process. Likewise, a governor may order the return of a person from Michigan to any other state whose justice process they have fled. These procedures are known as interstate rendition or extradition. While it seems clear in the U.S. Constitution that these exchanges are to be automatic, governors occasionally refuse to cooperate with each other. Finally, a governor can begin court proceedings (but not against the legislature) in order to secure compliance with, or enforcement of, the laws of the state.

Help For The Governor

The discussion of the roles of the governor indicates that the office has many responsibilities. Thus, it is necessary that the governor have assistance. The governorship, while a one-person office, includes many advisors and aides.

The following are typical staff offices for most Michigan governors:

Executive Office - usually headed by a very influential chief-of-staff, co-ordinates the work of all the other elements, and the day-to-day schedule of the governor

External Affairs- assists the governor in making appointments in the judicial and executive branches. Also provides services to constituents, responds to citizen mail.

Public Affairs/Communications- co-ordinates relations between the governor and the media, speech writing.

Legal Counsel -provides legal advice to the governor

Legislative Affairs-lobbies for governor's positions in legislature

Government Affairs/Strategic Initiatives-analyzes bills passed by legislature, helps develop the governor's program in bill form, coordinates lobbying efforts, attempts to coordinate the departments

S.E. Michigan, Northern Michigan and Washington Offices -coordinate relations with local government in the Detroit metro area, Northern Michigan and presents views of governor in national policy-making

These positions are funded in the state's budget. Appointees to these positions are not in the state's "civil service" but are appointed by and responsible to the governor. Most appointees have been associated with the governor a long time, and are part of his "personal team."

THE GOVERNOR AS EXECUTIVE

Article 5, section 1 of Michigan's Constitution says "The executive power is vested in the governor." The word "chief" used to appear before "executive" in that sentence, but was eliminated in the 1963 Constitution. "Chief" was removed because it was considered a limitation on the executive power. (In other words, if the governor was "chief" executive, then there must be others with some executive power.) With the word "chief" missing, the Constitution seems to indicate that the governor is the executive. One can get the impression that all

Figure 7.3

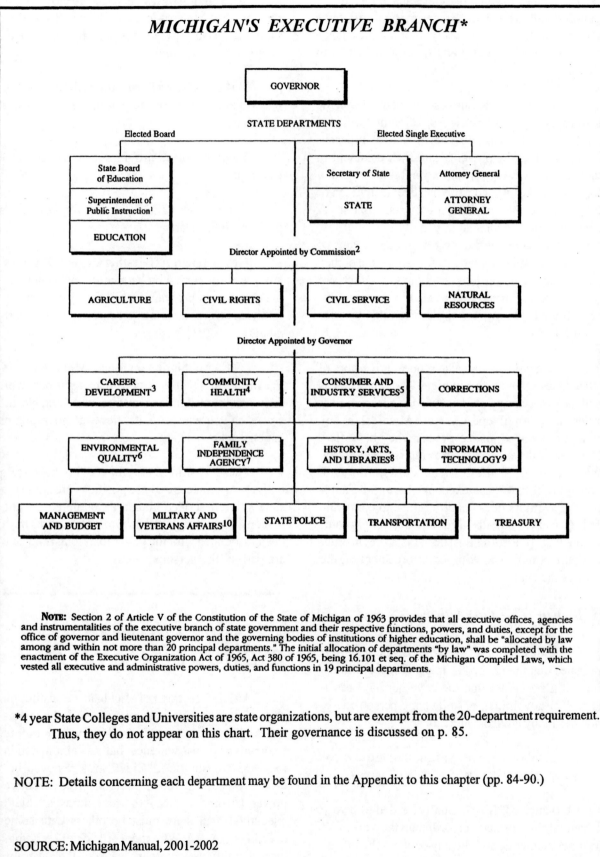

MICHIGAN'S EXECUTIVE BRANCH*

GOVERNOR

STATE DEPARTMENTS

Elected Board   Elected Single Executive

State Board of Education

Superintendent of Public Instruction[1]

EDUCATION

Secretary of State

STATE

Attorney General

ATTORNEY GENERAL

Director Appointed by Commission[2]

AGRICULTURE   CIVIL RIGHTS   CIVIL SERVICE   NATURAL RESOURCES

Director Appointed by Governor

CAREER DEVELOPMENT[3]   COMMUNITY HEALTH[4]   CONSUMER AND INDUSTRY SERVICES[5]   CORRECTIONS

ENVIRONMENTAL QUALITY[6]   FAMILY INDEPENDENCE AGENCY[7]   HISTORY, ARTS, AND LIBRARIES[8]   INFORMATION TECHNOLOGY[9]

MANAGEMENT AND BUDGET   MILITARY AND VETERANS AFFAIRS[10]   STATE POLICE   TRANSPORTATION   TREASURY

NOTE: Section 2 of Article V of the Constitution of the State of Michigan of 1963 provides that all executive offices, agencies and instrumentalities of the executive branch of state government and their respective functions, powers, and duties, except for the office of governor and lieutenant governor and the governing bodies of institutions of higher education, shall be "allocated by law among and within not more than 20 principal departments." The initial allocation of departments "by law" was completed with the enactment of the Executive Organization Act of 1965, Act 380 of 1965, being 16.101 et seq. of the Michigan Compiled Laws, which vested all executive and administrative powers, duties, and functions in 19 principal departments.

*4 year State Colleges and Universities are state organizations, but are exempt from the 20-department requirement. Thus, they do not appear on this chart. Their governance is discussed on p. 85.

NOTE: Details concerning each department may be found in the Appendix to this chapter (pp. 84-90.)

SOURCE: Michigan Manual, 2001-2002

executive activities in the state are under the complete control of the governor. Such a view is a bit oversimplified. It overlooks the fact that some executive responsibilities are given to other elected officials, and that there are some limits on the controls the governor has in other areas.

The Organization of Michigan's Executive Branch

Michigan's Constitution requires that the executive branch be organized by law into no more than twenty principal departments. The office of governor and lieutenant governor, the governing bodies of the University of Michigan, Michigan State University and Wayne State University and certain temporary agencies are not included in this limit. Within the departments, agencies are to be grouped as far as possible according to their major purposes.

Taken as a whole, we call this collection of agencies the state's "bureaucracy." A bureaucracy is a more or less organized group of offices with specialized responsibilities, a chain of command, a degree of permanence, and is involved in the production of goods (as in a corporation) or the delivery of programs or services (as in government). At the present time, the state executive branch is organized into 20 departments. Each of these is made up of a number of specialized offices, agencies, bureaus, and boards. This organization appears in figure 7.3.

The departments of state government differ from one another in many important ways. They each have responsibility in differing areas. Some of them administer state services only, while others are involved in relationships with local governments and their services. One of the most important differences between the departments concerns the manner in which the department is directed, or headed. Four different approaches are used in Michigan.

1) Two departments are headed by an elected official. These are Department of State and the Attorney General. These officials are chosen by the voters in partisan elections at the same time as the governor. They may be of a different party than the governor, and serve 4 year terms.

2) One department (Education) is headed by an elected, partisan board. The State Board of Education is an 8-person body. Two seats are filled every two years at the state-wide general election. Terms are 8 years. The board chooses the director of the department, the State Superintendent of Public Instruction. The governor is an ex-officio member of the board, with no vote. (You will note that Michigan elects many top bureaucrats. Currently, Michigan has 36 elected state administrators—the highest in the nation.)

3) Four departments are headed by an appointed commission. The governor appoints the commissioners as the terms expire, with the advice and consent of the state Senate, but the director of the department is chosen by the commission, not the governor. The Civil Rights department is established by the state Constitution and has an 8 member commission. The Civil Service department is established by the constitution and has a 4 member commission. Other commission departments, established by law, are Agriculture (5 members) and Natural Resources (7 members.)

In all of these, except Natural Resources there is a requirement that the two major political parties in the state be represented. The departments have bi-partisan commissions. Law requires that the parties be as evenly balanced as possible.

4) The remaining departments are headed by a single director appointed by the governor, with the advice and consent of the Senate. These are the Departments of Consumer and Industry Services, Corrections, Career Development, Management and Budget, Military and Veterans Affairs, Community Health, State Police, Family Independence Agency, History, Arts and Libraries, Information Technology, Transportation, Environmental Quality and Treasury.

In cases where the "advice and consent" of the Senate is part of the appointment process, the Senate has 60 days from the time the governor nominates a person to reject the nomination. If the Senate does not act to reject the nomination, the person nominated takes office.

The Governor--Chief Executive?

One key feature of the organization of Michigan's executive branch is that the governor's powers are somewhat limited. The governor is not in the same position as the president who may (in almost all cases) appoint persons of their own party to the top positions in all departments, subject to approval by the U.S. Senate. In Michigan, executive power is limited and divided in many ways. Some departments have elected heads, and others require people of both parties to be appointed. The terms of these officials do not expire at the same time and the Senate can reject the governor's nominees.

Furthermore, in the early 1960s, at the time the departments were created and the 120 or so then-existing agencies were folded into 19 (now 20) departments, some agencies were allowed to keep a considerable amount of independence. (These are called Type I agencies.) In this case, the authority of the governor to appoint the department head might not translate into genuine control.

These limits do not leave the governor powerless. Even in cases where the governor's power seems very limited, as in departments headed by elected officials or bi-partisan boards, the governor has many ways of influencing the actions of these departments. The governor has visibility and prestige. Laws affecting the department, including budget bills, are subject to the veto. The governor can inquire into the condition and administration of any public office, and receive written information from all executive officials, elected or appointed. The governor may suspend or remove any executive official for neglect or corrupt conduct in office.

What can we conclude? The governor is not an all-powerful executive. There are checks and limits on the authority of the office. Nevertheless, we can properly view the governor as the person with the ultimate responsibility to "take care that the laws be faithfully executed."

SUCCESSION TO THE OFFICE OF GOVERNOR

Michigan's 1963 Constitution provides (Article 5, section 26) that the order of succession to the office of governor is:

-the lieutenant governor
-the elected secretary of state
-the elected attorney general
-"such other persons designated by law"

By law, those others are:
-the president pro tem of the Senate, and
-the speaker of the House of Representatives

While this would appear to guarantee Michigan residents continuity in government, there may be serious flaws in the succession provisions. For example, law allows the governor to fill vacancies in the secretary of state and attorney general positions, but the appointee would not have been "elected." Would such appointees be eligible to become governor? Furthermore, those listed below lieutenant governor are not necessarily of the same party as the governor.

The most serious flaw lies in the uncertainty about the order of succession if the person elected as lieutenant governor leaves the office through death, removal, resignation or succession to the governorship. Until recently Michigan law (Public Act 44, 1981) seemed to allow the state Senate to appoint an "acting lieutenant governor." In 1995 however, the attorney general ruled that the law was unconstitutional and that there was "no constitutional authority to fill a vacancy in the office of lieutenant governor."

Thus, Michigan might be in a situation similar to that of the nation after the 1963 assassination of President John Kennedy. Vice-President Lyndon Johnson became president, and the vice-presidency was vacant until 1965. Had Johnson left office, the speaker of the U.S. House would have become president. This was corrected by the 25th amendment of 1967, which allows a president to nominate a person to fill a vacancy in the vice-presidency, with approval of the nominee by both houses of Congress. Michigan's Gerald Ford became vice-president this way in 1973 after Spiro Agnew resigned the vice-presidency. After Richard Nixon resigned the presidency in 1974, Ford became president and nominated Nelson Rockefeller as vice-president. This amendment provided continuity of position and party.

Recently there has been some controversy over succession to the governorship in the case of a recall. The Michigan Constitution specifies that the lieutenant governor takes over in case of a vacancy. However, the Michigan recall law requires a special election to fill an office vacated by a recall. Though the issue is still to be tested in court, most legal experts argue that the Constitution would take priority and that the lieutenant governor would take over.

Several years ago, the state legislature proposed a constitutional amendment (Proposal H-1980) which would have eliminated the lieutenant governor's role in the state Senate and allowed the governor to nominate a person to fill a vacancy in the lieutenant governorship, subject to the approval of both houses of the legislature. This would have assured party and succession continuity. The ballot was very crowded in 1980, and Proposal H was low on the proposal list. It lost, 1.9 million — 1.4 million.

MICHIGAN: BUREAUCRATIC BASICS

This chapter Appendix will provide an introduction to the activities of the various state departments. Readers interested in more detail should consult a recent edition of the Michigan Manual or the Executive Budget proposal. Both sources are rich in "bureaucratic" detail.

The basic organization of most departments dates to Act 380, Public Acts of 1965. In that law the legislature consolidated the many (over 120) agencies in state government according to the general requirements of the new 1963 Constitution (Article 5, sections 2 and 3.) More than any other recent governor, John Engler reshaped the bureaucracy, issuing over 100 executive reorganization orders during his 12 years in office.

Change in the organization of the departments is possible. This can be done by legislation, constitutional amendment or executive order. Under the executive order method, the governor submits to the legislature any plan for reorganization of the department(s) which is felt necessary or desirable. If the plan requires the force of law to be effective, the legislature has sixty days to consider the plan. If both houses disapprove, the change is not made. Otherwise, the order becomes effective on the date designated by the governor. All the departments are headquartered in Lansing and most maintain many offices throughout the state.

Department of State

Headed by the elected Secretary of State, this department (the state's oldest) has a wide variety of responsibilities. Among its many activities are:

-registering and titling motor vehicles and issuing license plates
-licensing vehicle operators, auto dealers, auto repair facilities, mechanics, and private driver education schools
-registering and titling watercraft, snowmobiles, and off-road vehicles
-supervising all elections in Michigan
-administering the campaign finance laws and assisting in the registration of voters
-keeping vital state and local government documents and records
-operating a system of branch offices in each of the eighty-three counties of the state.

Department of the Attorney General

Headed by the elected Attorney General, the chief law enforcement officer of the state, this department:

-may give opinions as to the meaning of laws; these formal opinions have the force of law unless overturned in court
-may serve as legal counsel for the legislature and any official or agency of state government
-may intervene in any lawsuit on behalf of the people of the state
-advises and supervises all county prosecutors.

Department of Education

The elected 8-member State Board of Education, is constitutionally responsible for leadership and general supervision of public education except for colleges and universities granting a bachelor's degree.

The board provides advice to the legislature regarding educational needs and policy. The board appoints the department's chief executive officer, the Superintendent of Public Instruction, who is responsible for carrying out the day to day activities of the department. Among the many areas of this department's activity are:

-distributing state aid funds to the schools as appropriated by the legislature
-certifying teachers and administering the state tenure law
-operating a state School for the Deaf and a School for the Blind (Flint)
-supporting statewide library services
-administering any special state or national school aid programs
-overseeing the state's local community colleges

PUBLIC FOUR-YEAR COLLEGES AND UNIVERSITIES

Public 4-year colleges and universities are part of the state's responsibilities. Currently, there are thirteen such colleges and universities in Michigan. They all grant baccalaureate (bachelor's) degrees and most provide additional educational levels (masters, doctoral, and professional degrees).

These institutions are:

University of Michigan (Ann Arbor and branches at Dearborn and Flint)

Michigan State University (East Lansing)

Wayne State University (Detroit)

Eastern Michigan University (Ypsilanti)

Michigan Technological University (Houghton)

Oakland University (Rochester)

Central Michigan University (Mt. Pleasant)

Northern Michigan University (Marquette)

Western Michigan University (Kalamazoo)

Ferris State University (Big Rapids)

Grand Valley State University (Allendale)

Lake Superior State University (Sault Ste. Marie)

Saginaw Valley State University (Saginaw-Bay City-Midland Area)

These colleges and universities have a considerable amount of independence. The state Constitution exempts them from supervision by the state Board of Education, and provides that each shall have its own governing authority. In the case of the three largest universities — Michigan, Michigan State and Wayne State — the governing bodies are elected in statewide partisan elections. All other colleges and universities are governed by boards appointed by the governor, subject to Senate veto.

The three elected boards each consist of eight members, two of whom are elected every two years to staggered 8-year terms. The appointed boards also consist of eight members, also serving overlapping 8-year terms. In all cases, the board selects the chief executive official of the institution — its president.

and helping plan for higher education.
    -conducting research
    -administering state laws affecting private schools.

Department of Agriculture

This department is headed by a 5-member, bipartisan Commission of Agriculture. The members are appointed by the governor to 4-year overlapping terms, subject to rejection by the Senate. The commission appoints the director of the department.

The major functions of this department are to:

-administer those laws intended to guarantee consumers safe, wholesome food supplies (meat, food and dairy inspection)
-encourage the development of the state's agricultural economy
-protect the state against establishment and spread of pests, and plant and animal diseases which threaten the public
-set standards for fair marketing of agricultural products
-administer the State Fair, County Fair programs, the Upper Peninsula State Fair
-encourage international agricultural exporting
-administer the state's Soil and Water Conservation program, including drainage districts
-establish regulations for horse-racing programs
-maintain the state weather service.

Department of Civil Rights

This department is headed by an 8-member, bi-partisan commission, appointed by the governor. The Senate may veto nominees. Members serve 4-year, overlapping terms, and the commission appoints the director of the department. This department is created by the Constitution, and:

-receives, investigates and seeks settlement of complaints of discrimination in employment, public accommodations, public service, education and housing
-may hold hearings for the purpose of gathering information on civil rights matters
-reviews the civil rights performance of contractors for state goods and services
-provides assistance to local agencies and other groups working in the field of human relations.

Department of Civil Service

The term "civil service" refers to the employees of government who have been hired based on their demonstration of job-related skills and knowledge. This merit concept is intended to substitute for "patronage" or "spoils" employment—being hired on the basis of political connections. The purpose of a civil service system is to attempt to guarantee that qualified career employees will carry on the work of government regardless of changes of elected leadership, and have considerable job security.

In Michigan, a civil service system applies to nearly all of the state's approximately 60,000 employees. The only state positions not covered are: elected officials, department heads, members of boards and commissions, employees of courts, the legislature, higher education institutions, certain positions in the governor's office, persons in the state's armed forces and up to five top policy making positions in each department.

The Civil Service department is headed by a 4-member, bi-partisan Civil Service Commission. Members serve overlapping 8-year terms and are appointed by the governor, unless vetoed by the Senate. The top executive in the department is the State Personnel Director, appointed by the commission on the basis of open competitive examinations. The commission is created by the state Constitution, and guaranteed a degree of independence by a requirement that 1% of the preceeding year's state payroll cost be appropriated to the commission to fund its work.

As the central personnel agency for state government, the department:

-classifies all positions in the civil service
-examines candidates for state employment on the basis of merit, efficiency and fitness
-provides lists of qualified candidates to state agencies when they fill a position
-develops policies, rules and procedures regulating conditions of employment in the classified service
-generally oversees the collective bargaining process and approves contracts with state employees. The legislature may, within sixty days, reject or reduce pay increases for employees. This requires

a 2/3 vote and must apply uniformly to all pay classifications.

Department of Natural Resources

This department is headed by a 7-member Natural Resources Commission. Commissioners are appointed to overlapping terms by the governor with the advice and consent of the Senate. The Governor appoints the Chair of the commission.

The department has wide-ranging responsibilities which include:

-preventing the destruction of timber and promoting the reforestation of state forests
-providing assistance to local communities in planning recreational facilities
-managing fish habitats, encouraging the propagation of fish through stream improvement and hatchery management
-developing and maintaining campsites, beaches, snowmobile areas
-planning public access and docking facilities
-improving shoreline control
-reviewing solid waste disposal plans, licensing facilities, and enforcing standards
-monitoring the state's water supply and investigating reports of contamination
-enforcing the state's hunting and fishing laws.

Department of Corrections

In 1991, this department changed from one headed by a commission to one headed by an appointed director. Previously this department had been headed by a five- member commission.

The Department of Corrections has grown significantly in recent years. Today nearly 20% of all state employees work for this department.

This department:
-operates nearly 40 correctional institutions and correctional camps
-oversees the Michigan State Industries, which consists of several plants and farms producing products for the state
-engages in research, development and evaluation of programs

-administers laws and regulations affecting local jail standards and procedures
-includes the Parole Board, the functions of which are discussed in chapter 9.

Department of Consumer and Industry Services

This department is headed by a single director appointed by the governor (unless the Senate rejects the nominee.) The director serves at the pleasure of the governor. The department's purpose is to contribute to the development of the state's economy, and its responsibilities include:

-regulating the state's insurance industry, financial and investment institutions, credit institutions, condominiums, cemeteries, and liquor distribution system
-regulating the state's public utilities through the Public Services Commission. This body has general authority over the development, investment decisions and rates of the state's privately owned utilities and motor carriers. The PSC consists of three members, only two of whom may be of the same party. They are appointed to six-year overlapping terms. The nominees may be rejected by the Senate.
-overseeing the Michigan State Housing Development Authority.
-licensing and regulating over thirty professional and occupational groups. Over 3000,000 licenses fall within the authority of the department.
-regulating certain types of subdivision land sales.
-acting as a tax tribunal to resolve disputes about property tax assessments.
-establishing state requirements for building and construction codes
-administering the Workers' Compensation laws, relating to employee illness and disability
-administering laws relating to occupational safety
-developing state programs for the training and employment of disadvantaged, unemployed and under-employed individuals
-providing unemployment insurance benefits and operating employment offices to assist workers in locating available jobs.
-mediating labor disputes within the state and administering laws governing the right to form unions.

Department of Career Development

In 1999 the Jobs Commission was split into two parts--The Department of Career Development and the Michigan Economic Development Corporation. The Economic Developmet Corporation became part of the Department of Management and Budget.

The Department of Career Development is headed by a director, appointed by the governor, subject to Senate veto. The department is a state workforce development agency that coordinates federal and state job-training programs which help workers find jobs and employers recruit and train skilled workers. The department also works with K-12 schools and community colleges to establish career preparations programs. Among its other functions, the department directs the School-to-Work program, the Corrections Parolee Training Program and the Welfare-to-Work Program. The Michigan Rehabilitation Services office and the Employment Services Agnecy are also in this department.

Department of Environmental Quality

Created in 1995 in concert with a reorganization of the Department of Natural Resources and others, this department is headed by a director appointed by the governor.

For the most part, the responsibilities of the department involve carrying out environmental regulatory programs. Among these are:

-shaping Michigan's relationships with other states and Canada through the Office of the Great Lakes.
-monitoring compliance with air quality standards.
-overseeing the clean up of various kinds of contamination. (e.g. underground storage tank leaks) and overseeing waste management/disposal practices.
-administering state policy relative to development/construction on or near shorelines, waterways and wetlands.

Department of Management and Budget

This department is headed by a director appointed by the governor (subject to Senate veto) who holds office at the pleasure of the governor. Its activities affect nearly all other aspects of government in Michigan. Among its many responsibilities are:

-to prepare economic analyses and forecasts and develop taxation options
-to prepare the executive budget for presentation to the legislature, and work closely with the legislature in developing appropriations bills
-to execute the approved budget and review the administration of state programs
-to plan, construct and maintain state government facilities
-to conduct the state's labor relations with classified bargaining units.
-to provide special assistance to the governor on issues affecting children and the aged in Michigan.
-to provide general management assistance to other departments, especially related to development of state databases and information technology.
-to direct the Economic Development Corporation.

Department of Community Health

This department is headed by a director appointed by the governor, subject to veto by the Senate. This department:

-operates facilities for the treatment of various types of mental conditions affecting adults and children. Recently a number of state facilities have been closed and the number of employees working in this area has diminished substantially as patients have been placed in community facilities, administered by over 50 community mental health boards.
-licenses private mental hospitals
-engages in research and planning for meeting the mental health needs of state residents.
-administers Medicaid health care coverage for people with limited incomes.
-administers health services for people who have a mental illness or a developmental disability, and services for people who need care for substance abuse.

-provides health needs assessment, health promotion, disease prevention, and accessibility to appropriate health care for all citizens, in conjunction with over 50 Public Health Departments throughout the state.

-encourages drug law enforcement, treatment, education and prevention programs.

-promotes independence and enhances the dignity of Michigan's older persons and their families.

-prevents and controls the spread of diseases in Michigan through research, laboratory testing and the distribution of vaccines

-works with local communities in licensing and inspecting private wells, mobile home parks, food establishments, public water supplies, schools and other facilities

-licenses and regulates hospitals, nursing homes, homes for the aged, emergency medical centers and other health facilities

-administers programs dealing with personal health, family planning, nutrition, and prevention of substance abuse.

Department of History, Arts and Libraries

This department was created by Governor Engler in 2001 to coordinate and oversee the Library of Michigan (formerly known as the State Library) which was transferred from the legislative branch to this new department. Other activities relating to the states' history and arts activities were transferred from the Department of State with the formation of this new deparment. The Michigan Council for the Arts and Cultural Affiars is now part of this department as is the Michigan Historical Commission.

Department of Information Technology

In 2001 Governor Engler Created a new department of Information Technology to centralize policymaing and coordinate the information technology of operations of the state. Among these are the operations of much of the state's computer systems, and telecommunications systems.

Department of Military and Veterans Affairs

Among other roles, the governor is commander-in-chief of the state's military establishment, which consists of this department. The director of this department is an appointee of the governor. This department:

-maintains programs to provide combat-ready forces to the United States (Army, Air National Guard)

-maintains forces to provide state law enforcement and the protection of life and property in natural disasters and other threats to safety and order

-administers over fifty armories, Camp Grayling, Custer Training Center (Battle Creek) and ANG bases-- Selfridge (near Mt. Clemens), Alpena and Battle Creek.

Department of State Police

This department is headed by a director appointed by the governor with the consent of the Senate. The director serves at the governor's pleasure and all officers have all the powers of a deputy sheriff in enforcing the criminal laws of the state. The department:

-enforces rules relating to fire hazards, which may include inspections of public buildings and other places of public gathering and investigating fires of suspicious origin. (The director of the department is the state fire marshal)

-develops policies and plans for civil defense

-develops a uniform system of traffic signs and signals, and establishes speed limits on any part of a state truck line highway

-provides the patrol of state highways

-provides assistance to local police agencies, when requested. Such help includes crime laboratory services, training programs, personnel and crime data. Recently the Tax Fraud division of the Treasury Department was transferred to the State Police.

Family Independence Agency

This department, formerly the Department of Social Services, is headed by a director appointed by the governor, subject to rejection by the Senate. The director serves at the pleasure of the governor. Generally, the department administers governmental programs providing economic and social assistance to the disadvantaged. The department does this through a network of FIA offices in each of Michigan's eighty-three counties. Some of its major activities are:

-administering the state-federal Aid to Families with Dependent Children program (AFDC).

-administering General Assistance programs providing income for those not eligible for other financial assistance

-providing other services to recipients, such as day care, rehabilitation services to the blind, housing, health and transportation services

-administering the federal Food Stamp program

-overseeing private child care agencies, summer camps, nursery schools, foster homes and adoption agencies

-providing services to neglected and delinquent children assigned to the department as state wards

-attempting to stimulate the development of housing for low-income persons and families through the activities of the Michigan State Housing Development Authority.

Department of Transportation

Once called the Department of State Highways, this department took its current form through law and constitutional amendment in 1978. The department is headed by a 6-member State Transportation Commission. Members are appointed by the governor, subject to disapproval by the Senate, for three year staggered terms. This commission establishes all policies and programs for the department, as required by the Constitution, but it does not appoint the director. The director is appointed by the governor, subject to veto by the Senate, and serves at the governor's pleasure.

The wide-ranging transportation duties of this department include:

-the general supervision of all aeronautics in the state, including airport location, design and operations, and oversight of schools of aviation

-operation of the International Bridge at Sault Ste.Marie and the Mackinac Bridge

-distribution of monies of the Michigan Transportation Fund according to requirements established by law (see part 5 for additional detail)

-administering funds related to urban and public transportation

-administering the construction and maintenance of state trunkline highways and the maintenance of interstate (federal) highways

-engaging in a variety of research and testing activities

-administering the payment of debt for state highways

-providing grants for many purposes, including freight and passenger rail activities, ferry, and intercity bus transportation services.

Department of Treasury

The office of State Treasurer is established in the 1963 Constitution (Article 5, section 3). The Treasurer is appointed by the governor, subject to Senate veto, and serves at the governor's pleasure. The department is responsible for:

-collecting state revenues

-safeguarding, depositing, investing and disbursing state monies

-selling any bonds issued by the state when it borrows and seeking the best possible interest rate on such debt

-supervising local property tax administration

-administering state laws regarding borrowing by local units of government

-setting accounting procedures for local units of government, periodically auditing counties, and reviewing the financial condition of other local units

-the Michigan Gaming Control Board.

-the Michgan Merit Award Scholarships and the Michigan Education Trust.

-statewide educational assessment tests.

-also contained within this department is the independent Bureau of State Lottery, headed by an appointee of the governor.

Profiles of Michigan's Recent Governors

Governor, Tenure, Party	Year/place of birth/family? veteran?	Higher education	Important positions before governorship.
Jennifer Granholm, 2003- D	1959, Canada, Married, three children	Berkeley, Harvard	Attorney General, federal prosecutor, Wayne county corporate counsel
John Engler, 1991--2002 R	1949 Beal City Married, Triplets	J.D. Cooley Law B.A. Michigan State	Majority Leader Michigan State Senate
James Blanchard, 1983-90, D	1942 Detroit Married, 1 child	BA, MBA Michigan State, J.D. Minnesota	Assistant to State Attorney General, 1969-74; Member, U.S. House of Representatives, 1975-82.
William Milliken, 1969-82, R	1922 Traverse City Married, 2 children WWII veteran	Graduate-Yale	Pres. J.W. Milliken, Inc. (Traverse City Retail firm) State Senator, 1960-64; Lieut. Gov. 1964-69.
George Romney, 1963-69 R	1907-1995, Mexico (Raised in Utah and Idaho) Married, 4 children	Attended Utah, George Washington	Chair and Pres., American Motors Corp. 1954-62; Head, Citizens for Michigan; Officer, 1961-62 Constitutional Convention.
John Swainson, 1961-62 D	1925-1994 Windsor, Ontario Married, 3 children WWII vet	BA, LLB, North Carolina	State Senator, 1954-58; Lieut. Gov. 1959-60
G. Mennen Williams, 1949-60 D	1911-1988 Detroit Married, 3 chidren WWII vet	BA, Princeton, JD, Michigan	Numerous state and national positions related to the administration of justice.
Kim Sigler, 1947-48 R	1894-1953 Nebraska Married, 2 children	Law degree, Detroit	Barry County Prosecutor, 1923-28; Special Prosecutor, 1944-47

Pay for Michigan's Elected Officials

A 1968 amendment to the Constitution (Article 4, section 12) establishes the State Officers Compensation Commission (SOCC) for the purpose of setting certain salaries. The SOCC is an autonomous agency within the Civil Service department. This 7-member body is appointed by the governor to overlapping 4-year terms.

Every two years, the SOCC is responsible for determining the salaries and expense allowances of the governor, lieutenant governor, Supreme Court justices, and members of the legislature. In 2002 the voters of Michgan gave the SOCC the power to set pay rates for the Secretary of State and the Attorney General as well and required that the legislature approve the salary changes by a majority vote

As of 2002, the respective salaries and expense allowances of the various officials are:

OFFICE		SALARY	EXPENSES
SOCC sets:	Governor	$177,000	$40,000
	Lt. Governor	123,900	12,000
	S. Ct. Justice	164,610	
	Legislators	79,650	12,000
	Sec. of State	124,900	
	Attorney Gen.	124,900	

Chapter 8

Michigan's Legislature

Development of Michigan's Legislature

General Powers and Duties of the Legislature

Basic Structure of the Michigan Legislature

Becoming and Remaining a Member of the Legislature

Internal Organization of the Legislature

How a Bill Becomes a Law

The Legislature and Other Branches

The Budget Process: an Overview

A Look to the Future

> *"The legislative power of the State of Michigan is vested in a senate and a house of representatives."*
>
> Article IV, Sec. 1, Michigan Constitution

Chapter 8

Learning Objectives

How has the Michigan Legislature changed since the early 1940's?
What is the number of members in the Michigan House and Senate?
What is the term of office for Michigan House and Senate Members?
What is the background of a typical member of the state legislature?
In recent years which party has been dominant in the legislature?
Why are committees important in the legislature?
What are the major roles for political parties in the legislature?
Why is most of the work of the legislature done in committee?
What is the purpose of a conference committee?
What is the process for impeaching a governmental official?
What checks does the legislature have on the courts?
What checks does the legislature have on the executive branch?
Besides legislators, who are the important actors in the legislative process?
What guidelines would you give a person seeking to influence the legislative process?
Summarize the budget process in Michigan.

Key Terms To Know

bicameral	caucus
majority leader	minority leader
floor leaders	party whips
bill	joint committees
standing committees	special committees
conference committees	appropriations committee
fiscal agency	auditor general
Legislative Service Bureau	immediate effect
Law Revision Commission	legislative oversight
pocket veto	impeachment
executive budget	appropriations
fiscal year	
Joint Committee on Administrative Rules	

As one enters the city of Lansing the most prominent feature of the landscape is the white dome of Michigan's capitol. When school classes "go to the capitol" to see the state government in action the usual stop is the legislature.

DEVELOPMENT OF THE MICHIGAN LEGISLATURE

At the time of the founding of Michigan and the formation of its institutions a very common slogan was "the government that governs best governs least." Thus in the Constitution of 1850 the legislature was permitted to meet only once every two years rather than every year as it had earlier. It met for forty days and members were paid three dollars per day. Many powers of the legislature in areas such as education, taxes, property and large capital projects were limited as well. In spite of the limits placed on the legislature some of its present features were in place as early as the 1850's and 1860's. By the early 1860's the Michigan Senate had 32 members and the Michigan House had 100 members. Both numbers are close to the present day size of the Senate (38 members) and the House (110 members). Many of the current rules for the Michigan House took shape during this period.

When the Constitution of 1908 was written other changes took place. The governor was given the power to veto individual items in the budget passed by the legislature. At about the same time provisions were made for citizen lawmaking by the use of initiative and referendum. In the view of many, the years that followed were the worst years for the Michigan legislature. Reapportionment (re-districting) of legislative districts was rarely done, and when it was it usually favored the party in power in a very obvious manner. Thus, in the early 20th century, while the state's population was becoming more urban, rural interests continued to dominate the legislature. As late as 1946 the lawmakers were still being paid three dollars per day.

In the early 1940's changes began to take place that would transform the Michigan legislature into its current form. In 1940 the legislature began to meet annually. At first the governors called extra sessions and then later the Constitution was amended to allow for yearly meetings. As the sessions got longer and the work became more complex the pay of the lawmakers gradually increased to reflect the nature of the work being done.

In the 1950's the Senate was redistricted for the first time in 27 years and the legislature began meeting in year-round session by the end of the decade. In 1962 the U.S. Supreme Court required states to redraw the state House and state Senate districts to equalize population (Baker v. Carr). These changes gradually made the Michigan legislature one of the more modern and progressive in the nation.

GENERAL POWERS AND DUTIES OF THE LEGISLATURE

The Michigan legislature is the basic policy making body in the state. It has the power to make laws for the state, levy taxes and appropriate funds to keep the government functioning. The state Constitution requires the legislature to do certain things and forbids it from doing other things. The Constitution requires the legislature to:

- provide for a system of free public education as defined by law.
- support a system of state colleges, universities and community colleges.
- provide for public libraries.
- regulate elections in the state.
- support the state's armed forces.
- provide an annual accounting of all public money spent, and appoint an auditor general.
- manage all state owned lands.
- carry out the declaration of rights of the Michigan Constitution.

There are some things that the state legislature cannot do. For example the legislature may not:

- enact a graduated income tax.
- restrain or abridge the freedom of press and speech.
- pass death penalty laws.
- support non-public schools.

Figure 8.1

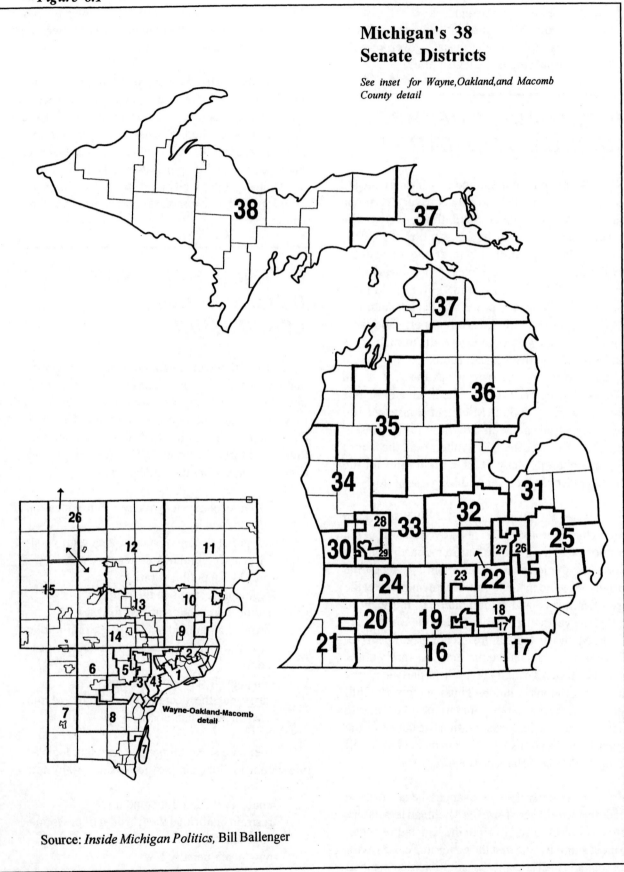

**Michigan's 38
Senate Districts**

*See inset for Wayne, Oakland, and Macomb
County detail*

Wayne-Oakland-Macomb
detail

Source: *Inside Michigan Politics,* Bill Ballenger

Figure 8.2

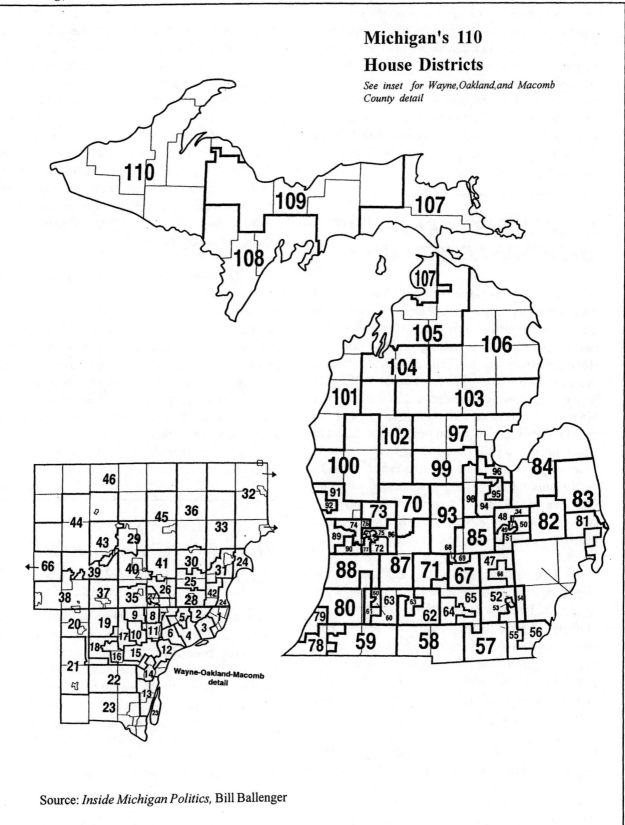

Michigan's 110
House Districts

See inset for Wayne, Oakland, and Macomb
County detail

Wayne-Oakland-Macomb
detail

Source: *Inside Michigan Politics,* Bill Ballenger

The legislature may also exercise some supervisory power over executive departments, override the governor's veto by a two-thirds vote in each house, play a role in determining the inability of a governor to serve and create judicial circuits and judicial posts. The Senate has the power to disapprove some appointments of the governor. In impeachments the House has the power to bring charges (impeach) and the state Senate has the power to decide whether or not the impeached official is guilty as charged.

BASIC STRUCTURE OF THE MICHIGAN LEGISLATURE

The Michigan legislature, like the U.S. Congress and all state legislatures except Nebraska's, is a bicameral system. A *bicameral* legislature has two houses—known in Michigan as the House of Representatives and the Senate. This bicameral system is derived from the early English parliament where one house represented the aristocracy (the House of Lords) and one house represented the people (the House of Commons). In the national government, the U.S. House of Representatives is based on population—so that each member speaks for the same number of people (about 625,000). The U.S. Senate consists of two senators from each state regardless of population. Bicameralism has deep roots in both American and English history.

Under a bicameral system a bill must pass both chambers to become law. Many things are done twice but mistakes may have a greater chance of being corrected. In the past the bicameral system meant that the state legislatures were based on both population (the House) and geography (the Senate). Since the redistricting decisions of the early 1960s, however, both parts of the state legislature have been based on population.

The size of the Michigan legislature is set by the state Constitution (Article 4, sections 2, 3). There are 38 members in the state Senate and each senator represents about 250,000 people. The Michigan House has 110 members and they each speak for about 84,000 people. (See Figure 8.3, p. 101)

Members of the state Senate are elected for four year terms concurrent with the governor's.

Thus, Michigan state senators are elected in 1998, 2002, 2006 etc., as is the governor. Members of the Michigan House face election every two years. This shorter term for House members is typical of many states and is based on the assumption that frequent election keeps the elected officials closer to the people. Elections for the Michigan legislature are partisan and the candidates for the November general elections are nominated at the August primary. Under the term limit amendment to the state Constitution, passed in 1992, state senators are limited to two four-year terms and state House members are limited to three two-year terms. Maps of the Michigan House and Senate districts appear on the preceding pages.

There is no limit on the legislature's time in session. Daily sessions of the House are usually held on Mondays at 5:00 p.m., Tuesdays and Wednesdays at 2:00 p.m. and Thursdays at 10:00 a.m. On Tuesdays, Wednesdays and Thursdays the Senate meets at 10:00. Sometimes the House and Senate will meet at 10:00 a.m. on Fridays. The meetings of the legislature are open to the public and visitors may view the proceedings from the balconies overlooking the two chambers. The proceedings of each day's meetings are published in the Journals of both chambers, as required by the Constitution.

BECOMING AND REMAINING A MEMBER OF THE LEGISLATURE

Any person 21 years of age or more, who is a registered voter, lives in the House or Senate district and has not been convicted of subversion or a major felony within the last 20 years can be elected to the Michigan legislature. A member of the legislature may hold no other governmental office. Obviously these qualifications make a great many people in the state eligible for the legislature. Only a few are chosen. Who are they? What are they like? How did they become members of the state House or Senate?

One becomes a Michigan state senator or state representative by being nominated in a party primary in August and then winning the general election in November. Individuals may choose to run for any of several reasons. Some run because they wish to represent the views of a particular pressure group such as labor or business. Others may choose to run because of party loyalty—to make sure their party is well represented at the polls. Some of them may be well known names from other fields such as the media or sports. Finally, there are those who run on their own initiative. These people may have some desire to change some particular part of public policy or they simply enjoy the challenge of trying to win political office as a personal achievement.

As one might expect, a great many of those elected to the Michigan legislature are attorneys. About one fourth of the legislators have law degrees. This is not surprising. The training that a lawyer goes through can be good preparation for a lawmaker's career. An even higher proportion of the U.S. Congress is drawn from the legal ranks. Other occupations well represented are teachers and businessmen. Generally those who have some flexibility in their jobs and career patterns are more free to enter the fray of politics. The average age of Michigan lawmakers is about 50. An increasing number of Michigan lawmakers are women. In 1972 less than 5% of state house and senate members were women. In 2002 nearly 23% were.

Though the job of being a lawmaker in Michigan is often a rewarding one and is now well paid ($79,650 plus about $12,000 in expenses in 2002) the turnover is often very high. In a typical year one-third or more of the state lawmakers will be new to the job for many reasons. Lawmakers may resign to go on to other pursuits, they may lose an election and some may die during their term. Lawmakers may also be recalled by the voters (see chapter 6) or may be expelled by their own house of the legislature by a two-thirds vote. When a vacancy occurs the seat is filled by a special election called by the governor. The rather high turnover rate for Michigan is not unique and has increased with term limits.

Thus it might be fair to say that a typical member of the Michigan legislature would look something like this: A white, 49 year old male, protestant, a professional who has had some prior political experience, though probably is in his first term or two in the state legislature. Term limits assure that he will serve only a limited time in Lansing.

HOW THE LEGISLATURE WORKS-INTERNAL ORGANIZATION

So far the focus has been on the legal and constitutional background of the Michigan legislature. The next section examines the way the institution really works. What makes the legislature tick?

The Political Party Caucus and the Leadership

One of the most important ways the political parties make their voices heard is through the *caucus*. A caucus is simply a meeting of lawmakers who belong to either of the two major parties. In Michigan's bicameral legislature there will be four caucuses—House and Senate Democrats and House and Senate Republicans.

A number of decisions are made in the caucus. Most importantly, the party members select their leadership. The respective caucuses in the Senate select the Majority and Minority leaders of that body. In the Michigan House the majority caucus selects the Speaker of the House. All caucuses will choose their own floor leaders, who help manage bills through the legislature, and party whips, who try to assure that all needed members will be present for important votes. In short, the leadership of the legislature is chosen along party lines. The Speaker of the House and the Majority Leader of the Senate belong to the majority party in their respective chambers. The top party leaders in each chamber are often called "The Quadrant." This group is a critical contact with the executive in planning legislative strategy.

The Committee System

Most of the work of the Michigan legislature, like that of the U.S. Congress, is done in committees. There are two main reasons for this; quantity and complexity. First, the number of bills (proposed laws) is so great that it would be impossible for any member to read all of the bills introduced. (There are about 4,400 bills introduced every two years.) Sec-

Table 8.1

Party Balance in Michigan's Legislatures

Year	Senators Dem.	Senators Rep.	Representatives Dem.	Representatives Rep.
1929	0	32	2	98
1931	1	31	2	98
1933	17	15	55	45
1935	11	21	49	51
1937	17	15	60	40
1939	9	23	27	73
1941	10	22	32	68
1947	4	28	5	95
1949	9	23	39	61
1951	7	25	34	66
1953	8	24	34	66
1955	11	23	51	59
1957	11	23	49	61
1959	12	22	55	55
1961	12	22	54	56
1963	11	23	52	58
1965	23	15	73	37
1967	18	20	54	56
1969	18	20	57	53
1971	19	19	58	52
1973	19	19	60	50
1975	24	14	66	44
1977	24	14	68	42
1979	24	14	64	46
1981	24	14	64	46
1983	20	18	63	47
1984	18	20	57	53
1985	18	20	57	53
1987	18	20	64	46
1989	18	20	60	50
1991	18	20	61	49
1993	16	22	55	55*
1995	16	22	54	56
1997	16	22	52	58
1999	15	23	52	58
2001	15	23	52	58
2003	16	22	47	63

Reapportionment increased the number of senators from 32 to 34 and the number of representatives from 100 to 110 in 1955. Again, in 1965, the number of senators was increased to 38 under the 1964 Constitution. (Stollman:32)

*Tied: Speaker and committee chairs alternated montly between parties. It worked better than most expected.

Figure 8.3

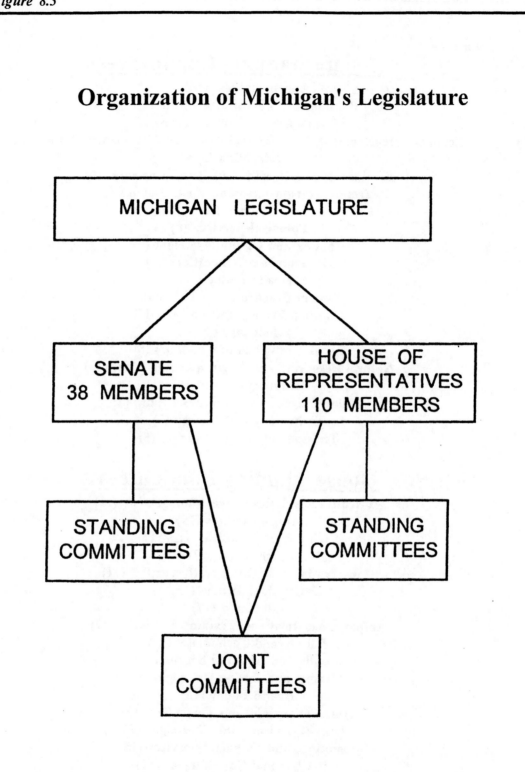

Organization of Michigan's Legislature

MICHIGAN LEGISLATURE

SENATE
38 MEMBERS

HOUSE OF
REPRESENTATIVES
110 MEMBERS

STANDING
COMMITTEES

STANDING
COMMITTEES

JOINT
COMMITTEES

Figure 8.4

<u>Senate Standing Committees</u>

Appropriations (16)
Banking and Financial Institutions (7)
Detroit Metro Airport Review (5)
Economic Development, International Trade and Regulatory Affiars (5)
Education (5)
Families, Mental Health and Human Services (6)
Farming, Agribusiness and Food Systems (5)
Finance (5)
Financial Services (6)
Gaming and Casino Oversight (5)
Governmental Operations (5)
Health Policy (5)
Human Resources and Labor (5)
Hunting, Fishing and Forestry (5)
Judiciary (7)
Local, Urban and State Affairs (5)
Natural Resources and Environmental Affiars (5)
Reapportionment (9)
Senior Citizens and Veterans Affairs (5)
Technology and Energy (7)
Transportation and Tourism (5)

<u>House Standing Committees</u>

Agriculture and Resourece Management (11)
Appropriations (29)
Civil Law and the Judiciary (11)
Commerce (17)
Conservation and Outdoor Recreation (11)
Criminal Justice (11)
Education (17)
Employment Relations, Training and Safety (7)
Energy and Technology (17)
Family and Children Services (9)
Gaming and Casino Oversight (5)
Health Policy (15)
House Oversight and Operations (5)
House Television and Oversight (6)
Insurance and Financial Services (15)
Land Use and Environment (11)
Local Government and Urban Policy (11)
Redistricting and Elections (9)
Regulatory Reform (9)
Senior Health, Security and Retirement (9)
Tax Policy (17)
Transportation (17)
Veterans Affiars (7)

ond, the bills introduced may require one to be an expert on law, highway construction, child care, pollution control and finance, among many other topics. Most bills are written in complex "legalese." Even if one person could read all of the bills there is no way one could be expert enough to understand them all.

Preliminary work is divided among committees where a small group of lawmakers can specialize on one area and read a few of the bills in great detail. The real fate of most bills rests with the 21 Senate and 23 House committees. These standing committees are the permanent committees of the House and Senate, and change little from year to year. They are the workhorses of both bodies.

There are, however, other kinds of committees that play special roles in the legislature. Some committees called *joint committees* are composed of members of both houses. Some of these joint committees may be permanent, like the standing committees. They deal with issues of concern to both the House and Senate and avoid the duplication that might otherwise occur. Currently there are four joint committees, Administrative Rules, Capitol, Legislative Council and Legislative Retirement.

Either the House or the Senate may create *special or select* committees for a specific purpose and a limited time. The purpose of these is to study a particular issue or problem.

A *conference committee* is a type of joint committee appointed to resolve the differences in a bill passed in slightly different form by both the House and Senate. The conference committee will work out the differences so an identical bill can pass both chambers.

The members and the chairs of the committees are appointed either by the Speaker of the House in the house or by the Majority Leader in the Senate. Seniority does play some role in assigning committee members but it is not as important in Michigan as it is, for example, in the U.S. Congress. With term limits, seniority is even less important in the Michigan legislature and many freshmen lawmakers chair committees. In choosing individuals to serve on committees the leadership will consider the expertise a lawmaker might have, his party loyalty,

loyalty to the leadership and personal interests. Each committee contains members of both parties, roughly in proportion to the party balance in the particular chamber. Thus the parties have great influence on the work of the committees.

Each of the standing committees contain from five to 29 members and each member of the legislature will sit on two to five committees within their own chamber. The exceptions are the appropriations committees in each chamber. Because these committees deal with any bill that proposes to spend a substantial amount of money they are very busy. For that reason, many of those who are on the appropriations committees in either the House or the Senate usually sit on no other or few other committees.

Legislative Staff

The job of a lawmaker is not an easy one. Individuals are often called upon to make decisions about many complex issues in a very short time. In order to make their task more manageable several sources of assistance have been created.

Not too many years ago the *staff* of the legislature was very limited. Today there is a good deal more staff aid to help the legislature do its job. There are over 900 staff members for the Michigan House and Senate. Some of them are clerks and pages for the House and Senate itself, others work for the party leaders and the party caucuses, some work for the various committees of the legislature and there are many who work for individual legislators as part of their personal office staff.

The *Secretary of the Senate* and the *Clerk of the House* take care of many of the daily administrative functions of the respective houses. These officials, elected by the membership of the House and Senate, prepare the daily journal, call the roll, announce a quorum, prepare a daily calendar (schedule) of bills and make sure that bills are printed and distributed in a timely fashion. These officials also act as chief parliamentarians within their own chambers.

Attached to the appropriations committee in each chamber is the *Fiscal Agency* which analyzes taxing and spending proposals. This agency also reviews the financial impact of all bills and estimates what costs or savings might be incurred if the bill should pass. The Fiscal Agencys are overseeen by a special committee of the legislature called the *Fiscal Agency Governing Board.*

The *Legislative Service Bureau* is the major source of legal advice for the legislature. It helps members of the legislature draft their ideas into formal legal language for bills. The bureau provides this assistance both to individual legislators and to the committees of the House and Senate.

The *Law Revision Commission* suggests changes in existing laws and tries to identify those laws which have become outdated or those that need revision because of recent legal changes.

The *Auditor General* is appointed by the legislature to audit the financial accounts of all state departments, boards, commissions and other agencies and submit annual reports to both the governor and the legislature. The auditor general can play a major role in *legislative oversight* of the executive branch.

Remember, finally, that legislators often rely on the expertise of lobbyists and officials from the executive branch.

HOW A BILL BECOMES A LAW

A bill (proposed law) may originate in either the House or the Senate and must be introduced by a member of the legislature. Senate bills are numbered beginning with "1" and House bills begin with the number 4000. Bills that are not passed in the first year of the legislature's term may be held over into the second session which meets in the even year. Ideas for bills may come from many sources. Interest groups, the governor, the bureaucracy, local governments, the courts, the public and the legislators themselves may all be sources for ideas for new laws.

Once the legislator forms the basic idea for the bill it is drafted into legal form by the Legislative Service Bureau. Assume that a hypothetical bill is introduced in the Senate first. Senate bill number 756 was introduced by a member of the Senate and quickly found a number of co- sponsors—other members of the Senate who were willing to indicate their initial support for the bills.

The bill is introduced at what is commonly called the first reading, where the title is read, and is then assigned to committee. In the Senate the Majority Leader will assign the bill to an appropriate committee (In the House the same job is done by the Speaker of the House). This is not an automatic process. Committees have life and death power over bills and a bill that might quickly find support in one committee might be killed in another. Thus, from the very beginning, the Majority Leader of the Senate or the Speaker of the House has a great deal of power over the fate of the bill.

The Committee

The committee stage is the most crucial step in the bill's path through the legislature. It is in committee that the bill may be studied, debated, changed or modified and finally given the breath of life or the kiss of death. At the committee stage many actors will enter the struggle. Lobbyists from the private sector, local governments, members from every state department affected, other legislators, perhaps the governor and others may get involved in this most important decision making process. Many of the groups mentioned will prepare a detailed analysis of the bill and present their findings and arguments to the committee.

The committee, usually acting on the basis of majority rule, can take many actions on the bill. If they choose to hold hearings on the bill and take action they can:

1. Report the bill out of committee with a favorable recommendation, which will give it a good chance of passage in the full House or Senate.
2. Report the bill out with no recommendation one way or the other. At best this will give the bill a rather poor chance of passage in the legislature.
3. Report the bill out with an unfavorable recommendation. This usually means that the bill has practically no chance of passing.

The committee may, however, do other things as well. It may:

1. Amend the initial bill in many ways.
2. Replace the bill entirely with another "substitute" bill.
3. Recommend that it be referred to another committee.
4. Take no action on the bill at all, and refuse to report the bill out of committee.

The committee stage is the basic filtering process of the legislature. Among other things its job is to weed out the bills it considers inappropriate or those that duplicate other legislation. In each session between 2,000 and 4,000 bills are introduced into the legislature. Only about 10-20% of them become law. Most of those which fail are stopped at the committee stage. Assume that a bill did have a favorable trip through the committee and was reported out with a positive recommendation. If the bill has substantial financial implications it will also have to face a similar hurdle in the appropriations committee of the chamber.

Committee of the Whole (Senate)— Second Reading (House)

At this stage the bill may be debated, the committees recommendations will be considered and additional amendments may be offered and adopted. All members of the chamber may participate at this point.

Third Reading

The formal decision stage in both the House and Senate is called the third reading. At this step there may be more debate or possibly more amendments. The chamber may refer the bill back to committee, postpone the bill or table it, any of which will probably have the effect of killing the bill. If the bill can avoid all of these roadblocks it will be voted on by the full Senate or the full House. If it passes the Senate (where this example began) it will then go to the House and face the same obstacle course as indicated above. It is important to note that a bill must pass by a majority vote of the total membership of each house.

If it passes the house in identical form the bill is then "enrolled" and sent to the governor for his signature or veto. If, however, the bill has been changed in any way by the House then it will go back to the Senate. If the Senate agrees with the changes then it will be sent to the governor. If not, a conference committee is formed, composed of members of both houses. The job of the conference committee is to iron out the differences in the two versions of the same bill. Each chamber must approve the conference report. If they do, the bill is then enrolled and goes to the governor.

The Governor's Role

Once the governor has the bill on his desk he has fourteen days to deal with it. He has several options.

First, he may sign the bill. If he does, it will become law. A bill signed by the governor can become law either immediately or 90 days after the adjournment of the legislature. The state Constitution specifies that a bill will not go into effect until 90 days after the end of the legislative session that passed it. This means that when the legislature adjourns late in December a bill will not go into effect until the following March. This might be too long a waiting period. Thus, there is a procedure, which requires a 2/3 vote of the legislature, whereby a bill can take *immediate effect* upon the signature of the governor. About 90% of the bills passed by the legislature take effect immediately.

Second, the governor could veto the bill, and return it along with his objections to the house of origin. The legislature can then, if it chooses, try to override the veto. If two-thirds of the members elected and serving in both the House and Senate vote to override the veto then the bill becomes law without the governor's signature. Of course, if the bill fails to gather the required two-thirds vote then the veto stands and the bill doesn't become law.

It is also possible that the bill could be tabled in an attempt to override the veto at a later date. The bill could also be referred to a committee again where it might be rewritten to accomodate some of the governor's objections.

Third, the governor could refuse to either sign or veto the bill. If the legislature is still in session at the end of fourteen days the bill becomes law without the governor's approval. If, however, the

Figure 8.4

How a bill becomes a law in Michigan

BILL DRAFTED
Ideas may come from governor, executive agencies,
 interest groups,legislators or local governments.

FIRST READING
Bill introduced and assigned to committee
by either Majority leader of the Senate or Speaker of the House

COMMITTEE ACTION
Committee may:
-report bill out
        -with favorable report
        -with unfavorable report
        -without recommendation
-offer amendments to bill
-replace bill with substitute bill
-refer to another committee
-postpone action

SECOND READING-HOUSE
COMMITTEE OF THE WHOLE-SENATE
At this stage:
-bill is debated
-committee amendments are considered
-amendments from floor considered

THIRD READING
At this stage:
-limited debate
-amendments considered

IF PASSED
Bill is sent to the other chamber to follow the same path

CONFERENCE COMMITTEE
If bill has been changed by the second chamber, a conference committee composed of
members of both houses, works out the differences. Both houses must approve the
conference action.

GOVERNOR
-may sign bill-it becomes law
-may veto bill-requires 2/3 vote to override
-may do neither: After 14 days
        -becomes law if legislature is in session
        -fails if legislature is adjourned.

legislature has adjourned and isn't in session at the end of the 14 days then the bill doesn't become law. This practice is commonly called the "pocket veto."

Citizen Lobbying

Professional lobbyists often have a great deal of contact with the legislature and they are often the source of many ideas for new laws. The professional lobbyists, however, are not the only ones who can have contact with the Michigan legislature. An ordinary citizen can often have substantial impact on the lawmaking process. The Michigan legislature publishes a free booklet called *A Citizen's 'Guide to State Government."* It describes the legislature, tells who sits on the various committees, when and where they meet and many additional current details of the legislature. This booklet, available from your state senator or representative, also describes some of the techniques that an average citizen should use to have his or her voice heard. What follows are a few of the suggestions contained in the booklet. Make it a point to pick up a copy for more details.

If you contact your legislator personally:

1. Be informed. Know what you are talking about. Do some research on the full scope of your concern. Be sure your facts are correct.
2. Use correct timing. The best days to find your legislator in his or her office are Tuesday, Wednesday and Thursday. It is always easier if you have made an appointment in advance.
3. Be constructive, brief and to the point. If you don't like a law being proposed, can you offer an alternative? Keep your comments short and related to the matter at hand.

If you decide to contact your lawmaker by letter:

1. Include your name and address.
2. Know when to write. If you can, write before a decision has been made in committee. Often letters arrive too late to have an impact.
3. Use your own words. Avoid form letters. Your own words and ideas will have more impact and meaning than a form letter

provided by an organization.
4. As with personal contact, be informed, brief and state your reasons clearly.

If you should testify in front of a committee in the legislature some similar rules also apply:

1. Write your legislator ahead of time and notify him or her of your desire to testify. Keep track of the bill.
2. Be prepared. Know your facts well and be ready to answer questions about your position. If you are suggesting an amendment to a bill, have it prepared ahead of time.
3. Have a clear, concise written statement ready for the committee.
4. Keep your testimony short and to the point. If the committee hearing is a long one, summarize your major points and ask to present more detailed material in the record—to be read at a later time by the lawmakers.

THE LEGISLATURE AND OTHER BRANCHES OF GOVERNMENT

The checks and balances of Michigan's government means that the legislature will have many contacts with the other parts of the government.

Legislative Oversight

One of the most significant checks that the legislature has is the power of *legislative oversight* of the bureaucracy. The legislature keeps an eye on the bureaucracy in several ways. One of the most important "watchdog activities" is carried out by the *Auditor General.* This official, appointed by the legislature, is a certified public accountant who audits the accounts of all the state boards, commissions, authorities and institutions (with the exception of the major universities in the state). The auditor general submits annual reports to both the legislature and the governor. Clearly the ability to keep an eye on the funds a bureaucracy spends gives the legislature a strong oversight power.

Another major legislative control over the bureaucracy rests with the *Joint Committee on Administrative Rules*. This committee, composed of both House and Senate members, has power over the rules and regulations issued by a governmental agency. As a result of the Administrative Procedures Act of 1969 an agency that wants to develop new rules and regulations must:

1. Draw up the proposed rules.
2. Hold public hearings where those affected will have a chance to be heard.
3. Submit the proposed rules to the Attorney General for a legal opinion.
4. Send the proposed rules to the Joint Committee on Administrative Rules. If the proposed rules are approved by the committee within two months they become law. If the committee doesn't approve the rules then the legislature may act to change them.

In addition to these powers the legislature has a great deal to say about the budget of any agency. An administrator in the state bureaucracy would pay a great deal of attention to the concerns of the legislator because of this financial control.

Other Checks on the Executive

There are other powers that the legislature can exercise as part of the check and balance process. The Senate has the power to "advise and consent" to many of the governor's appointments (except for judicial appointments). The Senate has the option of rejecting an appointment within sixty days. If the Senate doesn't disapprove, the appointment stands confirmed.

The legislature may also play a role in the impeachment of the governor and other civil officials. The House has the duty of impeaching, or bringing charges against an individual, by a majority vote. Once the House has impeached an official then the Senate determines whether or not the individual is guilty of the charges. The Senate will listen to the evidence against the official and must support the charges by a 2/3 majority in order to convict. An official who is impeached and convicted is removed from public office and may face criminal charges later.

Checks on the Courts

The legislature also has several checks against the court system. The laws that are interpreted and applied by the courts are passed by the legislature (though the courts may find them unconstitutional). The legislature may provide for new courts, may define (within the limits of the Constitution) the powers of the courts, may determine the election procedures for state judges and may request the governor to remove a judge by a two-thirds majority vote in each chamber. In turn, through their power of judicial review, the courts may define the limits of legislative power.

THE BUDGET PROCESS— AN OVERVIEW

There is perhaps no quicker way to evaluate the details of a government than by reviewing its budget. In those dry rows of numbers is the story of what the government is doing. It is, in short, the pulse of the government. Though the budget is not the total responsibility of the legislature, the lawmakers play a major role in forming the state's financial blueprint. There is an old saying about budgets: "The executive proposes and the legislature disposes."

The Governor's Proposals

Michigan's financial (fiscal) year runs from October 1 through the following September 30. However, the process of drawing up the budget begins long before that time. In the executive branch, many departments begin a year ahead of time in developing plans, estimating costs and submitting proposals. The budgetary work of the executive branch is coordinated by the Department of Management and Budget, which combines all of the many requests and proposals into a single comprehensive executive budget.

The state Constitution (Article V, sections 18-20) requires that there be no deficit for an operating budget. However, the state may borrow for long term purposes. The Constitution also requires that the governor's proposed budget be in the form of appropriations bills. The governor, with the aid of the Department of Management and Budget, must also estimate what revenues the state will need to pay for the expenditures to insure a balanced or surplus operating budget. Once the governor has assembled all of these elements he will present his proposed *executive budget* to the legislature in January. From this point the legislature may begin to change and modify many parts of the budget.

The Legislative Budget

Once the governor has submitted the appropriations bills that make up his budget to the legislature, the usual legislative process takes over. The appropriations bills go to the most important and powerful committees in the legislature-the appropriations committees of the House and the Senate. These committees review the governor's proposals in light of their politics and their view of the state's needs. In each house its fiscal agency assists the appropriations committee in making independent assessments of the needs and resources of the state. By custom some of the appropriations items begin in the House and others begin in the Senate. The appropriations committees are divided into subcommittees to consider separate parts of the budget.

Usually the legislature changes the governor's budget as it wends its way through the lawmaking process. The appropriations bills go through the legislature as all bills do and they must face the governor's approval or veto. The governor may veto any item in an appropriation bill. Thus the process that began with the governor and went to the legislature returns again to the executive office.

As the fiscal year proceeds, changes in the approved budget might be necessary. Increases in spending levels occur as supplemental appropriations bills, which are approved in the same manner as above. If it is necessary to reduce state spending, the governor initiates the process by proposing cuts. Such proposed cuts take effect if approved by the appropriations committees of both the House and Senate.

A LOOK TO THE FUTURE

A little over ten years ago a study compared all fifty state legislatures. Though one often reads a good deal of negative coverage about the Michigan legislature, compared to other states Michigan ranks fairly well. Among the fifty states Michigan's legislature ranked eighth in overall quality. Michigan's legislature was rated as being very well informed and representative. At the same time the study made a number of suggestions for future improvement. It recommended that the state legislature reduce the number of committees, publish uniform rules for the House and Senate, publish proceedings of committees, support offices in the home districts and improve the physical facilities for the members and their staffs.

In short, compared to only a few decades ago, the legislature has come a long way but there is still room for improvement. Yet, compared to those of most other states Michigan's legislature is considered representative and effective.

The Fiscal Year

Month/Year	Action Taken
April 2003	Department of Management and Budget (executive branch) develops program guidelines.
June 2003	Guidelines sent to departments to draft their budgetary requests.
September 2003	Departments return budget requests to DMB
October-November 2003	Departments meet with Governor's budget office.
December 2003	Governor's decisions made.
January 2004	Governor's recommendations prepared for submission to legislature. State-of-State and Budget message prepared.
February 2004	Legislative action begins.
March-July 2004	Legislative action--committee hearings, floor votes, conference committees.
July-August 2004	Governor signs (or vetoes) bills (May include line-item vetos.)
October 1, 2004	Fiscal Year 2005 begins.

Chapter 9

Michigan's Judiciary

History and Background

Relationship of the State Courts to the National Courts

Organization of Michigan's Courts

Becoming and Remaining a Judge in Michigan

The Criminal Process in Michigan

The Courts and Other Decision-Makers

Michigan's Courts-Problems and
Prospects

*"The judicial power of the state is vested
exclusively in one court of justice which shall
be divided into one supreme court, one court
of appeals, one trial court of general jurisdiction..."*

Article VI, Sec. 1, Michigan Constitution

Chapter 9

Learning Objectives

Outline several ways in which the Federal and State courts differ.

What are the basic courts in Michigan? Are they independent or related to one another?

How many members are on the Michigan Supreme Court? How long is their term?

How many members are on the Michigan Court of Appeals? How long is their term?

What is the major job of the Circuit Courts?

What are the major duties of the District Courts?

What do Probate Courts do?

What does the Judicial Tenure Commission do?

Summarize the major steps in a typical criminal case.

What is plea bargaining?

What are the major barriers to an appeal?

Distinguish between the different types of trial juries and the grand jury.

Key Terms To Know

common law	Supreme court
statute law	Probate court
constitutional law	District court
Court Administrator	Circuit court
plea bargaining	Judicial Tenure Commission
preliminary hearing	parole
trial jury	grand jury
voir dire	judicial discretion
injunction	

In Michigan's government one part of the system makes the law (the legislature), one part enforces the law (the executive), and one part interprets the law (the courts). This chapter examines the third branch of the government.

The courts do more than interpret the laws. In some ways they make laws. In some ways they enforce the laws. They determine who has violated the laws and the punishment they will face, and they determine the damages to be awarded in civil cases. None of us can escape the impact of the judicial system. In a typical year in Michigan more than 150,000 individuals will take their civil cases to Circuit Court, 55,000 criminal cases will be heard at the same level and nearly 400,000 individuals will have civil disputes resolved in District Courts. Furthermore, thousands of estates will be handled through Probate Court and over two million traffic offenses will be dealt with in District Courts.

HISTORY AND BACKGROUND

The American legal system originated with King Henry II of England (1154-89) who developed a system of laws known as the common law. King Henry wanted to guarantee a uniform system of justice throughout his realm to reflect the customs and habits of the people at the time. As the king's judges went from town to town and tried cases, records were kept. The number of records grew with the passing years and certain patterns of justice developed. In some areas of England it might be a very serious crime to steal a loaf of bread and might be punished accordingly. In other areas it might be a trivial offense. Thus the common law began to reflect the habits and customs of the people. Today much of our legal system finds its roots in the common law. Our judges apply the legal principle of *stare decisis* (Latin for 'let the decision stand'), a basic principle of common law. It means court rulings are based on past decisions. Today where no other law covers a situation, judges may apply the common law. Though the common law is the oldest basis for our legal system, it isn't the only one or the most important. Several other kinds of law exist.

Constitutional law, as the term indicates, is law derived from a constitution, either national or state. This is the law which establishes government, assigns powers to certain parts of the government and limits the government. In our legal system constitutional law supercedes any other form of law. A constitution (particularly the national constitution) is often called the "supreme law of the land."

Statute law is law spelled out in legislation passed by legislatures—national, state or local. The great bulk of our laws today such as those dealing with murder, robbery, rape, no fault insurance or zoning are statutory laws. Local laws are commonly called "ordinances." There are two major kinds of statute law, criminal and civil. Criminal law defines those actions considered crimes against the people and prosecution is brought by the government against a defendant. The individual who is wronged does not initiate the prosecution. In contrast, civil law deals with the rights of one individual in relation to another. If a dog bites you no criminal law may be violated. However, you could sue the dog's owner as a result of your injury. Such action—one individual against another—would be a civil suit.

Finally, the law of equity allows the courts to (among other things) prevent a wrong before it occurs by issuing injunctions. If a mean, nasty, rabid dog were running loose and if it were obvious that it would bite someone, one wouldn't need to wait until they were bitten to take action. They might obtain an injunction that would order the dog's owner to keep the dog tied up.

THE RELATIONSHIP OF THE STATE COURTS TO THE NATIONAL COURTS

The United States has what may be the most complex system of courts in the world. There are at least 51 different court systems in this nation. Each state has its own court system and all live under the federal court system. Each state court system is similar to that of other states, but is also unique— each has its individual variations and characteristics.

The federal courts are usually considered superior to the state courts. Sometimes that is true, but it is probably more accurate to think of the federal and state courts as different types of courts, with different laws to apply and different rules and procedures. Generally, federal courts will deal with violations of federal law, such as counterfeiting, postal fraud, draft law violation or treason. Civil suits must be over $10,000 or involve citizens of two different states to be brought to federal court.

The great bulk of legal activity in this country takes place in state courts where most civil and criminal suits are resolved. Thus, for example, state courts would deal with burglary, assault, arson, divorce or traffic violations. Some federal matters may even be tried in state courts (civil suits under $10,000 for example). The average individual is far more likely to be involved with the state courts than the federal.

This complex dual court system leads to many significant consequences that would not occur if we had a single unified court system. First, a single criminal act may violate both federal and state law, and the defendant may be tried in either federal court or state court or both. In certain civil actions, a litigant may choose one court over another because he expects a more favorable hearing for his case. For example in the 1950's and 1960's many civil rights activists in the south took their cases to federal courts, which were more friendly to their cause than the state courts. Second, our dual system of courts means that the interpretation of both the statute law and of higher court decisions will vary from state to state. In part, this may be the result of local political pressure and custom. However, this variation in interpretation may simply be the result of several thousand individual judges trying to apply a general rule to tens of thousands of individual cases. Third, the existence of our dual system of courts gives both the individual states and the federal government the tools to expand (or retain) their share of authority. Often the federal government will initiate legal action, with the intention of expanding federal power (e.g. desegregation) while the states will use their own courts to block what they see as a loss of their own power (e.g. busing).

THE ORGANIZATION OF MICHIGAN'S COURTS

Michigan has three basic elements in its court system. First, there is an appeals system, (the Michigan Supreme Court and Court of Appeals) to review lower court decisions. Second, there is a system of general trial courts, (the Michigan Circuit courts). Third, Michigan has a network of lower courts to deal with other minor and specialized matters (the Probate and District courts). It is important to realize that these courts all form one system (as illustrated in Figure 9-1). Michigan is said to have a unified court system. The 1963 Constitution makes this clear. In Article VI, section 1 it says:

> "The judicial power is vested in one court of justice which shall be divided into one supreme court, one court of appeals, one trial court of general jurisdiction known as the circuit court, one probate court, and courts of limited jurisdiction that the legislature may establish by a two-thirds vote of the members elected and serving in each house."

The Michigan Supreme Court

The highest court in the state, the Michigan Supreme Court, has "general superintending control" in supervising administration of all the lower courts in the state. It is also the final court of appeals in the state.

In 1805 the Supreme Court consisted of one chief judge and two associate judges appointed by the president of the United States. In 1824 their terms were limited to four years. Early state Constitutions modified the Supreme Court several times. The Constitution of 1835 provided that judges would be appointed by the governor, with the consent of the state Senate, for seven year terms. By 1838 the court was composed of a chief justice and three associate justices. The Constitution of 1850 set terms at six years and required the judges of the five circuit courts to also be judges of the Michigan Supreme Court. A few years later, in 1857, as a result of legislative reorganization, the Supreme Court consisted of a chief justice and three associate justices elected for eight year terms. In 1887 the number of justices was increased to five and in 1903 the number was increased to eight. In 1908, the state Constitution required Supreme Court judges to be nominated at partisan conventions and elected at non-partisan elections, as is done today.

The court today is composed of seven jus-

Figure 9.1

THE MICHIGAN JUDICIAL SYSTEM

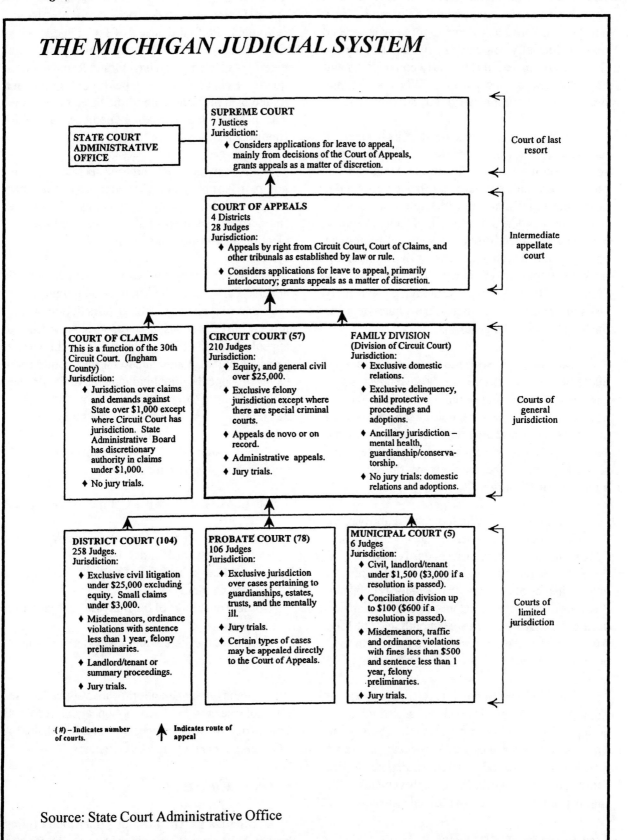

SUPREME COURT
7 Justices
Jurisdiction:
♦ Considers applications for leave to appeal, mainly from decisions of the Court of Appeals, grants appeals as a matter of discretion.

Court of last resort

STATE COURT ADMINISTRATIVE OFFICE

COURT OF APPEALS
4 Districts
28 Judges
Jurisdiction:
♦ Appeals by right from Circuit Court, Court of Claims, and other tribunals as established by law or rule.
♦ Considers applications for leave to appeal, primarily interlocutory; grants appeals as a matter of discretion.

Intermediate appellate court

COURT OF CLAIMS
This is a function of the 30th Circuit Court. (Ingham County)
Jurisdiction:
♦ Jurisdiction over claims and demands against State over $1,000 except where Circuit Court has jurisdiction. State Administrative Board has discretionary authority in claims under $1,000.
♦ No jury trials.

CIRCUIT COURT (57)
210 Judges
Jurisdiction:
♦ Equity, and general civil over $25,000.
♦ Exclusive felony jurisdiction except where there are special criminal courts.
♦ Appeals de novo or on record.
♦ Administrative appeals.
♦ Jury trials.

FAMILY DIVISION
(Division of Circuit Court)
Jurisdiction:
♦ Exclusive domestic relations.
♦ Exclusive delinquency, child protective proceedings and adoptions.
♦ Ancillary jurisdiction – mental health, guardianship/conservatorship.
♦ No jury trials: domestic relations and adoptions.

Courts of general jurisdiction

DISTRICT COURT (104)
258 Judges.
Jurisdiction:
♦ Exclusive civil litigation under $25,000 excluding equity. Small claims under $3,000.
♦ Misdemeanors, ordinance violations with sentence less than 1 year, felony preliminaries.
♦ Landlord/tenant or summary proceedings.
♦ Jury trials.

PROBATE COURT (78)
106 Judges
Jurisdiction:
♦ Exclusive jurisdiction over cases pertaining to guardianships, estates, trusts, and the mentally ill.
♦ Jury trials.
♦ Certain types of cases may be appealed directly to the Court of Appeals.

MUNICIPAL COURT (5)
6 Judges
Jurisdiction:
♦ Civil, landlord/tenant under $1,500 ($3,000 if a resolution is passed).
♦ Conciliation division up to $100 ($600 if a resolution is passed).
♦ Misdemeanors, traffic and ordinance violations with fines less than $500 and sentence less than 1 year, felony preliminaries.
♦ Jury trials.

Courts of limited jurisdiction

(#) – Indicates number of courts.

↑ Indicates route of appeal

Source: State Court Administrative Office

tices, one of whom is chosen chief justice every two years by the other members of the Supreme Court. The justices are elected for eight-year staggered terms in formally non-partisan elections. In reality, they are nominated at state party conventions and are endorsed by the parties. When a vacancy occurs, the governor may fill it by appointment.

With few exceptions, most of its business is taken on appeal from lower state courts. However, some cases may go directly to the Michigan Supreme Court, such as final orders from the State Bar Grievance Board that require discipline or dismissal of attorneys, orders of the Judicial Tenure Commission that recommend discipline, removal, retirement or suspension of a judge, and certain questions of law pending before lower courts. The Michigan Supreme Court, unlike the U.S. Supreme Court, may also render advisory opinions at the request of either the legislature or the governor.

Like the U.S. Supreme Court, the Michigan Supreme Court has discretionary power over which cases it will accept and which it will reject. After it has accepted a case, the court receives written briefs and hears oral arguments from the attorneys. Then it decides the case with a majority vote of the seven justices. The opinions of the court are published in *Michigan Reports*.

The opinions may include: the majority opinion, which decides the case; concurring opinions, in which a justice agrees with the majority's conclusion for different reasons, and dissenting opinions, in which a justice disagrees with the majority decision. Sessions of the Supreme Court are held in Lansing during the first week of every month, except July, August and September. (See p. 126 for information on current Michigan Supreme Court justices.)

The Michigan Supreme Court appoints a State Court Administrator. This official assists the court in supervising courts throughout the state. The administrator examines court dockets, monitors workloads, assigns judges to courts that need extra help and makes suggestions for improvements in the administration of the state's judicial system.

The Courts of Appeals

The Michigan Constitution of 1963 created the Court of Appeals as a new intermediate level of appeal for lower court decisions. The appeals court is divided into four districts of seven judges each. Each appeals court has panels of three judges each meeting in Detroit, Lansing, Grand Rapids or Marquette. Decisions of the appeals courts are determined by a majority vote of the three judge panel. The panels have a rotating membership, which should help eliminate conflicitng rulings.

Each judge is elected for a six year term on a non-partisan ballot, though the non-partisan primary and general elections often involve significant partisan activity. A map of the appeals regions and election districts appears in figure 9.2.

Except for a few matters which may be appealed directly to the Michigan Supreme Court, the Court of Appeals exercises jurisdiction over all lower court decisions. A person has the right to appeal almost all final judgements of the Circuit Courts, Court of Claims and Recorder's Court to the Court of Appeals. Final judgements of the Probate Courts, District Courts and other minor courts may be appealed at the discretion of the higher court.

Some administrative actions that go directly to the Court of Appeals are:

-action of the Worker's Compensation Appeal Board.
-license suspensions or revocations by the state licensing board for dentistry.
-some license revocations by the State Insurance Commissioner.
-orders or rulings of the State Labor Mediation Board.
-orders of the State Municipal Finance Commission.

Some other agencies may also appeal certain kinds of issues to the Court of Appeals. The formal written opinions of the appeals court are published in *Michigan Court of Appeals Reports*.

Circuit Courts

Michigan's Circuit Courts trace their origins back to 1824 when three judges of the state Supreme Court held annual term in a number of counties in the state. Later, in 1835, the Circuit Courts were

Figure 9.2

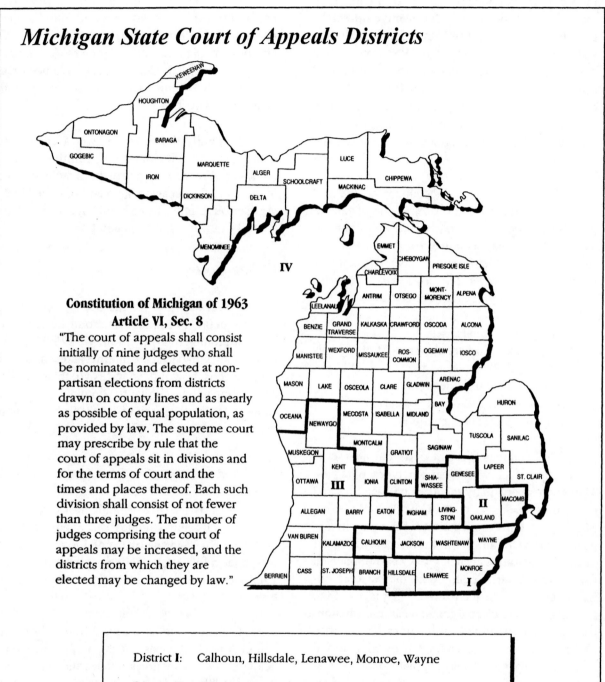

Michigan State Court of Appeals Districts

Constitution of Michigan of 1963
Article VI, Sec. 8

"The court of appeals shall consist initially of nine judges who shall be nominated and elected at non-partisan elections from districts drawn on county lines and as nearly as possible of equal population, as provided by law. The supreme court may prescribe by rule that the court of appeals sit in divisions and for the terms of court and the times and places thereof. Each such division shall consist of not fewer than three judges. The number of judges comprising the court of appeals may be increased, and the districts from which they are elected may be changed by law."

District **I**: Calhoun, Hillsdale, Lenawee, Monroe, Wayne

District **II**: Genesee, Macomb, Oakland, Shiawassee

District **III**: Allegan, Barry, Berrien, Branch, Cass, Eaton, Ionia, Jackson, Kalamazoo, Kent, Muskegon, Newaygo, Ottawa, St. Joseph, Van Buren, Washtenaw

District **IV**: Balance of counties for State of Michigan

established by name but were still presided over by the Supreme Court judges. The Constitution of 1850 made the office of circuit judge elective and set the term at six years. The 1908 Constitution divided the state into judicial circuits. The 1963 Constitution made no basic change and today there are over 50 separate judicial circuits covering from one to four counties. A map of the Circuit Court boundaries appear as figure 9-3. The number of judges in each is stipulated by the state legislature and varies from one to over thirty.

The Circuit Courts of Michigan are the trial courts of general jurisdiction. As a court of general jurisdiction, the Circuit Courts follow the common law tradition of having power over all matters not specifically forbidden by law or allocated to another jurisdiction. However, the cases which comprise the bulk of the Circuit Court docket are:

-All felony criminal cases.
-All civil cases where the amount claimed is over $25,000.
-Some serious misdemeanors.
-Cases involving title or real estate.
-Injunctions and similar actions.

The Michigan Circuit Courts may also serve as an appeals court for certain types of cases. Though there are many specific qualifications and exceptions, decisions made by the Probate Courts, Municipal Courts and District Courts may be appealed to the Circuit Court. Further, the rulings of most administrative agencies may also be appealed to the Circuit Court. Circuit Courts may also naturalize aliens (make them citizens). The judges of the Circuit Court are elected for six year terms in non-partisan primary and general elections. The salaries of the Circuit Court judges are paid by the state and each individual county may supplement those salaries.

Family Division of the Circuit Courts

In 1997, as part of a state-wide court reform, the legislature established a Family Division of the Circuit Court throughout the state. The new Family Court has jurisdiction over some traditional Circuit Court areas such as divorce, but also includes many areas that once belonged to the Probate Courts.

Some of the major jurisdictions for the Family Courts are: divorce, adoptions, name changes, juvenile criminal offenses, child custody, paternity, child support, personal protection orders, consent waivers for abortions and emancipation of minors. A number of Probate and Circuit Court judges have been reassigned to the Family Court to accomodate the heavier workload.

Generally, those under 17 who are accused of committing a crime are tried in Family Court and could possibly be sent to one of the juvenile facilities in the state. On occasion, a juvenile charged with a very serious crime may be bound over by a judge to Circuit Court for trial as an adult.

Cyber Court

A recent innovation has been the creation of a "cyber court" to conduct electronic hearings that deal with commercial litigation over $25,000. Communication will be via the internet and similar electronic means. Use of the court is voluntary and the proceeding will be similar to Circuit Court. Circuit Court judges will be assigned to the Cyber Court by the Supreme Court for terms of at least three years.

Probate Courts

As early as 1818, Michigan had a Probate Court in each county. Judges were appointed by the governor. In 1838 the office of Judge of Probate was made a four year elective position. Under the 1963 Constitution Probate judges are elected for terms of six years.

Probate Courts are very different from Circuit Courts. In the past Michigan Probate Courts dealt with two major areas: estates and many issues involving "those who couldn't take care of themselves"--particularly juveniles. With the recent court reforms (PA 388, 1996) the Probate Courts retain jurisdiction of wills and estates but have shifted most of the cases that involve families and children to the Family Division of Circuit Court. Some Probate judges are assigned to the Family Courts.

One of the major functions of the Probate Court is the "probating" or processing of wills. The court makes sure that the provisions of a will are

Figure 9.3

Michigan's Circuit Courts

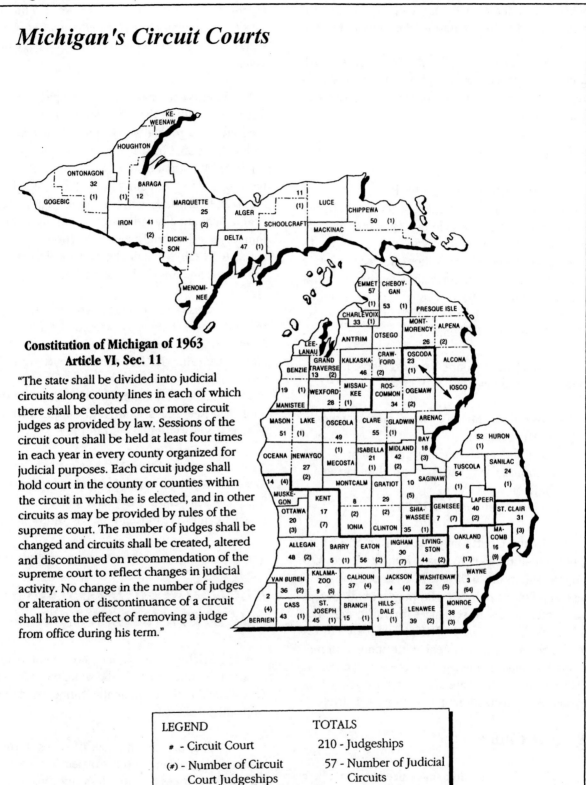

Constitution of Michigan of 1963
Article VI, Sec. 11

"The state shall be divided into judicial circuits along county lines in each of which there shall be elected one or more circuit judges as provided by law. Sessions of the circuit court shall be held at least four times in each year in every county organized for judicial purposes. Each circuit judge shall hold court in the county or counties within the circuit in which he is elected, and in other circuits as may be provided by rules of the supreme court. The number of judges shall be changed and circuits shall be created, altered and discontinued on recommendation of the supreme court to reflect changes in judicial activity. No change in the number of judges or alteration or discontinuance of a circuit shall have the effect of removing a judge from office during his term."

LEGEND	TOTALS
# - Circuit Court	210 - Judgeships
(#) - Number of Circuit Court Judgeships	57 - Number of Judicial Circuits

119

carried out and applies the appropriate state law when a person dies without a will. The court also supervises the administration of estates and trusts.

The Probate Court also deals with guardianships and mental health commitments. Currently there are nearly 80 Probate Courts, based on county lines.

District Courts

The District Court is the basic court of limited jurisdiction. In 1969, the state legislature abolished a variety of minor courts in most parts of the state and established a system of 98 District Courts. As required by the 1963 Constitution, the District Courts replaced the Justice of the Peace Courts and Circuit Court Commissioners in 1969. Many Municipal Courts were also abolished at that time but a few cities chose to retain them.

The District Courts have exclusive jurisdiction over certain categories of cases:

- most misdemeanor offenses (most commonly traffic-related).
- the initial arraignment (arraignment on the warrant), fixing bail and the preliminary exam in felony cases.
- all civil litigation up to $25,000.

District Courts may create a Small Claims Division that allows individuals, without attorneys, to litigate matters of $3000 or less. District Courts may also appoint magistrates who may set bail, accept guilty pleas and issue sentences for traffic and other minor violations. These officials, who are not required to be attorneys, deal with minor criminal cases and under some conditions act as a coroner. District Court judges are elected for six-year terms in non-partisan elections held within the districts.

Special Courts

Over the years there have been several other types of specialized courts within the state. Today they include only the Court of Claims and Municipal courts.

Since the state cannot be sued without its own consent, Michigan, like most states, has created a *Court of Claims* to deal with legal claims made against the state. When the Court of Claims is in session in Lansing, one of the Ingham county Circuit Court judges acts as administrator and judge of the court.

In the years that followed the passage of the 1963 Constitution the *Municipal (city) Courts* of the state were gradually to be phased out according to local option. In the late 1960s there were 28 separate Municipal Courts. Since then the number has dropped to five courts (all in the Grosse Pointe area) and may be less in the future. These courts deal with minor city ordinance violations, hold preliminary hearings, and have jurisdiction in civil matters up to $1750. Municipal judges are elected for six year terms and are paid by the cities.

Because Detroit is the largest city in the state, the legislature long ago created the *Recorder's Court* to handle all felony criminal cases within the city of Detroit. The Recorder's Court's criminal jurisdiction was similar to that of the Circuit Courts in other parts of the state. The 1996 court reforms abolished Recorder's Court and merged it with the Wayne County Circuit Court in 1997.

At one time Detroit had a Court of Common Pleas that dealt with minor criminal and civil matters. Since September of 1981 that court has been a District Court like those in the rest of the state.

BECOMING AND REMAINING A JUDGE IN MICHIGAN

In Michigan, all judges are required to be licensed to practice law in the state, be under 70 at the time of their election or appointment and live in their judicial district.

Michigan, like a number of states, formally holds a non-partisan election to select its judges. But the election process is often less significant than it seems. In the first place, elections are infrequent because judicial terms are long (six to eight years). Secondly, the campaigns are usually issueless and rather invisible, resulting in the regular return of incumbents to office. It is rare for an incumbent

Figure 9.4

JUDICIAL ELECTIONS IN MICHIGAN

COURT	NUMBER OF JUDGES NUMBER OF COURTS TERM OF OFFICE	NOMINATION AND ELECTION	ELECTION AREA
Supreme Court	7 justices 1 court 8 years	nomination by party convention, non-partisan general election	state-wide
Court of Appeals	28 judges 7 from each of four districts 6 years	non-partisan primary and general election	districts (see map)
*Circuit Court	210 judges 57 courts 6 years	non-partisan primary and general election	districts following county lines
Probate Court	106 judges 78 courts 6 years	non-partisan primary and general election	by county (a few counties combine to form district)
District Court	259 judges 104 courts 6 years	non-partisan primary and general election	districts along city or county lines
Municipal Court	6 judges 5 courts 6 years	non-partisan primary and general election	within city

NOTE: Any incumbent judge may nominate himself or herself for the same position by filing an affidavit of candidacy.

* Detroit Recorders Court became part of the Wayne County Circuit Court (3rd Circuit) on October 1, 1997.

judge to lose an election. Thirdly, Michigan, like many of the nearly two-thirds of the states that elect judges, allows the governor to appoint a replacement for a judge when a vacancy occurs or when a new position is created. This often means that the initial selection of many judges is made by the governor's office usually from "applicants" in the governor's own party and not by the electorate. After the governor has made the appointment, the person serves until the next state-wide general election. Then they face the voters for the remainder of the term or a new term. However, the governor's choice is rarely overturned by the voters.

Michigan governors have adopted the practice of using a committee of lawyers and judges to screen candidates for appointment to a vacant judicial position. This does not eliminate partisan politics from the process, but it may substitute the politics of the bar association for the politics of the voting booth.

Michigan has a curious way of nominating its "non-partisan" Supreme Court justices. Supreme Court candidates are nominated by state party conventions in the late summer and then face non-partisan elections in November. For all other judicial positions, nomination takes place in non-partisan primaries in August. Incumbent judges can nominate themselves by filing an "affidavit of candidacy" and will be noted as incumbents on the ballot. In the November election judges are elected within their respective districts in non-partisan elections.

Judicial vacancies can occur through death, resignation or retirement. Though these are the most common ways of creating judicial vacancies, there are more formal methods of removing judges who may be incompetent or corrupt.

In 1968 the Michigan Constitution was amended to establish a Judicial Tenure Commission. This commission investigates complaints against judges in the state. In a typical year several hundred complaints against judges will be heard. The commission may recommend disciplinary action to the Supreme Court. A judge disciplined by the Supreme Court may be censured, suspended, retired or removed from office. The grounds for action must be based on a felony conviction, physical or mental disability, misconduct in office, failure to perform judicial duties or "conduct prejudicial to the administration of justice." The nine-member commission is composed of four judges—one each from the Appeals, Circuit, Probate and District Court levels. Three lawyers, one of whom must be a judge, are chosen by the State Bar Association and two non-lawyers are chosen by the governor.

Judges must be removed if two-thirds of each house of the legislature recommends removal to the governor. Furthermore, any civil officer of the state (including judges) may be impeached by the state House of Representatives, tried by the state Senate, convicted and removed by a two-thirds vote of that body. Unlike all other elected officials in Michigan, judges may not be recalled by the voters. The recall of judges is prohibited by Article 2, section 8 of the state Constitution.

THE CRIMINAL PROCESS IN MICHIGAN

The judicial system in Michigan deals with a multitude of issues and it would be impossible to explore all of them here. However, a brief outline of a typical criminal case can demonstrate the workings of the Michigan criminal justice system.

Assume that an individual is arrested for a typical 'street' crime— let's say an armed robbery of a "7-11" convenience store. Shortly after his arrest he will begin the path through the Michigan criminal justice system. One of the first stops will be in the district court for what is commonly called the "District Court arraignment." At this point the county prosecutor will file formal charges against the defendant and bail will be set by the District judge. This will usually occur within hours of the arrest. Usually within 12 days of the arrest the defendant will face a preliminary hearing, also in District Court, where the court will determine if there is "probable cause" to bind him over to Circuit Court for trial.

The next (and usually very important) step will take place outside the formal courtroom procedures. Most criminal cases in Michigan (as well as other states) are settled by plea bargaining between the defendant (or his lawyer) and the prosecutor. Per-

JURIES IN MICHIGAN

Jurors are chosen by random selection from drivers license and state identification card lists. They can serve up to several weeks but increasingly jurors are asked to serve just a few days. The hope is to have a better cross-section of the public if individuals only had to serve for the duration of one trial, (usually no more than a few days). Many kinds of persons who might have other compelling obligations (e.g. doctors, dentists, attorneys, firemen, state and county officials) and those who might have health reasons for not being able to serve may be exempted from jury duty at the discretion of the judge. Those over 70 may also be exempt from jury duty at their own request. Sometimes, an extra juror or two is chosen to reduce the chance of a mistrial due to absence of a juror.

After the jurors are chosen for the general jury panel they must then be selected to serve on a particular case. The jury selection process (called the Voir Dire) allows for dismissal of jurors on two grounds. First, jurors may be dismissed "for cause." If they have any bias in the case, have formed an opinion about the guilt or innocence of the accused or have any personal ties with any of the trial participants they may be dismissed "for cause." Jurors may also face a "preemptive" dismissal where they can be dismissed without either attorney giving a reason. The number of preemptive dismissals varies with the offense, but for a serious offense like armed robbery the defense usually has twenty and the prosecution fifteen.

Once chosen, the twelve jurors must be unanimous is their verdict in a felony criminal case. Jury rules are a little different for minor criminal (misdemeanor) cases and civil matters compared to felony trials. In misdemeanor cases, juries consist of six persons and a verdict must be unanimous. Such cases are usually tried in District Court. In civil cases in Circuit and District Court, juries consist of six persons and five of them must agree in order to render a verdict. Juries are rarely used in Probate Courts.

Grand juries can be used in Michigan as they are at the federal level. They do not decide guilt or innocence but determine whether or not charges should be brought against an individual. The main duty of a grand jury is either to bring charges against an individual or to investigate criminal activity. Grand juries have wide ranging powers to investigate crime. A citizens grand jury is usually composed of 13-17 individuals. On occasion judges may act as a "one man grand jury" and investigate certain complex crimes. A grand jury should not be confused with a trial jury, which determines guilt or innocence.

PAROLE: RELEASE FROM SENTENCE

Once a defendant has been convicted and sentenced much of his fate rests with the seven member Michigan Parole Board. The board has the duty of making parole recommendations to the governor. Those serving life terms must have the approval of the sentencing judge (or the judge's successor) before parole is granted. Those granted parole must have a job and home and report regularly to a state parole officer. Since they are no longer confined in jail, they may resume voting.

Under normal conditions the parole board is the major decision maker. The governor usually accepts their recommendations. However, on occasion, the governor may override the parole board and grant reprieves (delay in sentence) or commutations (reduction in sentence). Usually these are granted only with the recommendation of the parole board.

haps 75% or more of all criminal cases are settled by the "plea bargain" process where the prosecutor offers the defendant reduced charges in exchange for a guilty plea.

The prosecutor often prefers the plea bargain system since it offers a speedy and more certain method of convicting individuals. Because of the great case backlog there is often pressure on the prosecutor to "keep the line moving" and deal with cases quickly. Plea bargaining is speedier than taking a defendant to trial. The defendant may also find the plea bargain tempting. If he did commit the crime, he will probably jump at the chance to face a lesser penalty. A "bargain" can be reached at any time until the jury returns the verdict.

The next step is the formal arraignment in Circuit Court. At this stage the defendant will be formally notified of the final charges filed against him by the prosecutor. These may or may not be the same as those in the District Court arraignment. He will enter a plea. This defendant is charged with armed robbery and pleads not guilty.

Perhaps six or eight months later he will face trial in a Michigan Circuit Court. At the trial the prosecution will have the burden of proving him "guilty beyond a reasonable doubt." The prosecutor will present the evidence of the arresting officer, the victim of the crime and any physical evidence available. In turn, the defense will try to undermine the case of the prosecution and raise a 'reasonable doubt' about his guilt in the minds of the jurors.

During the adversary contest between the defense and prosecution, it is the duty of the judge to:

-rule on legal motions regarding evidence and testimony.
-guarantee an impartial trial, where each side can fully present its side of the case.
-instruct the jury about the law in the case and the jury procedures to be followed.

The state Constitution guarantees the right to a trial by jury in criminal cases, though a defendant can choose to be tried by a judge. A felony jury is composed of twelve people and a misdemeanor jury is composed of six persons. In any criminal case, such as the felony in this example, all jurors must agree in order to convict or acquit a person. Other-

wise, the jury is considered "hung" and there could be a new trial. If this case is like most, the defendant will be convicted by the jury. About 70% of all defendants are found guilty by juries. He will usually be sentenced about a month after the trial.

If the defense felt that there was some flaw in the trial (for example, that the judge gave improper instructions to the jury) then they might try to appeal the case through the Michigan court system and beyond. A felon convicted at trial has a guaranteed right to one appeal in the Michigan Court of Appeals. Since this right is guaranteed, the right to a state-provided attorney is also guaranteed. (Since a 1994 ballot proposal passed, those who plead guilty are no longer guaranteed an automatic appeal with the Court of Appeals.) Assume that the Michigan Court of Appeals rejects the defendant's claim and reaffirms his conviction.

In nearly all real cases that is the last chance for the defendant. As one goes up the appeals system two barriers emerge. First, both the Michigan Supreme Court and the U.S. Supreme Court exercise what is commonly called "judicial discretion." This means that the supreme courts may decide which cases they will hear. Usually they hear only one case out of ten. Thus, for a defendant trying to appeal to the state or U.S. Supreme Court, the odds are great that his case will not even be accepted for a full hearing.

In addition to this barrier, as one appeals the costs mount. There is, of course, a guarantee of legal counsel at the trial stage. If the defendant can't afford his own lawyer the state will pay for the defense. The same is true at the first appeal stage, in the Michigan Court of Appeals. However, since there is no guaranteed right to appeal to the Michigan Supreme Court there is no guarantee that the state will provide an attorney. Thus the defendant must provide for his own legal expense, or find some group like the American Civil Liberties Union (ACLU) to pick up the cost. Appeals can be very expensive. Taking a typical case from an ordinary state Circuit Court to the U.S. Supreme Court can cost from $50,000 to several hundreds of thousands of dollars. Few defendants have such resources. Appeals are very time consuming. It may take two years or more for a case to work its way through to the U.S. Supreme Court. By that time the defendant may have served his time in prison.

Assume that this defendant does appeal to the Michigan Supreme Court and loses there—the Supreme Court reaffirms his conviction. Then, and only then, may he appeal to the U.S. Supreme Court. Finally, after so much time and money have been invested, he wins his case—the U.S. Supreme Court agrees that there was some flaw in his trial. Does this victory in the top court of the land mean that he goes free? Not necessarily!

When a person appeals he is usually claiming that there was some legal error in his trial and is asking for a new trial. Appeals courts usually do not decide issues of guilt or innocence. They usually decide whether or not the first trial was correct. If they decide that the first trial wasn't correct, the case returns to the local prosecutor, who may decide to try the defendant again, with the flaw corrected. Thus our defendant may still face a second trial and a second conviction. The local prosecutor may decide against trying the defendant again if the ruling of the higher court has undermined the case or if the defendant has served most of his sentence.

THE COURTS AND OTHER DECISION MAKERS

Because of the system of checks and balances the Michigan courts come into frequent contact with the other two branches of the government. How do the courts affect the legislature and the executive? How do those branches impact on the courts?

The courts may act like the executive branch when they issue writs of mandamus or injunctions. A writ of mandamus is a court order commanding an official (for example, the governor) to do a particular act. An injunction is a court order forbidding a certain action. In either of these ways the courts may limit the action of a governor or other members of the executive branch.

In contrast, the governor may have an impact on the courts through the appointment power. As mentioned earlier, the governor may appoint judges when a vacancy occurs. Besides filling vacancies, a governor may exercise judicial-like powers in granting pardons, reprieves and commutations of sentences. The governor is also officially responsible for returning criminal defendants to and from Michigan for judicial processing.

The legislature and the courts also interact in many ways. Most important is the ability of the courts to declare laws unconstitutional or interpret the meanings of the laws passed by the legislature. In turn the legislature may create new courts and define the powers of those courts, as it did with the Family Courts in 1996. Many operating procedures of the courts, such as the manner of electing judges, are also decided by the legislature. The legislature may also act in a court-like manner when it is involved in the impeachment and removal of elected officials.

The state courts often affect the national government as well. Most U.S. Supreme Court cases have their origins in the state courts. Thus, the state courts play a role in "setting the agenda" for the U.S. Supreme Court. State courts as well as federal courts may interpret the U.S. Constitution, though the interpretation of the federal court is supreme.

As the U.S. Supreme Court has grown more conservative, civil liberties groups have turned to the state courts more often. For example, recently the U.S. Supreme Court found Michigan's "drug lifer law," which required a life sentence for those convicted of possession of more than 1.4 pounds of cocaine, to be constitutional under the U.S. Constitution's "cruel and unusual" provision. Later the State Supreme Court found the law to be a violation of the "cruel or unusual" provision in Michigan's Constitution.

MICHIGAN'S COURTS - PROBLEMS AND PROSPECTS

Since the court system at some time or another touches every aspect of government, all governmental problems can become judicial issues. However, certain problems, such as crime and punishment, are usually deemed to be a major concern of the judicial system. State courts deal with the great bulk of criminal activity in the country. As the crime rate has risen and the public has become more concerned about it, there have been many efforts to modify parts of the criminal justice system in an attempt to control the crime problem.

In recent years various groups, either through lobbying, the initiative, or referendum, have tried to:

-deny parole to those convicted of certain violent crimes.
-require minimum sentences for some crimes.
-deny bail to certain types of defendants.
-prohibit 'early release' from prison under certain conditions.
-reinstate the death penalty in Michigan.
-build new prisons in the state.
-deny automatic appeal to those who plead guilty.

Whether any of these measures have much effect on the crime problem is a matter of great debate, but the appearance of such issues on the Michigan ballot is an indication of the obvious concern about crime.

Because of the increasing case loads throughout the state there have been calls for more judges and courts. Curiously, in spite of their importance, states average only three percent of their total expenditures on the courts. Michigan has a complex system of financing its courts. The Supreme Court has the duty of creating a budget for the state court system and the legislature sets the basic salaries for the various levels of state judges. However, local units of government may supplement the salaries of Circuit, Probate and District court judges, up to a certain level. The State Supreme Court has favored complete state financing of the judicial system to equalize the administration of justice throughout the state.

Figure 9.5

MICHIGAN SUPREME COURT JUSTICES (2003)

Name	Party Nominating**	Term ends on Jan.1:
Clifford Taylor	R	2009
Marilyn Kelly	D	2005
Robert Young, Jr.	R	2011
*Maura Corrigan	R	2007
Stephen Markman	R	2005
Elizabeth Weaver	R	2011
Michael Cavanagh	D	2007

*Chief Justice. Chosen by the other justices every two years.
** Supreme Court justices are nominated by political party conventions but run on non-partisan ballots.

Part 4

Local Government in Michigan

Introduction

Township Government in Michigan

Village Government in Michigan

City Government in Michigan

County Government in Michigan

Local School Government in Michigan

Local Government: Problems and Prospects

Introduction to Part 4

Learning Objectives

Why are local governments "creatures of the state"?

Explain how local governments are limited by the U.S. Constitution.

What are some reasons for having local governments?

Give examples of general-purpose and special-purpose local governments in Michigan.

Summarize conflicts about the independence of local governments from the state.

Key Terms To Know

residual power
general-purpose government
special-purpose government
overlapping local governments

The United States Constitution mentions only two levels of government— the nation and the states. There is no requirement that local governments exist, and no constitutional right to have such governments. How does it turn out that there are over 86,000 units of local government in the U.S.?

The power to create local governments is not specifically granted to the states by the national Constitution, but it is not denied them, either. The power to establish local governments is a residual power of the states. (See chapter 2.) Any state may establish local governments within its boundaries if it desires. All the states have done so, although the forms and powers of local governments differ from state to state. Thus, local governments are "creatures" or "children" of a state, or its people. Local governments may be established by state law (the usual approach) or by language in the state's Constitution.

As "creatures of the state" locals can and sometimes are 'taken over' by the state in some circumstances, such as serious financial difficulties. When the state takes over a local government the state administrator's powers are very great and supercede local elected officals. Recently, the cities of Highland Park, Hamtramick and Flint have been taken over by the state.

Since local governments are created by the state, they may only exercise those powers allowed by the state, and their internal organization may be limited by the state. A state may not allow its local creatures to do anything which the national Constitution prohibits the state itself from doing. Thus, by interpretation, even though local governments are not mentioned in the U.S. Constitution, they are bound by it.

WHY HAVE LOCAL GOVERNMENTS?

An obvious reason for the existence of local government is the large geographic size of most of the states and the fact that the typical state is not the same throughout. Some areas may be urban, others rural. The economy of one region may be based on one kind of activity, the economy of some other region on something else. Individuals in one area

may develop different values and lifestyles than those in another. Residents of different areas will likely have different needs. For example, those in a built-up urban area will have a greater need for services such as public water supply, police and fire protection, and sanitary sewage disposal than those in a sparsely-populated rural area. Local governments allow meeting these different needs in the most suitable fashion.

Local governments are often defended because they allow the residents of an area to tailor services to their desires. With local government, voters can adjust the cost and mixture of services to whatever they desire. While a person within the community will be compelled to accept the decision of the community, that is not the same as being forced to accept a decision made in other communities or the whole state.

Some feel that when important decisions are made by small numbers of people, citizens each have a more powerful role. In the mathematical sense, a voter in a group of 10,000 has more "vote power" than if the group numbers 100,000 or 1,000,000. Furthermore, if a citizen is unhappy with the decisions of the community, ("we needed the sewer and it was voted down" or "the cost of schools is too high for me") a system of local governments allows choice. Disgruntled citizens have many political options, including moving to a community where decisions better match their own preferences. If votes at the polls are not effective, individuals may "vote with their feet." Having many local governments allows choice.

MICHIGAN LOCAL GOVERNMENT IN GENERAL

Michigan's Constitution (Articles 7 and 8) mentions many local government forms: counties, townships, cities, villages, school districts and special districts, for example. For the most part the Constitution's language is very general. The precise features of local governments—their organization and powers—are primarily determined by state law.

Over the 20th century four major themes hve emerged.

- Michigan has a large number of local governments.

- The structure of many local governments, reflect the 19th century preference for a weak executive. This is especially true of counties and townships.

- Some powers exercised by cities are now being exercised by townships. Incorporation of new cities has been very low in recent years.

- Increasingly local units, while still relying on the property tax, are receiving more revenues from the state.

As of 2002, there were over 2900 local governments in Michigan. The number in each major category was as follows:

Counties	83
Cities	272
Villages	261
Townships	1242
K-12 School Districts	519
K-6/K-8 School Districts	36
Public School Academies	150
Intermediate School Districts	57
Community College Districts	28
Special Districts	263
Planning/Development Regions	14
Total	**2925**

Michigan ranks 14th highest out of the 50 states in terms of the number of local governments. These governments can be classified according to the number of functions they perform. A general purpose local government provides a variety of services to its residents. Counties, cities, villages and townships are general-purpose governments. School districts and community colleges are special-purpose governments providing a single service, education. There are many other forms of special-purpose local governments. Examples are: airport authorities, intermediate school districts and downtown development authorities. As you can see in Figure I-4.1 a wide variety of activities are shared by many local governments. Figure I-4.2 shows the population range of Michigan's local governments.

It is important to realize that these governments overlap each other. If your home is in a very rural area of Michigan you are simultaneously under the authority of a township, a school district, the county, the state and nation. If you live in a village,

its authority is added to those. If you live in a city in an urbanized area, you are subject to the authority of the city, a school district, a county, the state, the nation and (probably) a community college district and a number of other special-purpose local governments.

Striking the Proper Balance

The "parent-child" relationship between the state and its local governments is often controversial. Local officials frequently complain that the state does not provide local government with enough authority, or enough flexibility in administration, or enough money to carry out state-required programs, or enough taxing power. They see the state as an overly strict parent. The state's point of view is that it has created these governments, is responsible for them, contributes money to support their services and thus is entitled to a considerable amount of control over them.

These kinds of conflicts continue despite the fact that Michigan's 1963 Constitution modernized local government somewhat and allows the state legislature to strengthen the local level. Among other local-related changes, the Constitution requires the legislature to allow local governments to cooperate with each other in the solution of shared problems (Article 7, section 28). It also requires the "liberal construction" (broad interpretation) of the state Constitution and laws regarding counties, townships, cities and villages in their favor (Article 7, section 34).

Furthermore, the (Headlee) Tax Limitation Amendment of 1978 (Article 9, sections 6 and 25-34) requires the state to pay the localities for their cost in complying with any new state-required activity. The amendment also requires the state to keep the proportion of its revenues which are shared with local governments at the same level as in 1978-9. This requires the state to share about forty-two percent of its revenue with the local governments!

While local governments are creatures of the state, they can be as strong or weak as the legislature allows by statute or the people require by the Constitution. The following chapters will examine the main features of local governments in Michigan.

Figure I-4.1

Duplicative Functions of Levels of Government in Michigan

Function/Unit	State	Counties	Cities	Villages	Townships	Special Dist.	School Dist.
PARKS & RECREATION	X	X	X	X	X	X	X
LIBRARIES	X	X	X	X	X	X	X
ROADS & HIGHWAYS	X	X	X	X	X/+		
WATER		X	X	X	X	X	
SEWERAGE	+	X	X	X	X	X	
POLICE	X	X	X	X	X		
PUBLIC TRANSPORT.	+	X	X		+	X	
REFUSE DISPOSAL		X	X	X	X	X	
REFUSE COLLECTION			X	X	X		
FIRE			X	X	X		
CORRECTIONS	X	X					

The plus (+) indicates a role in financing or regulating specific services. Each type of governmental unit with an "X" has the authority to provide that governmental service.

Citizens Research Council Report No. 326, *A Bird's Eye View of Michigan Local Government at the End of the Twentieth Century.* August 1999, p.20.

OPEN MEETING ACT (Act 267, 1976)

This law requires open meetings of virtually all governmental bodies in Michigan. It guarantees every person in Michigan the right to know in advance, by public notice, when and where a public body is meeting, and gives each person the right to peaceably address a meeting of that body.

A meeting can be closed to the press and public only by a two-thirds vote of the members (in a recorded roll call vote) for a stated specific purpose. The only exceptions to this are for times when discussions are on sensitive matters that might allow someone to benefit from the information talked about. Examples are: labor negotiations, employee or student discipline, an option to purchase property, a pending lawsuit, a confidential job application, or material exempted by either state or federal law.

Moreover, the Act guarantees that copies of the public meeting minutes can be purchased from a public body, at only the reasonable estimated cost of printing and copying.

Source: Ferris E. Lewis, *State and Local Government in Michigan*, Hillsdale Mi., Hillsdale Educational Publishers Inc. 1979.

Figure I-4.2

Govermental Units in Michigan by Population, 1990

	Townships	Charter Townships	Villages	Cities	Counties
Less than 5,000	1044	34	260	134	1
5001--10,000	53	35	2	51	8
10,001--25,000	17	42	1	44	22
25,001--50,000	0	12	0	20	17
50,001--100,000	0	5	0	17	16
100,001--1,000,000	0	0	0	7	16
Over 1,000,000	0	0	0	1	2

Source: Citizens Research Council of Michigan, Report # 326, *A Bird's Eye View of Michigan Local Government at the End of the Twentieth Century*, August 1999, p.3.

Chapter 10

Township Government in Michigan

The Origins of Township Government

The Organization of Township Government

The Powers of Township Government

> *"In each organized township there shall be elected for terms of not less than two nor more than four years...a supervisor, a clerk, a treasurer and not to exceed four trustees..."*
>
> Article VII, Sec. 18, Michigan Constitution

Chapter 10

Learning Objectives

Summarize the creation of townships through the survey.

When and why were the earliest township governments created?

Are township powers spelled out mainly in the state Constitution or by state laws?

What is the principal governing body of township government? How are members selected?

Identify the major responsibilities of the township supervisor, clerk and treasurer.

What is the township annual meeting? Is it as powerful today as in the past?

Compare a charter township to a general law township.

Summarize township public safety services.

What are the economic and physical development powers of townships?

What are the functions of zoning boards? Boards of Review?

Key Terms to Know

Survey (congressional) township
Civil township
Township board
Supervisor
Clerk
Treasurer
Trustee
Annual meeting
General law township
Charter township
Zoning
Board of Review

Townships are the most numerous form of Michigan local government. As of 1999, there were 1241 townships and 44% of the state's citizens lived under township local government. Although a few cities and counties existed at statehood, through the action of the territorial legislature, the township could also be considered Michigan's oldest local form.

THE ORIGINS OF TOWNSHIP GOVERNMENT

Township government blends local government traditions of England and New England with a set of boundaries created as the state's land was surveyed in the early 19th century.

Townships originated in England during Anglo-Saxon times. The word "town" comes from the Anglo-Saxon TUN and "ship" from the word SCIPE meaning "the bounds of." So we get the words tun-scipe or township. In early English days the king's forces were far away and raids on the coast by foreigners from the European continent were fairly common. It became the obligation of each town to defend itself. Later townships became a local area of English government.

The early settlers that came to New England brought this custom of local government with them. From it grew what we now know as the New England town and the town meeting where problems of government were discussed. The geography of New England aided the growth of towns and thus kept alive the town meeting as a unit of government.

Today townships operate in 20 states, primarily the New England, Mid-Atlantic and Midwestern states. Outside the Midwest, townships often function like cities. Generally, in the Midwest they emphasize basic rural services. There are however, many exceptions to this pattern.

Creating Township Boundaries: The Survey

A congressional, or geographical township, is a unit of land survey and not a unit of local government. This system of land survey was set up in the Ordinance of 1785 to give settlers moving into the region a definite description to their land. Land was to be divided into townships each six miles square, each township thus containing thirty-six square miles. Each of these one square mile areas in a geographical township was called a section and given a definite number.

The survey of Michigan was begun in 1815 in the southern area of the state. Work proceeded northward, and was completed in 1847 at the Michigan - Wisconsin border. As the survey progressed, people to the east began to respond to the low land prices in Michigan and to the availability of surveyed land with clear title. The state's population, theretofore centered in Detroit, began to grow in size and become more dispersed.

While Michigan did not grow as rapidly as other places in the Northwest Territory until the mid 1830s, its growth was significant, as the following table indicates.

Table 10.1

Michigan's Population 1810-1840	
1810	4,764
1820	8,765
1830	31,639
1840	212,267
Source: *Santer, Michigan: Heart of the Great Lakes*, pp. 166-169.	

From Boundaries to Governments

Immigrants to the territory brought the idea of local government with them from eastern states, especially New York. Most of the new settlement was rural and the need arose for a local government to provide such services as public meetings, burials, building and repairing roads, providing relief for the poor, and regulating fences on property lines.

The territorial legislature responded to this need in 1827 by converting the survey township boundaries into governmental boundaries. Thus civil townships (units of government) were formed, and names, as well as numbers, were given to them. There is not always a perfect correspondence between the boundaries of survey and civil townships, because adjustments to local circumstances and desires were often made. In general, though, today's township boundaries are based on the survey boundaries.

We will soon see that these township boundaries will be changed if a city is formed within the township. A civil township may even go out of existence if all of its land becomes a part of one or more cities or villages. (The survey township would still exist.)

Township government, then, has its origins in lines drawn on maps for the main purpose of keeping land records. This set of survey boundaries was converted to governmental purposes by the legislature. In a sense, the survey boundaries served as a ready-made framework for rural local government. This form of government has been adapted to changing needs as time has gone by.

Today, Michigan townships range in size from tiny 300 acre Novi Township in Oakland County to 380,000 acre McMillan Township in Luce County. Population ranges from the 10 people in Point Aux Barques Township in Huron County to the 95,648 in Macomb County's Clinton Charter Township.

Michigan Constitutions and Townships

Michigan's 1835 Constitution contained a few references to townships but did not deal with them in any great detail. The Constitution of 1850 did have some provisions of importance for townships. Township officers were mentioned, and townships were recognized as "corporate" bodies, able to enter into contracts, sue and be sued. Furthermore, the township supervisors (chief executives) were to serve as the governing body of county government (see chapter 13 for more detail on this) and the county board was given the responsibility of organizing new civil townships.

Michigan's Constitutions of 1908 and 1963 had little direct effect upon township government. Constitutional provisions affecting townships included the elimination of justices of the peace (1963)

and the spread of initiative and referendum procedures (1908). A pattern was in place whereby laws, not constitutional language, were used to clarify township powers.

THE ORGANIZATION OF TOWNSHIP GOVERNMENT

Michigan's Constitution says "In each organized township there shall be elected for terms of not less than two nor more than four years as prescribed by law a supervisor, a clerk, a treasurer and not to exceed four trustees, whose legislative and administrative powers and duties shall be provided by law," (Article 7, section 18).

Most of the details of township organization are determined by state law. The overall effect of state law has been to create a rather simple organization pattern, as will be seen below. Also, it should be noted that township organization is quite standardized — most townships are organized in about the same way.

The Township Board

Most of the powers granted by state law are exercised by the Township Board. This body has either five or seven members: the supervisor, clerk, treasurer and two or four trustees. The board thus combines officials with some executive responsibilities (the supervisor, clerk and treasurer) with legislators (trustees) and is the governing body of the township, exercising administrative and legislative powers.

Members of the Board are chosen in at-large elections in the fall of presidential years. The election sequence involves a partisan primary (August) and partisan election (November). The term of office is four years. Only two trustees are elected unless a township has over 5,000 residents, or over 3,000 registered voters, and has opted to choose four trustees. All "charter townships" (see below) have four trustees.

Candidates for a township office must be voters in the township, and designate a particular position they wish to fill. One does not run for the board and then become, say, clerk. Instead, one seeks a particular position. Voters in the township can thus evaluate candidates with reference to the particular post they are seeking. In most townships, nearly all offices are held by members of the same political party.

Vacancies in any elective township office must be filled by the township board within forty-five days after they occur; if not, the governor must call a special election. If the vacancy arose because of a recall, it must be filled by a special election. (For a review of recall procedures, see chapter 6.)

The compensation of Township Board members may be set by the township residents at an annual meeting, by the Township Board (subject to referendum) or by a compensation commission. In this last approach, the commission consists of five township residents, appointed by the board, who set compensation unless overridden by the board by a two-thirds vote.

As noted earlier, some board members have special administrative responsibilities (the supervisor, clerk and treasurer) while others (the trustees) perform only legislative responsibilities. The sections below provide some detail on the special responsibilities of township executives.

The Township Supervisor. The chief executive officer in the township is the township supervisor, who acts in many ways like the mayor of a city or the president of a village. Unlike some mayors, the supervisor has no veto power over actions of the board. The supervisor is a member of the Township Board and chairperson of that body. He or she is also in charge of assessing taxable property in the township, enforcing township ordinances and, working with the township clerk, transacting all legal business for the township. Public Act. 90, of 1972 permits townships to employ a township manager to whom some of the supervisor's responsibilities can be assigned.

The Township Clerk. The township clerk is the secretary of the township and keeps a record of township business. The clerk also keeps records of registered voters in the township and conducts all elections held in the township. The clerk also keeps the minutes of the township meetings, financial records and copies of all township ordinances. The clerk also serves as a member of the Township Board, the Election Board and the Board of Health.

The Township Treasurer. The township treasurer is the custodian of the township's money and must be bonded. He is a member of the Township Board, the township Election Commission, and the township Canvassing Board. The treasurer is in charge of collecting taxes paid to the township and paying out money on order of the Township Board. The treasurer also keeps records of all financial tranactions.

Other Elected Officials

A township may elect up to four constables. A constable is not a member of the board. Constables have powers of arrest for misdemeanors committed in their presence and for traffic violations, may serve various writs and legal notices and perform some business inspections. In the past, all townships were required to have at least one constable, but the office is now optional.

Townships may also have an elected Park Board and/or Library Board and may join district library systems.. A favorable vote by the township voters is required to create these. Such boards each consist of six members chosen for six-year staggered terms. The establishment of such boards is often coupled with special taxes to fund park or library activities.

The Annual Meeting

The annual meeting of township residents allows township citizens to exercise "direct democracy" regarding some township matters. At one time, citizens in townships could do anything the township government could do. As time has gone by, the powers of citizens at this meeting have been limited. The annual meeting is no longer a legal requirement, as it had been before.

If an annual meeting is held, the supervisor chairs it and conducts any voting. As mentioned above, the powers of the citizens at the annual meeting have been limited over time. While the meeting may have an important role in setting compensation, most of its other actions are advisory to the township board. Today's meetings are quite different from those of the past, when township residents set budgets, passed ordinances, and elected township officials.

Appointed Township Officials

Many services of townships will be administered by departments headed by a person appointed by the township board. Other services might be administered by a board or commission appointed by the township board. Generally, these officials serve at the pleasure of the board. Details on many important appointed positions will be provided in the sections below dealing with township powers.

Charter Township Organization

So far, the discussion has been limited to the standard form of township government in Michigan—the so called general law or regular law township. There is another type of township government, called the charter township. There are about one-hundred and thirty charter townships in Michigan, and the number is increasing, especially in populated areas.

In 1947 the state legislature passed the Charter Township Act, in response to the desire of township officials in urban areas to increase the powers of townships. This act does *not* allow the people of a township to write their own charter, detailing the powers and structure of township government. A charter township does *not* have a locally written charter, as does a home rule city or village. Instead, the state law which allows a charter township to be formed from a regular law township specifies the organization and powers of the charter township. All charter townships have the same powers and are permitted the same organizational options. In effect, the state law is the charter.

Any township of more than 5,000 residents can become a charter township by action of the Township Board. The board would pass a resolution of intent to switch, which would become effective unless challenged by citizen referendum petitions. A referendum on charter township status can be forced by signatures of 10% of the number of electors last voting for supervisor, and must be filed within sixty days after passage of the resolution of intent. A township with a population of at least 2,000 residents, but fewer than 5,000, may also become a charter township, but there must be a public vote on the question at a regular or special election. The question may be placed on a ballot by the Township Board or by the initiative petition process. In the latter, signatures of registered voters equal to 10% of the number of votes cast for the office of supervisor are required to force the election.

A change to charter township status may bring minor changes in the organization of the township's government. A charter township's board may appoint a township superintendent and delegate to that office many of the functions of the supervisor. The superintendent does not replace the elected supervisor, but as an appointee would presumably guarantee more professional administration of township policies. In a charter township, there must be four trustees elected rather than the usual two. As of 1999 there were 128 charter townships in Michigan.

Generally, the organization of charter townships is the same as that of regular law townships. Later, it will become clear that the major differences between charter and regular townships is in terms of their powers, not organization. Charter townships have more protection than general law townships against loss of territory by annexation (see chapter 15) and also have greater property taxing power than the regular township (see chapter 16).

THE POWERS OF TOWNSHIP GOVERNMENTS

As in the case with governments at all levels, the powers of townships have expanded as time has gone by. Much of this expansion of authority has been in response to urbanization, and the need for more public services.

The growth of township powers has not been without controversy. At various points in the past, some students of government have argued that townships should be abolished. These critics of townships usually suggest that the county assume most of the township's functions in rural areas. They point to the fact that in most states no equivalent to the township exists, and that counties are stronger than in Michigan. Others have suggested that township territory be reduced by allowing cities and villages to easily expand their boundaries.

Township government has successfully resisted such pressures. Township powers have expanded. Township territory is now somewhat protected against encroachment by cities and villages. The ability of general law townships to convert to charter township status has allowed even greater powers to be exercised. While the local taxing power of townships is weaker than that of cities and villages (see chapter 16) the townships receive substantial state aid in meeting costs, and thus can provide a wide range of services. The following sections review the major township services and the officials responsible for them.

Public Safety Services

Township boards may appoint a Building Inspector to enforce the construction code in effect within the township. Townships may also establish fire and police departments and provide for school crossing guards, ambulance service, street lighting or other emergency preparedness services. Townships may also contract with nearby governments to provide any of these services.

Townships can also regulate garbage and refuse disposal and regulate many kinds of business through zoning and licensing laws. Enforcement of liquor laws is also done by the township.

Economic and Physical Development Powers

Townships may exercise many powers related to the uses of land. In doing so, the township government influences growth (or lack thereof) in the township.

Many of the most important powers relate to "zoning." Townships may pass zoning ordinances, which determine the kind of use to which particular land in the township may be put. An appointed zoning board is in charge of this process. Township zoning boards consist of four to seven members appointed by the township board to four-year staggered terms.

Decisions of the Zoning Board, or other officials charged with enforcing zoning ordinances, may be appealed to a Zoning Board of Appeals.

Townships may establish a Planning Commission, consisting of five to nine electors of the township. The staggered terms are three years long. The function of a planning commission is to establish a comprehensive plan for orderly township development.

A township also may establish a Building Authority, to aid in developing township public facilities such as buildings, parks and parking lots.

Townships have authority to enter into agreements with other local governments in order to provide water supply and sanitary sewage disposal systems. Under one approach, two or more governments form an authority, which in turn contracts with the units for the establishment of the system.

A Township Board may also create industrial development districts and land rehabilitation districts. Property in such districts is given favorable tax treatment: new industry, plant expansion and remodeling are encouraged by a twelve-year, 50% tax waiver. Townships may also create Economic Development Commissions, which may establish commercial and industrial projects, lease them to private business, and grant certain property tax waivers.

Townships may provide sidewalks, and through contracts with the county Road Commission, build and maintain roads in the township. The role of the county in township road development is discussed in chapter 13.

Other Township Activities

The role of townships in providing library and park services has already been noted, as have the very important activities of the township clerk in conducting elections. There are numerous other township actions of importance to residents.

Townships have important roles in property tax administration. The supervisor is responsible for setting the taxable value of property in the township, and other assessors are often appointed. Sometimes, townships employ an independent appraiser for this purpose. Townships must have a Board of Review, a body of three members serving two-year terms, appointed by the township board. The function of this board is to hear appeals of assessments and make such adjustments in taxable value as it sees fit. Additional detail on the property tax is provided in chapter 16.

Townships may employ an attorney to provide legal advice to the board and prosecute township ordinance violations in district court. Townships must arrange for an audit of township finances at least every two years or annually if larger than 2,000 residents.

Thus, the township form of government is able to provide a wide range of services. Once considered by many to be declining in importance, or even fit to be put out of business, the township has grown in significance, even in urban areas. It is likely that township powers will continue to expand and some have suggested that the powers of townships in urban areas be expanded greatly.

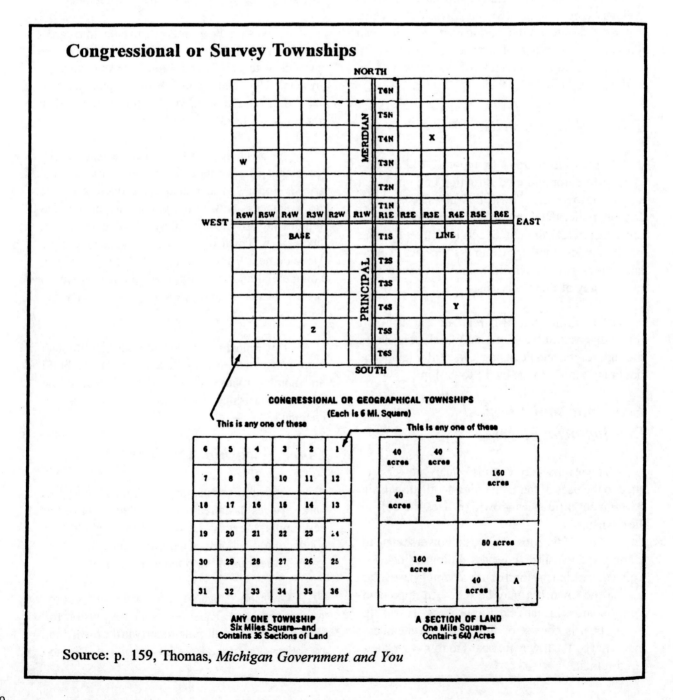

Congressional or Survey Townships

CONGRESSIONAL OR GEOGRAPHICAL TOWNSHIPS
(Each is 6 Mi. Square)

This is any one of these

This is any one of these

ANY ONE TOWNSHIP
Six Miles Square—and
Contains 36 Sections of Land

A SECTION OF LAND
One Mile Square—
Contains 640 Acres

Source: p. 159, Thomas, *Michigan Government and You*

Chapter 11

Village Government in Michigan

Powers of Villages

Forming a Village Government

General Law Villages

Home Rule Villages

> *"The legislature shall provide by general laws for the incorporation of... villages."*
>
> Article VII, Sec. 21, Michigan Constitution

Chapter 11

Learning Objectives

Are all small settlements commonly known as villages actually a government?

Describe the process for forming a village government. Why are fewer villages being formed now, compared to in the past?

Describe the relationships between a village and a township in terms of voting, taxes and boundaries.

Describe the basic organization of a general law village.

Describe the basic organization of a home rule village.

Which form of village government has the most flexibility in terms of internal organization and powers?

Summarize the election process in villages.

What future would you predict for village government in Michigan?

Key Terms To Know

incorporation
charter
general law village
home rule village
village officers

In some rural areas small communities of people live in a single area and are governed by townships. These are commonly called unincorporated villages. Such settlements often have names, highway signs and may even have separate listings in the telephone directory. However, they are not governments and have the township as the local government. There are other kinds of villages which have governmental powers. These incorporated villages are the topic of this chapter.

POWERS OF VILLAGES

The reason people choose to create villages is to provide greater governmental services for themselves. Some of the general powers that villages have are:

-to develop and enforce building codes and zoning regulations.
-to license and regulate a wide variety of activities such as taverns, motels, hospitals and others.
-to establish its own water supply and to protect the public health by requiring sanitation.
-to control and maintain streets, highways and sewers.
-to maintain a police and fire department.
-to condemn private property for village use. Villages may own buildings, parks, cemeteries, hospitals etc.

Finally, villages may levy and collect property tax and charges to pay for the services provided.

FORMING A VILLAGE GOVERNMENT

Villages are often created because a concentration of people living in a certain area (usually rural) decide that they need more services than the township can offer. Those living in a heavily populated part of the township may need a water system, building regulations, street lighting, better police and fire protection and, of course, more taxing power to pay for these services.

The earliest village governments in Michigan were formed by the state legislature or the county supervisors in response to the wishes of the people in the settlement. Since 1909, people have been able to form a village at their own initiative, under guidelines set by state law.

Under current law a village may be incorporated with a minimum population of 150 people and a minimum density of 100 people per square mile. Most of Michigan's villages are very small. Most have fewer than 750 people and none are over 5000 population. The boundaries of a village may cross over township or county boundaries.

When the people living in a certain area decide to form a village they can choose one of two types. The first, called the general law village, is governed by the general laws of the state. The other, called the charter village or home rule village, can develop its own charter to reflect the special needs of those in certain areas.

A charter is like a local constitution. It is a document drafted by people within the community and approved by the voters. It spells out the organization and powers of the village government and its officials. The charter must not, however, violate state law. In the final analysis, state law determines the options the community may have and the community picks from among these options.

The powers of townships have expanded in modern times. As townships became more able to meet urban needs, the number of villages being formed has dropped. During the 1970's, only one new village was formed. Since 1930 more than 100 villages have become cities, to take advantage of greater powers allowed in a city form of government.

The Village and the Township

Villages remain a part of the township or townships in which they are located. This can often cause some confusion for those living in the village, especially at election time. Since villagers vote in both the elections held by the township (which include township, state, school board and other elections) and those of the village, they must register twice—in the village and also in the township. The village registration is for village elections only. Those living in villages will pay taxes to the village as well as their usual taxes to the township, schools and others. Property in the village remains in the township too. Thus the formation of a village does not reduce the property tax base of the township. If a village includes the entire township, the township no longer exists as a government. Residents of the township outside of the village do not pay village taxes, and do not have a vote in village elections.

GENERAL LAW VILLAGES

As of 2002 there were 261 villages in Michigan. Of these about 213 are general law villages. If an area desires to become a general law village a petition signed by qualified voters equal to one percent of the population (but at least 100 voters) must be presented to the State Boundary Commission. The commission can either accept or deny the request for proposed incorporation. If the boundary commission accepts the request then the question of incorporation is presented to the voters of the proposed village. If the voters approve, then the area becomes a general law village. It has no separate charter and operates under the general laws of the state regarding villages.

Officials of General Law Villages

According to state law, general law villages are to elect a village president, a clerk, a treasurer and six village trustees to serve on the village council. Though there are some exceptions, most villages nominate their officials in odd-numbered years by petitions or at a partisan primary on the third Monday in February and then elect them at a partisan village general election on the second Monday in March. The terms of office are usually two years. The president and the six trustees form the village council.

The village president is the chief executive of the village and the presiding officer at village council meetings. He informs the council of items that should be brought to their attention, recommends measures, votes in case of a tie and sees that ordinances are enforced, officials appointed and that the books and records of the village are kept in order.

He may also exercise, within the village, powers like those granted to sheriffs.

The village clerk has powers similar to that of the township clerk. The clerk keeps the records and documents of the village. He or she may act as an accountant for the village, keep records of all property belonging to the village, register and countersign licenses and report to the council on money paid out. The village treasurer keeps track of money taken in and spent by the village.

General law villages sometimes appoint other officials. Some villages appoint a village marshall who acts as a police officer to enforce ordinances. He has the same power as a sheriff within the village. Other villages may also appoint a surveyor and a street commissioner. As the title indicates the surveyor surveys the lands and makes plats of subdivision lots and other maps for village use. The street commissioner is in charge of repair and upkeep of the streets, bridges, sewers and parks of the village.

HOME RULE VILLAGES

About 50 villages in the state are home rule villages. This means that the villages are able to draft their own charters to reflect their own local needs and desires. The charters drawn up by home rule villages may not violate the state Constitution or state law. The process of incorporating a home rule village, like that for the general law village, requires that a petition for incorporation be signed by qualified voters equal to one percent of the population of the area to be incorporated. At least 100 voters must sign. The petition is reviewed by the State Boundary Commission as outlined above. If the voters approve incorporation they must also elect a five member commission to draw up the charter for the village. Then, after the charter is approved by the governor, the voters of the proposed village must approve the document.

The home rule village (sometimes called the charter village) may adopt somewhat different election procedures and has greater taxing power than a general law village. Typically, the home rule charter indicates the village officers to be elected and appointed as well as the dates of election and the salaries. It also outlines a basic system for collecting and appropriating tax money. Villages also must provide public records of all official village preceedings.

The home rule charter may be amended at any time if the village council proposes an amendment by a two-thirds vote and the public approves the amendment at the next general election. Charters may also be amended by citizen initiative petitions followed by a vote of the public.

Officers and Elections in Home Rule Villages

The precise operating details of home rule villages will vary as their charters vary. However, a home rule village must elect a village president, a clerk, a treasurer and a council. The size of the council may vary from three to seven members. Most villages (either home rule or general law) have a local government similar to the weak mayor-council form of government. Some (about 13) home rule villages operate with a council-manager form of government. (chapter 12 provides details on these forms.) Elections in home rule villages can be either partisan or non-partisan. Home rule villages usually hold their general elections in March of odd-numbered years.

VILLAGES AND THE FUTURE

Villages can provide some very important governmental services at the local level. Historically, villages have been an important transition between rural settlements and urban development. Today, as we become an increasingly urbanized society, small settlements of people in rural areas are often skipping the village stage and incorporating as a small city because cities have greater governmental power and more independence than villages. Other areas that were once villages are finding it to their advantage to become cities. In recent years few new villages have been formed and many existing ones have become cities. Furthermore, the expansion of the powers of township government has reduced the need for the formation of new villages. In a 1999 report on Michigan local government, the Citizens Research Council recommended that villages be eliminated and their functions be taken over by either cities or townships. This may or may not take place, but it will be interesting to see what happens to the village form of government in the future.

PREAMBLE

We the people of the Village of Holly in order to enjoy to the fullest extent the advantages and benefits of local self-government, as authorized by the constitution and laws of the State of Michigan, do hereby establish this Home Rule Charter.

CHAPTER 1. BOUNDARIES AND SUBDIVISIONS OF THE VILLAGE

Section 1.1. Boundaries.

The village shall embrace the territory constituting the Village of Holly on the effective date of this Charter, together with such annexations thereto and less any detachments therefrom that may be made from time to time. Upon annexation or detachment of territory, the boundaries shall be deemed thereby to be changed without amendment of this section. The clerk-treasurer shall maintain and keep available in his/her office for public inspection an official description of the current boundaries of the village.

CHAPTER 2. GENERAL MUNICIPAL POWERS

Section 2.1. Powers of the village.

(a) All powers, privileges, and immunities not inconsistent with the provisions of this Charter, possessed by the Village of Holly by virtue of its incorporation as such and enumerated in Act No. 3, P.A. 1895, the former Charter of the village which is hereby superseded, are hereby expressly retained by the village and shall constitute a part of the police power of the village even though not expressly enumerated herein.

(b) Further, unless otherwise provided or limited in this Charter, the Village of Holly and its officers shall be vested with any and all powers, privileges and immunities, expressed and implied, which villages and their officers are, or hereafter may be, permitted to exercise or to provide for in their charters under the constitution and laws of the State of Michigan, and of the United States of America, including all the powers, privileges, and immunities which

Chapter 12

City Government in Michigan

Powers and Duties of Cities

Creating a City

Elected and Appointed Officials of City Government

City Government Organization

> *"Each city... shall have the power to adopt resolutions and ordinances relating to its municipal concerns, property and government, subject to the constitution and law."*
>
> Article VII, Sec. 22, Michigan Constitution

Chapter 12

Learning Objectives

What is the procedure for creating a city form of government?

What is a charter? Do all cities have one?

Can a city's charter be changed?

Identify some of the services likely to be performed by a city government.

How can the office of mayor differ from city to city?

Summarize the duties of a city council and discuss different methods of council selection.

Identify the major departments in a typical city's government.

Summarize the features of the major forms of city government organization.

Which form offers the best guarantee of strong leadership in city politics?

Key Terms to Know

incorporation
charter
strong-mayor form
city manager
city council

charter commission
council-manager form
weak-mayor form
mayor

The first cities were formed at the very dawn of recorded history. Much of what we call civilization is based on the formation of cities. The term "city" has many meanings. Centuries ago it referred to the place where the bishop of the church lived. Today the word brings to mind the crowded streets of New York, Chicago, Spokane and Detroit. Areas that are homes to millions of people are cities of course, but so are Michigan's communities of Au Gres, Beaverton, Mackinac Island and Fennville, each with a population of about one thousand.

Care must be taken not to confuse the social-economic city with the legal city. When one says "Detroit," the reference might be to the more than four million people living in the entire metropolitan area of southeastern Michigan, or to the legal Detroit, with about one million people and a very small share of the land area of the total metropolis. Likewise, many small communities do not have the social complexity of a Flint or Muskegon, but are cities in a legal sense. (Today almost one-half of Michigan's cities have fewer than 5000 residents.) The focus of this chapter is on the legal city—the city as a governmental body.

A city is one of the basic units of local government in the state. Local governmental powers are assigned to either cities, villages, or townships. (Villages remain part of the township and exercise limited governmental authority.) Cities do not remain part of the township but rather are separate governmental units. The city form could be considered the most powerful and independent local government in Michigan. As populations have grown within the state, the city has become a far more significant local unit of government. More and more villages are incorporating as cities and many settlements are becoming cities directly, without going through the village stage. Today a majority of Michigan's population lives in cities.

POWERS AND DUTIES OF CITIES

The city is a subdivision of the state and like the township has several basic duties. Cities are required by the state to assess property as the basis for county and school taxes, collect taxes for the counties and the schools and conduct county, state and national elections.

In doing each of these things a city may be taking over some of the work that was previously done by the township. A city that was once a village will take over these duties from both the township and the village. When the people of an area decide to incorporate as a city they must weigh the pros and cons of taking over the extra duties that were once done either by the township or the village.

These required duties are not the only things that cities do. Depending on the size of the city and the needs of the population a city might provide many other services.

Fire control is an obvious need for urban areas, where a single fire may threaten the homes of many people. Cities provide fire department, electrical inspectors, fire inspectors, establish building codes and zoning regulations to prevent serious fires.

Most cities provide a dependable supply of safe water for their residents. Many cities maintain their own pumping stations though some purchase their water from larger cities in the state. Cities must provide for the disposal of waste materials. Cities commonly provide garbage collection and storm and sanitary sewer systems.

The streets and alleys must be installed and maintained by the city. This is often one of the more costly parts of the city budget. State gas and weight taxes are shared with cities for this purpose.

In an age of great worry about crime, cities are expected to provide more and more police protection. The local city police find that their duties range from enforcing minor traffic violations to investigating murder.

Some larger cities provide public transportation systems. In Michigan buses are the most common form of public transportation, though in other large cities, subways, rail and other types of public transportation may be provided.

Cities may provide many other services such as city planning and zoning regulation, recreation facilities, libraries, cemeteries, museums, zoos and parks. The type and range of these services varies greatly. What the nearly one million people in Detroit want and need will be quite different from what the 1500 people in Frankfort need and want.

CREATING A CITY

The earliest city governments in Michigan were created by the state legislature, or, as in the case of Detroit, established by the French in 1701, the territorial legislature. Many of today's cities were first villages, established by either the legislature or the county board of supervisors. Whatever their origin, most of today's cities have a form of government which has been selected by the people in the city. The first methods of creating cities were replaced in the early 20th century, when the state implemented the "home rule" approach to creating city (and village) governments.

Cities may be formed in areas where the population is at least 750 persons. However, county seats may become cities without regard to population and villages in more than one township may become cities with only 600 persons. If the people living in an area desire to become a city the first step requires a petition to the State Boundary Commission, which deals with many types of boundary changes in the state. If the commission accepts the proposed incorporation then the question is submitted to the voters of the area.

If the voters in the area approve the idea of becoming a city they then elect a nine member charter commission to draw up the charter. Charter commission members may be elected at the same time as the election on the question of incorporation or at a later time. The charter commission drafts a proposed charter. After review by the governor, it is submitted to the voters of the area for approval. If approved, the charter takes effect according to a schedule included in the proposal. Once in effect, charters can be revised. The process of revision is essentially the same as that outlined above. An elected commission develops a revised charter and it is submitted to voters for their approval.

Types of City Incorporation

Home Rule Cities. All but eight of the 273 cities in Michigan have developed and written their own charter based on the **Home Rule** Act of 1909. This act permits the people of an area to draw up a charter, within the limits of the state laws and Constitution, which will meet their own needs. Thus the details of the organization and operation of home rule cities will vary a great deal. Home rule cities must have a population of 2000 and a population density of 500 per square mile.

The *charter* is the basic law of the city. It lays out the structure and, to some extent, the process of the government. It describes the powers to be granted to the legislative branch (the city council) and the executive (the mayor or manager). It may also detail the terms of office for city officials, when and how they are to be elected, regulations regarding finance and taxation and policies for city employees.

Charters may be changed by a majority of the public voting on an amendment, which can be proposed by the city council or through citizen initiative. The charter may even be entirely revised if the citizens desire. This would require electing a charter commission and later approval of its proposed changes. Generally home rule cities have much greater flexibility than those cities governed by general state laws.

Special Charter Cities. One city in the state (Mackinac Island) was incorporated by special act of the state legislature before the Home Rule Act was passed in 1909.

Fourth Class Cities. These cities are organized under the general law of 1898. About eight of these cities currently exist in the state. Most of the governments are of the weak council-mayor variety and partisan elections are held in April for city offices. Principal officers elected are the mayor, city clerk, treasurer, assessor and members of the city council.

ELECTED AND APPOINTED OFFICIALS OF CITY GOVERNMENT

Though cities vary considerably, there are several offices that are common to most cities in Michigan. The patterns of city elections were reviewed in chapter 5. It should be kept in mind that most cities hold elections in odd-numbered years, and that non-partisan elections are common in cities.

The Mayor

In general, the mayor is the chief administrative officer of the city, though like other executives he may also exercise some legislative powers. He has the duty of enforcing state laws and city ordinances. In many larger cities he must prepare and submit a budget to the city council. The mayor is expected to make recommendations to the council for action and may often mobilize public opinion for his goals. In some cities the mayor will preside over the city council and will usually have the power of vetoing the measures passed by the council. Typically, that veto may be overridden by the council—often by a required 2/3 majority. The mayor is also the ceremonial head of the city and is the individual who personally greets visiting dignitaries. He is often a lobbyist for the city, appearing before legislative committees in Lansing and other groups to attract new funds and programs to the city. Like almost all elected officials in the state he may be recalled by the voters.

The City Council

The city council is the legislative branch of city government. It is a unicameral body (though there are a few bicameral city councils elsewhere in the country) usually composed of five to nine members. They are typically elected for two year terms, though the charter may provide for different length terms, and may stagger the terms. The city council can often be the principal policy making body for the city—particularly in the manager or weak mayor arrangements. The council may pass ordinances (laws) dealing with a variety of matters such as zoning, health and safety regulations, licensing regulations and traffic safety. The annual budget of the city is also approved by the council.

Members of the council must be registered voters and live in the city (and often the ward) in which they seek election. City councils may be elected either on a ward basis or at-large. The difference in election systems can be significant and there are certain advantages and disadvantages to each.

Electing individuals at-large (where the voters of the city vote on all of the members of the city council) may select individuals who are the most skilled at administration and government. Those who are attorneys, accountants or who have had prior governmental experience are more likely to be chosen in an at-large election. This kind of election, however, may select members of the council from only one part of the city—often the upper middle class area. Though it may produce expertise it can leave many parts of the city with the feeling that they are not represented at city hall. Electing members of the council by wards should produce a more diverse city council and does give those living in each of the city's wards the feeling that they are being represented.

The city council may, within any limits set by the charter, set its own internal operating procedures, meeting times and other details of operation. The council may also investigate activities of the mayor or other officials. In those cities where the mayor does not preside over council meetings, the council will choose a presiding officer. Council meetings are open to the public. Members of the city council may be recalled by the voters in accordance with state law and the charter provisions.

Other Officials

Many cities elect several other officials, though other cities may appoint them. The most significant of these are the city clerk and the city treasurer.

The *city clerk* is the major record keeper of the city. The clerk keeps a record of the proceedings of the city council, keeps records of the monies spent by the city. Clerks issue licenses for many activities. In larger cities as many as seventy different types of licenses are administered. Clerks keep records of all registered voters in the city and prepare the voting machines and ballots for election day. (See chapter 5)

The *city treasurer* is in charge of the financial matters of the city. The treasurer collects city and county taxes, pays the bills of the city and makes regular reports to the city council on the financial status of the city.

City Departments and Commissions

These agencies carry out much of the day-to-day work of the city. City departments function under either a single director appointed by the mayor or manager or under appointed boards or commissions. The number and type of these agencies vary from city to city but some of the most common are:

Personnel/ Human Relations Department. This department is in charge of filling jobs for the city. It develops job descriptions, deals with city unions, negotiates contracts and manages many complex matters inherent in employing a number of people. This department must be certain that the employees of the city are treated in accordance with the city charter, state law and federal law. In many cities, some or all of the personnel practices may be kept independent of control by elected officials by a Civil Service Commission. If a city has a Civil Service system, its organization usually resembles that of the state's, which is described in chapter 7.

Department of Finance. This department is in charge of preparing a city budget in accordance with the wishes of the council and the mayor. This department may also do much of the city's purchasing.

Department of Assessment . This department assesses the property in the city in order to make up the city tax roll. Property must be assessed in accordance with state law in a fair manner.

Board of Review. This board's duty is to listen to citizens who feel their property has been incorrectly assessed and make any adjustment they feel is appropriate. Usually the board of review meets in March.

City Planning Commission. This commission plans the future growth of the city and may provide zoning for certain types of economic activity. In some cities appeals of rulings on current zoning may be taken to this commission.

Department of Law. This department provides legal advice to the city and its officials. It may look into land titles, defend the city or its officials in court and help in writing city ordinances.

Complaint Department. Cities often have a department that reviews citizen complaints against various city departments. Sometimes this official is called an *ombudsman* and may investigate city departments in response to citizen complaints.

Police Department. The police department is charged with maintaining peace and order in the city. The police enforce city ordinances and state laws. The size and organization of the police force will vary with the size of the city.

Fire Department. The obvious function of the fire department is to put out, control and prevent fires. Departments conduct fire safety inspections, investigate the cause of fires and other programs.

Department of Public Works. This is often one of the larger departments of the city. The Department of Public Works repairs and maintains streets, sewers, city parks and many other basic facilities of the city. In some cities this department also does inspections of dwellings for safety. Some cities will include services for rubbish disposal under this department (called the Department of Sanitation in other cities). In short, this is one of the most visible and active departments in the city.

These departments are typical for many cities. Not all cities will have them, and many smaller cities may have only a few. The names and titles of the departments will also vary from one city to the next.

This concludes the discussion of the organization of city government in Michigan. The financing of city services will be reviewed in chapter 16. While the city is Michigan's most powerful form of local government, there is concern about the ability of some cities to survive financial stress. The main questions facing some of Michigan's are not about their powers or internal organization, but whether they can afford to deliver the services desired by their residents.

CITY GOVERNMENT ORGANIZATION

There are several ways to organize a city government. Some methods give great power to the executive (mayor or manager), others grant most power to the legislature (city council or commission). The three basic types of city government are: The weak mayor-council, the strong mayor-council and the council-manager plan. Each of these plans has certain advantages and disadvantages and over the years each plan has emerged as a popular form of city government. These forms are summarized in Figure 12-1.

Currently the *council-manager* form is the most popular among the cities of the state. Of Michigan's 273 cities, 176 are council manager and 97 are mayor-council. In this system the people of the city elect the city council and the city council appoints a city manager to administer the laws and policies established by the council. The city manager is trained to effectively manage the daily affairs of a city. City managers are often experts in the areas of law, public administration, finance or civil engineering.

The manager is typically appointed for an indefinite term by the city council. He or she serves at the pleasure of the city council, though some charters require certain procedures before the city manager may be fired. The average city manager stays in one job for about seven years. The manager reports to the council and carries out its policies. Frequently friction develops between the manager and the city council. The council may feel the manager is entering the realm of policymaking and often the manager feels that the council is interfering with the day-to-day administration of city government.

In spite of its problems there are several advantages offered by the council-manager type of city government. The daily operation of the government is centered in a single professionally trained individual. The plan is fairly simple and easily understood by the voters. Governmental and political responsibility may be enforced by the voters upon the council and by the council on the manager. Some of the deadlocks and delays with other forms of government are avoided.

This form is not without its critics, however. The chief charge directed against this form is that it fails to develop strong leadership on the city council. Strong political personalities, such as a dominant mayor, are usually absent. It also has been argued that too much power is placed in the hands of a person (the manager) who is not directly responsible to the voters.

In the council-manager city the council will usually choose a presiding officer who may hold the title of mayor but will have few significant powers. The manager usually appoints department heads and the mayor's roles are largely ceremonial.

The *mayor-council* form is the next most common form of municipal government in Michigan. It is also the oldest type of city government. Throughout the nation it is the most popular with very small and very large cities. There are two general types of mayor-council governments—the "strong" mayor and the "weak" mayor systems. In actual practice a government may blend a little of each.

The *weak mayor* form provides for a strong city council and a mayor with few powers. The council, usually elected on a ward basis, has the greatest amount of power. The mayor has relatively few appointments to make they must be confirmed by the council. The mayor may have a veto but the council can often override it. Administrators of city boards and commissions are either appointed by the council or independently elected. The administration is often decentralized. The power to organize and develop a budget is shared with the council and other administrative agencies. In Michigan the weak mayor system is still used in a number of small cities, particularly fourth class cities developed under the general law of 1898.

The weak mayor system has a number of problems. Since there is no single strong official, central direction of the government is often lacking. The responsibility of government is diffused among the mayor, the council and a number of rather independent boards and commissions. Under this plan, since many officials are elected, the voters face a long and complex ballot and may be required to vote for offices that they have little knowledge of.

On the positive side, the weak mayor system does provide a very good check and balance system, making it difficult for any individual to dominate the government. Because it has so many elected officials it allows much public involvement.

The *strong mayor* form of government eliminates some of the problems of the weak mayor arrangement by giving more power to the mayor. Usually much of the power that was scattered among several agencies under the weak mayor form is centralized in the mayor's office. The mayor can appoint and remove the heads of major departments. The mayor has a veto power over most acts of the council. It is difficult to override—a 2/3 vote of the council is usually required. In some smaller cities the mayor may be the presiding officer of the council and vote in case of a tie. The mayor is separately elected and is not a member of the council, but does have the power to recommend legislation and call special meetings of the council. In short, the mayor really is the chief executive of the city. The mayor is elected at large, is responsible to the voters for his acts, and may be recalled by the voters at any time. This approach to city organization most resembles the "separation of powers, checks and balances" model in use at the state level.

There are five major advantages to the strong mayor-council system. It gives the mayor the power to give central direction to the management of the city. The mayor is chief executive and may direct the city government. With the elimination of many independent boards and commissions the council's command of policy is also strengthened. Eliminating independent boards and commissions shortens the ballot and allows the average voter to be better acquainted with the merits of those running for office. The lines of responsibility are clearer since the basic administration of government rests with the mayor. This form allows for aggressive city leadership.

There are a few possible problems with this system. The mayor may be a popular political figure who has little experience with administration. To counter this, some strong mayor charters require that a professional chief administrative officer (CAO) be appointed—a kind of assistant mayor a blend with the "manager" concept. Further, the separation of powers between the mayor and the council can lead to conflict and deadlock, making it difficult for the government to take any action.

Figure 12.1

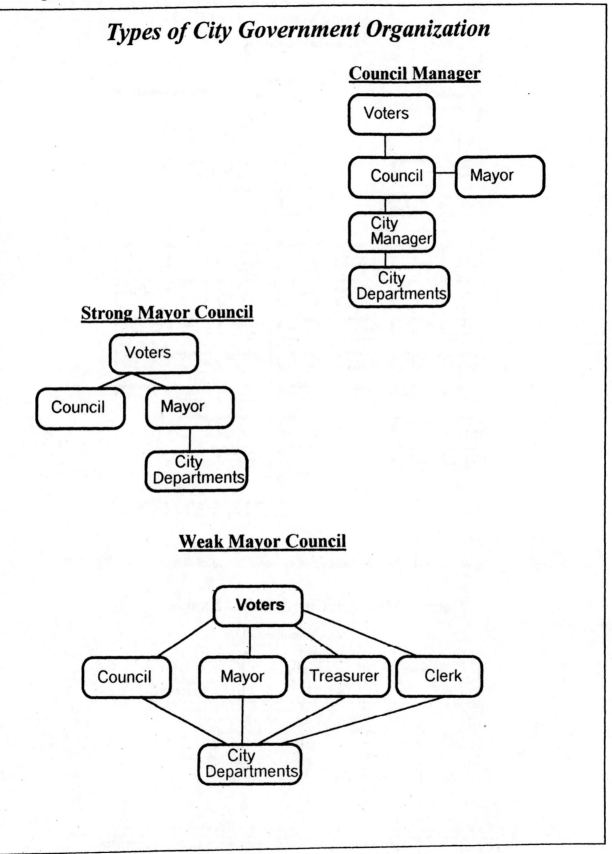

Types of City Government Organization

Council Manager

Voters

Council — Mayor

City Manager

City Departments

Strong Mayor Council

Voters

Council   Mayor

City Departments

Weak Mayor Council

Voters

Council   Mayor   Treasurer   Clerk

City Departments

Organizational Structure
Strong Mayor: City of Flint

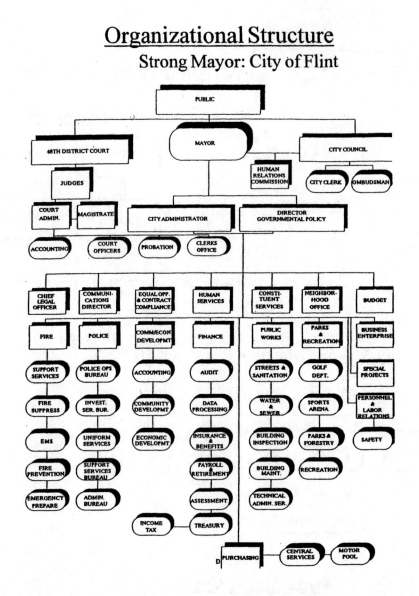

Source: City of Flint, Mi. *Comprehensive Annual Financial Report, FY 97* **p. 1-D**

Council Manager: City of Grand Rapids

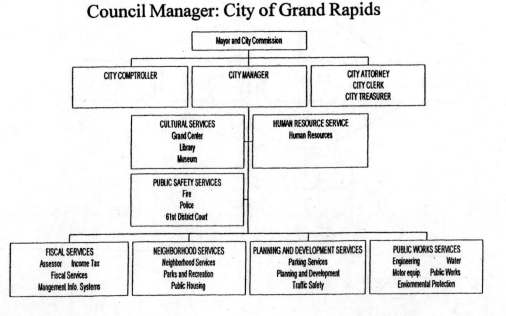

Chapter 13

County Government in Michigan

The Origins of County Government

County Organization in Michigan

Options/Alternatives in County Government

> *"There shall be elected for four-year terms in each organized county a sheriff, a county clerk, a county treasurer, a register of deeds and a prosecuting attorney, whose powers and duties shall be provided by law."*
>
> Article VII, sec. 4, Michigan Constitution

157

Chapter 13

Learning Objectives

Was the county level created mainly as a local government or as an arm of the state?

How do county boundaries relate to those of other local governments?

What are some major features of county government organization?

Identify the major elected officials in county government and discuss their responsibilities.

Identify the major boards, commissions and departments of county government.

Summarize the organization and powers of the County Board of Commissioners. How does it compare with the old board of supervisors?

Compare the local government powers of the county to those of cities, villages and townships.

Summarize the kind of changes which would come about in the "optional unified form" of county government.

How is a "home rule county" created?

Is the executive stronger in a home rule county than in the optional unified form?

Key Terms to Know

county seat	DPW	optional unified form
county clerk	planning commission	home rule county
register of deeds	social services board	county executive
county treasurer	tax allocation board	sheriff
board of health	prosecuting attorney	mental health board
drain commissioner	controller	road commission
medical examiner	county board of commissioners	

More than 3000 county governments exist throughout the United States, 83 of them in Michigan. A common view of the county is that it is a mixed government, partly local and partly state. Sometimes it is viewed as close to the people, sometimes distant. For quite a long time the county did not receive much attention from students of government. This situation is changing for a number of reasons.

In some states, counties have become much more powerful than in the past and more powerful than in Michigan. There have been some recent changes in county government in Michigan and these have made counties more important. Many people believe that a streamlined and more powerful county may be helpful in dealing with problems which "spill over" city, village and township lines in urbanized areas.

This chapter will examine the past and present of county government. Chapter 15 will look at its possible future(s).

THE ORIGINS OF COUNTY GOVERNMENT

The roots of county government can be traced through the first states (especially New York), to the colonies (Massachusetts had counties in 1643) and to England. In England the county equivalent was called a "shire" and its law enforcement officer a "shire-reeve." Today's equivalent? The "sheriff"!

The formation of counties was intended to allow a central government (the state) to carry out its activities by creating administrative centers within its boundaries. In this sense the county, more than any other general purpose local government, is an "arm" or "agent" of the state. The main purpose of the early county was not so much to deliver local services but to carry out state functions such as conducting elections, prosecuting state law violators, and keeping vital records. This helps explain why county boundaries are quite large compared to those of cities, villages and townships.

The Evolution of County Boundaries

It took about a century for the existing boundaries of Michigan's 83 counties to take shape. Michigan's first county, Wayne, was created by Congress in 1796 under the terms of the Northwest Ordinance. It originally included nearly all of what is now Michigan, and parts of all the other Northwest Territory states. The present boundaries of Wayne County date to 1815.

As time went by, new counties were formed by dividing up the older larger counties. The maps on the following page illustrate this, and show how the creation of counties followed the survey and settlement. As Kenneth VerBurg summarizes: "the legislature would designate and name an area as a county and, for a time, it would be attached to an organized county for governing purposes. After the number of settlers became large enough, the legislature would pass an organization act to establish the county permanently." (VerBurg, 1972, p.I-7.) This process was completed in the 1890s, and county boundaries have stayed the same since then.

In developing county boundaries care was taken to relate them to township boundaries. County boundaries include groups of townships. Village and city boundaries can cross township lines, and may also cross county lines. The most striking feature of county boundaries is that they are linear. A glance at the map will show how many are square or rectangular. The square counties would consist of 16 townships, 4 high and 4 wide, or 24 by 24 miles, for a total of 576 square miles. Only a few Michigan counties have fewer than 16 townships within their boundaries. Benzie, the smallest county, has only 10 survey townships and 316 square miles. Marquette, the largest, has 1,841 square miles and over 50 survey townships. Most of the variations in county land area or shape can be explained by coastline irregularities or by local desires at the time of the organization of the county.

All counties have a *county seat,* a city or village in which the county's offices are headquartered. These locations were selected by the people in the county and are frequently the city or village largest at the time of organization. There was often heated competition for "seat" status because of the economic benefits expected and some county seats

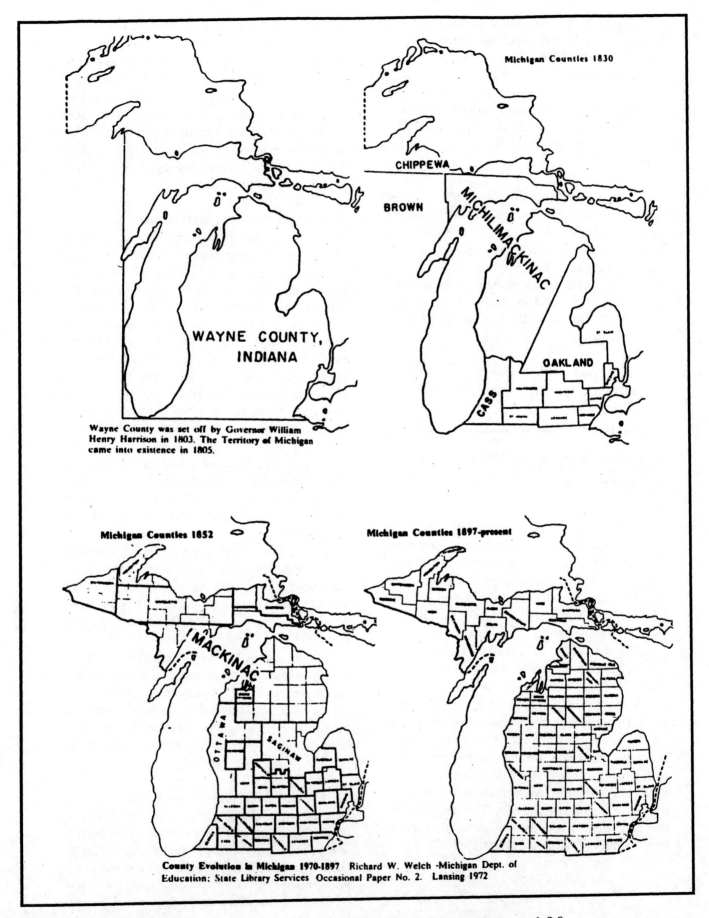

Michigan Counties 1830

CHIPPEWA

BROWN

MICHILIMACKINAC

WAYNE COUNTY, INDIANA

OAKLAND

CASS

Wayne County was set off by Governor William Henry Harrison in 1803. The Territory of Michigan came into existence in 1805.

Michigan Counties 1852

MACKINAC

OTTAWA

SAGINAW

Michigan Counties 1897-present

County Evolution in Michigan 1970-1897   Richard W. Welch -Michigan Dept. of Education: State Library Services Occasional Paper No. 2. Lansing 1972

Source: Appears in VerBurg; *Guide to Michigan County Government* pp.1-8,9.

have been relocated from time to time, by majority vote of those in the county. Since today's county boundaries have been in place for such a long time we should probably not expect them to change. However, the legislature could alter the county map, or two or more adjacent counties could combine into one if voters in each affected county approved.

The Evolution of County Organization and Powers

County government in Michigan is very complex. Its internal organization is much less streamlined than that of other governments. County powers have expanded, although the county does not have the strong local government powers of cities, villages and townships. Such a situation did not arise overnight.

The earliest powers of counties were related to land development, tax collection, vital records, and law enforcement. Michigan's 1835 Constitution required each county to elect a clerk, treasurer, sheriff, register of deeds and prosecutor. That Constitutuion also established many county-based courts, but did not specifically mention an overall governing body for the county. An 1827 act of the legislature of the Northwest Territory established that the governing body of the county would be a "board of supervisors" consisting of the supervisor of each township.

Since there were hardly any cities or villages in existence at that time, a die was cast. The county was to be a service agency for the state and its activities were to be coordinated by local governments—the townships. Note also that there was no one single head of county government. Many officials were separately elected, and the governing body was a board which would combine legislative and executive activities.

The 1850 Constitution provided that each county would be a body corporate, able to act in its own name, sue, and be sued. It provided that cities, which were becoming more numerous, would be entitled to representation on the board of supervisors, and placed some limits on the taxing power of counties. Michigan's 1908 Constitution continued the same basic organization of the county, established tax limits in connection with county road

systems and set limits on borrowing for non-road uses. The 1908 Constitution did make reference to an emerging role for counties in the areas of public health and support of the "indigent poor and unfortunate."

In the 1963 Constitution's provisions regarding county government, few fundamental changes were made. Debt limits were raised, terms of office of most county officials were lengthened to 4 years, a "charter county" status was allowed, and changes were made in the court system. Yet, on the whole, county organization and powers remained the same—complex, with a great many elected officials and a governing body based on the governments within the county. County powers were those permitted by the state and did not include the usual powers of local government. Cities, villages and townships were the "strong" local governments, having the police power, ability to zone land, regulate businesses and so forth.

It is important to realize that county government functions were growing throughout this time. While some county services were mentioned in the Constitution, most of them were spelled out in state law. As new needs arose in a changing society the state often made the county responsible for meeting them. Many new county departments were created by law and the state defined the powers of these offices in ways that made them quite independent of any local control. These constitutional and statutory actions created four major features in county government:

-Many independent officials, some elected and some appointed.
-The lack of a central executive.
-A strong state role in defining county powers.
-The lack of most local government powers.

Such a pattern results from the kind of patchwork development which characterizes the county. This led to confusion in the minds of the voters about who had responsibility for certain governmental activities. These patterns will be examined in more detail in the next section.

COUNTY ORGANIZATION IN MICHIGAN

Nearly all counties in Michigan are organized in the same fashion. Many departments are headed by elected officials and there are many departments headed by appointed officials or boards, some of which are quite independent. All counties have a Board of Commissioners, which combines administrative (executive) and legislative functions.

Elected Department Heads

This section examines a number of county elected officials (such as sheriff, prosecutor, treasurer, clerk and register of deeds) who have major responsibility for the administration of a particular department. All these officials are elected county-wide, for terms of four years. (Terms were two years until the 1963 Constitution.) Their terms follow the presidential sequence. These offices are all filled through partisan primary and general elections. Individuals holding these offices usually have a strong political base in the county electorate and close ties to one or more factions in their political party.

The compensation for these offices varies from county to county and is set by the County Board of Commissioners. In nearly all cases these are "constitutional officers." They are required by the state Constitution, although their duties are defined by law. Except for clerks and prosecutor, vacancies in these positions are filled by a committee consisting of the probate judge with the longest service in office, the prosecuting attorney and the county clerk. In the case of the clerk and prosecutor, a vacancy is filled by the county's circuit judge or judges.

With the exception of the prosecutor, the qualifications for these positions are minimal. One must be a registered voter within the county, and remain so in order to stay in office. Prosecutors must be attorneys in good standing. All of these officials are subject to removal by the governor, or recall by the voters.

The County Clerk. Nearly all of the duties of the county clerk are set by state law and concern the keeping of important records. In about 20 counties, this office is combined with the register of deeds, as the state Constitution permits.

The clerk serves as record keeper for many boards and commissions in county government, including the board of commissioners, tax allocation board and board of canvassers. The clerk also serves the Circuit Court, being responsible for maintaining records of pleadings and decisions.

The clerk issues many kinds of permits and licenses, keeps records of business incorporations, marriages and divorces, assumed names, and births and deaths. The clerk has major responsibilities in the administration of national, state and county elections, as outlined in chapter 5. Members of many licensed professions are required to file proof of license with the clerk.

The Register of Deeds. As noted earlier, the Constitution permits the County Board of Commissioners to combine this office with the office of county clerk. Most counties have not done so. If combined, the new office is usually called clerk-register.

Like the clerk, the register of deeds has record-keeping responsibilities of major importance. Unlike the clerk, the register's work falls into one category: property records. The register of deeds keeps a record of the ownership of all property within the county. Transfers of ownership are also recorded, as are mortgages and other claims against a property (such as past taxes due, or an easement allowing use of the property by a utility.) Plats (subdivisions) of land in villages and townships are kept in this office.

The County Treasurer. The duties of the treasurer involve receiving county funds, and the safeguarding and depositing of such funds. The treasurer must be "bonded": insured for the safety of county funds.

The treasurer receives money belonging to the county, pays out money when legally authorized to do so, and sells land on which taxes are delinquent. The treasurer pays moneys to the state treasurer received from the Probate Court such as moneys received from deceased people whose identity is unknown, or from the sale of land where there is no known heir. (Such moneys are said to "escheat" back to the state.) The treasurer also pays moneys received from various forms of state aid to city, township, and school treasurers, reports to the County Board of Commissioners each year the amount on money received and disbursed by him and serves on the county board of allocation and on the plat board.

The County Sheriff. The office of sheriff began in Anglo-Saxon times, when there were many small independent kingdoms in England like Kent, Essex, and Sussex. When they became united into one kingdom they became known as shires. In each shire there was a shire-reeve, who was appointed by the king. It was their duty to collect the king's income, enforce the law, and see that the king's government was carried on. From these early English shire-reeves comes the modern county sheriff.

Every Michigan Constitution has required this office at the county level. The sheriff is responsible for the employment of deputy sheriffs and other employees, as the county budget permits. Sheriffs perform a number of services in the operation of courts. For example, they may serve summonses, subpoenas, and execute various court orders.

Sheriffs are also responsible for the operation of the jail which each county must maintain or contract with another to do so. They have custody of and responsibility for a variety of prisoners. Some people in jail are awaiting trial while others are convicted but awaiting sentence. Some are waiting to be transferred to state penal institutions to serve sentences greater than a year, while others are serving less than a one year sentence in the jail. The construction of the jail, and the appropriation of money to maintain it, are responsibilities of the county board of commissioners. Thus the sheriff can be viewed as jail administrator. The state department of corrections and state and federal courts monitor county jail facilities for "overcrowding" and other health and safety problems.

The sheriff and deputies act as police officers, and are charged with enforcing state statutes, from criminal laws to traffic law, and their duties often include civil defense and animal control. The law enforcement duties of the sheriff are complicated if there are other police agencies in the county. Cities have police departments and their officers have the same authority as the sheriff. In practice, sheriffs do not police cities unless some cooperative arrangement is worked out. Townships may also have police departments and, if so, the sheriff usually serves in a back-up capacity. Areas of a county without a police department depend entirely on the sheriff. How much patrol and investigation the sheriff actually can do is determined by the County Board of Commissioners through the county budget. To guarantee itself protection a community without a police force may contract with the sheriff for services if it does not want to create its own police force.

The Prosecuting Attorney. The most important duty of the prosecuting attorney is to see that persons accused of violating state laws receive trial and punishment if convicted. In doing so, prosecutors occupy an important stage between the police and the courts. When the police arrest someone in the belief they have committed a particular crime, the evidence is reviewed by the prosecutor or his assistants. If satisfied that the person did commit the crime the prosecutor may then authorize legal proceedings. If not satisfied, the prosecutor is free to refuse to process the case. Thus, there is much discretion in this role.

Some prosecutors have implemented deferred prosecution programs where an accused person is not prosecuted, but not fully released either. In these programs the prosecutor's office supervises the person's participation in counseling programs. These programs are usually used in first-offense, non-violent crimes.

The prosecutor may petition circuit judges to appoint a grand jury. These grand juries do not try cases as would a court, or give verdicts. They are used to gather evidence which might lead to charging (indicting) a person of a crime. There can be either the "one man" grand jury, where an individual (usually a judge) can investigate complex crimes, or the traditional citizens grand jury, composed of 13-17 persons.

Prosecutors have responsibilities in connection with the enforcement of support orders in divorce cases if public assistance is involved, in consumer protection, and may be called upon to assist the state's attorney general. County prosecutors may act as attorney to the County Board of Commissioners, although county boards may choose

163

to appoint their own counsel. In larger counties, the elected prosecutor usually has a staff to assist in the responsibilities of the position.

The Drain Commissioner. This position is a statutory office not required by the Constitution. In a few smaller counties there is no elected drain commissioner and the responsibilities of the office are undertaken by the road commission.

This office is of great importance in urbanized counties and in those which have a very productive agricultural economy. In response to petitions by citizens or local governments, this office establishes "drainage districts" (a form of special-purpose government) and conducts engineering studies to determine how to best control drainage problems. The construction of a drain is authorized by a "board of determination", a panel of disinterested county residents. Costs are apportioned between residents of the drainage district and government bodies. (These are special assessments). The drain commissioner oversees construction and maintenance of the drain system. Drain commissioners may also become involved in the management of flood control projects in multi-county areas and in the management of inland lake water levels within the county.

In urban counties one of the most important functions of the drain commissioner is the coordination and development of facilities for water supply, and sewer and waste disposal services. State law allows counties to use the road commission for these functions, but most do not do so. Since much of the work of the drain office is done near roads, coordination of these two offices is highly desirable. As "county agent" for water and sewer services, drain commissioners act to plan, finance and construct facilities upon request by the road department or local units of government. Financing is usually through bonding (borrowing) by the county and/or local communities, and the bonds are paid off by property taxes, special assessments or user charges. Occasionally, state and/or national moneys are available for these projects.

The Judges. It was pointed out in chapter 9 that judges in Michigan are part of a unified *state* court system. However, many relationships exist between judges and county government.

Judges (other than Supreme or Appeals Court judges) are elected within county boundaries. Their salaries may be supplemented by the county. The staff of courts is paid for by the county. The sentencing decisions of judges can affect the sheriff's ability to administer the jail, which is also funded by the county.

Major Appointed Boards and Commissions

One of the most distinctive features of county government in Michigan is the great number of boards and commissions which administer services. State laws frequently require (or allow) a county to undertake a service and often require that the department be headed by a group of people. There are examples of this in the state executive branch as well.

Most of the time members of these executive bodies are appointed by the County Board of Commissioners and serve staggered terms of office. In a few cases specific qualifications exist but as a rule the county board has full discretion as to whom to appoint. These appointments are commonly viewed as "patronage"—the distributing of political rewards. Compensation is determined by the County Board of Commissioners.

These boards and commissions often have a degree of independence from the County Board of Commissioners. The activities of the departments are often financed by funds over which the county board has little if any control, and the activities of the department are often limited to those required or allowed by state law. Once appointed, members of these boards serve long terms and can only be removed after a public hearing.

This section will survey the more important agencies in this category.

The County Road Commission. State law allows a county to elect this body, but most road commissions are appointed. The three members serve overlapping 6-year terms, whether elected or appointed.

The activities of the road commission are of great significance. Residents desire a safe and

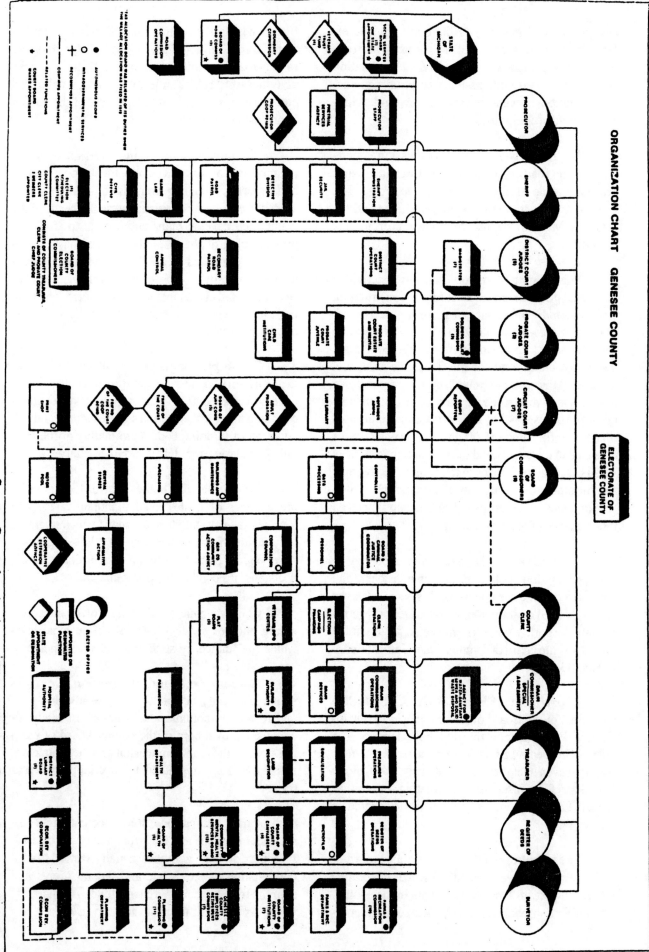

ORGANIZATION CHART GENESEE COUNTY

Source: *Comprehensive Annual Financial Report, Genesee County, Mich. 1987*

165

convenient road system and there are obvious effects of the road system on the physical and economic development of the county. Coordination between the road commission, the drain commissioner and other agencies concerned with development would seem highly desirable.

The authority of the road commission extends to non-state roads in townships. Cities and villages are responsible for their own non-state roads. The commissioners are to hire a superintendent and the state encourages the use of an engineer in this position.

Road commissions coordinate their activities with local government as plans for the construction, widening and maintenance of roads are developed. These activities are almost entirely paid for by state gas and weight taxes which are distributed to state agencies, county road commissions, and cities and villages. Most gas and weight revenues are devoted to road uses, while some are used for other transportation purposes. The key factors in the distribution of funds are the amount of gas and weight taxes collected in the county and the mixture of "primary" versus "secondary" roads in the county. Some road commission projects are partially financed by township or county taxes or special assessments levied on those whose properties benefit.

As noted earlier, the road commission may be assigned the duties of the drain commissioner, and may also operate the county park system. Wayne County's road commission operates Detroit Metropolitan Airport. Airports may also be operated directly by the board of commissioners, as is the case in Kent County.

Department of Public Works. State law allows a County Board of Commissioners to establish a "DPW" and more than half have done so. The DPW is headed by a board of public works—three, five or seven members appointed by the County Board of Commissioners to rotating three year terms. The road commission may be designated as the DPW.

The activities of DPWs are confined to water and sewer systems, and usually involve cooperative relationships with local governments in the county. The DPW approach can be considered an alterna-

tive to having the drain commissioner involved in water and sewer activities. If the DPW is assigned to the road commission, important public works activities would all be under one agency, but the road commission is somewhat independent of the county board of commissioners.

Planning Commission. The purpose of planning is to assure that development is coordinated and orderly. Planning commission staffs usually study the economic, physical and social needs of the county and develop plans and criteria to guide the process of growth. County boards may, by an ordinance approved by a 2/3 vote, establish a planning commission. These commissions have between five and eleven members, a majority of whom must hold no county office. Members serve 3-year overlapping terms.

County planning commissions primarily serve in an advisory capacity to county government and to local governments. The most important controls over land use (the zoning and subdivision of land and adoption of building codes) are mainly at the city, village and township levels, not the county.

County planning bodies provide local governments types of professional planning advice and services such as statistics and maps which might be very costly if each local unit developed its own. Also, county planners attempt to coordinate zoning decisions of neighboring governments.

County planners are often involved in coordinating and reviewing programs at the local level which are funded by state and/or federal monies.

County Park and Recreation Commissions. A county or counties may establish a park and recreation commission. Members usually include some members of the county board of commissioners, the road commission and the drain commission and are appointed for overlapping 3-year terms.

Park commissions study recreation needs, may acquire lands and construct and operate parks. Funding for park activities usually comes from a combination of fees, state and federal grants and support from the county general fund. A separately voted tax for park purposes may be used.

Family Independence Agency (Social Services) Board. In Michigan, the county occupies a critical position in the delivery of social welfare and income assistance programs. Unlike many other states, Michigan's cities, villages and townships are not involved in many social welfare services, but the county has long had such a role. Today's county responsibilities were determined by the state in response to needs dramatized by the Great Depression of the 1930's.

The state Family Independence Agency, formerly the Department of Social Services (discussed in chapter 7), is responsible for administering state and state-federal assistance programs. Each county has a Family Independence Agency to deliver these services. The employees of the department are state employees.

The governing body of the department is the county Family Independence Agency board. It consists of three members, two appointed by the board of commissioners and one by the director of the state department. The term is three years. The duties of the board are mixed. It functions as an advisory body to the state department, but does not have much authority over programs originating at the state level. On the other hand, the board has some policy-making responsibilities in social services provided by the county, which may include emergency relief, hospitalization and foster care.

Tax Allocation Board. Since the Great Depression, the Michigan Constitution has limited the total property tax which may be levied without a vote of the people to fifteen mills (1.5 percent of taxable value). These fifteen mills must be divided between many local units of government which depend on the property tax. The tax allocation board does this. In effect, this board levies property taxes.

The governments affected by the board's action are townships (except charter townships), K-12 school districts, intermediate school districts, and the county. Cities, villages and charter townships have their tax limits and powers set in their charter or by law. Voters in townships, school districts and the county may raise taxes above fifteen mills by vote and may also vote to make a fixed division of the fifteen mills among governmental units. They may also raise the limit on unvoted property taxes to eighteen mills and adopt a fixed allocation. If the distribution of taxes to the township, school district and county is made permanent, a county does not have an allocation board.

In counties having a tax allocation board, it consists of the county treasurer, the chairperson of the county board's finance committee or the chair of the board of auditors if the county has one and the superintendent of the intermediate school district (see chapter 14). Other members include a private citizen chosen by the county board, a township board member chosen by the supervisors of the townships in the county, a board member of one of the three smallest school districts chosen by the intermediate district board, a resident of a city and a member of a school board both chosen by the probate judges, unless there is a school district in a city of more than 10,000 people, in which case the board of the largest school district selects the board member.

The board examines tax needs of the various governments in the county. State law guarantees each a certain minimum tax levy, unless they cannot show need. The tax allocation board divides up the rest. Tax allocation board decisons may be appealed to the state tax commission.

More details on the operation of the property tax in Michigan can be found in chapter 16.

County Board of Health. The county has a very important role in delivering health services. It has virtually replaced the cities, villages and townships in this function. Since 1965 all counties must have a health board and department or join together in such. Boards of health consist of five persons appointed to five year terms by the board of commissioners. Regional health boards have a number of representatives from each participating county.

Much of the responsibility of the health department involves environmental matters. The state health department sets standards to be met with reference to private sewage disposal, garbage and refuse disposal, sanitation in food establishments and resorts, among other things. The county health department will enforce these standards.

Other areas of county health department activity include maternal and child health programs, tuberculosis control programs, programs related to the identification and elimination of communicable diseases, for example diphtheria, smallpox, rubella, dental health and health education service.

In addition to these activities, counties may also operate hospitals. A separate board operates county hospitals. These boards, known as hospital boards, are appointed by the county board.

Community Mental Health Boards. During most of its past, Michigan's policy and services regarding mental illness relied heavily upon large institutions such as the state mental hospitals in Pontiac and Traverse City. Beginning in the 1960's, the state developed a different emphasis and brought the county into this field for the first time.

By majority vote of its board of commissioners any county may establish a community mental health program. Counties may also join with one another to do so. The principal governing body of the program is a 12-member community mental health board, appointed to 4-year terms by the county board chairperson. This board, according to state law, is to be broadly representative of the community.

The mental health board is responsible for identifying mental health needs in the community. It must attempt to develop local sources of financing from governments and private institutions (the state also participates), and attempt to establish coordinated mental health services. A comprehensive set of local services would include emergency services, in- patient and out-patient services, and close coordination with local health, judicial and other social services institutions.

The Cooperative Extension Service. This office is an arm of Michigan State University, part of that institution's mission as the original land-grant college. The office provides professional assistance to citizens in matters dealing with agriculture, horticulture, forestry, 4-H, home economics, nutrition and energy. Professional "extension agents" are MSU employees, and others are county employees. The county board has no appointive authority over the service, but usually tries to keep in touch with its activities, which are funded by the nation, state and county.

The County Board of Commissioners

The County Board of Commissioners is considered the principal governing body in county government. It has authority which affects the operations of county departments whether they are headed by an elected official or an appointed board.

Each county has a "county board." This body replaced the Board of Supervisors in 1969. The manner of choosing the Board of Supervisors was found to violate the "one-person, one-vote" norm required by the U.S. Constitution's 14th Amendment "equal protection" clause. Under the old Board of Supervisors, communities (cities and townships) were guaranteed representation regardless of population size. A populous township had only as many votes on the Board of Supervisors as a very sparsely settled one. There was also a tendency for county boards to become quite large.

Now, under state law, each county must be divided into between five and thirty-five county commissioner districts, based on the equal population principle. The number of districts in a county can vary according to the total county population, as follows:

County Population	No. of Commissioners
Under 5,001	Not more than 7
5,001 to 10,000	Not more than 10
10,001 to 50,000	Not more than 15
50,001 to 600,000	Not more than 21
over 600,000	25 to 35

These districts are created after each census by a county apportionment commission, consisting of the county clerk, prosecutor, treasurer and the chairpersons of the two major political parties in the county.

Elections to the county board involve partisan primary and general elections held in the fall of even-numbered years. The term of office is two years. Vacancies are filled by appointment by the rest of the board or by special election in the district if more than one year of the term remains. A vacancy caused by a recall would be filled by election. In most Michigan counties, one political party dominates the board quite decisively.

One of the members of the board is elected chairperson of the group by the other members. The county clerk is the clerk of the board and keeps a record of the meetings. Much of the work done by county boards is done by committees that are appointed by the board chairperson.

Powers of the County Board. In addition to selecting a chairperson and organizing their committees, county boards exercise a number of important powers. The board has appointive, supervisory, rulemaking, budget and legislative powers.

Some of the most important powers are *appointive.* As pointed out in the preceding section, many semi-independent county agencies are headed by boards appointed by the county board. In addition, the county board appoints many people to head other county departments. In most of these cases, the department is headed by a single official, who serves "at the pleasure of" the county board. (Removal is fairly easy.)

Some of the more important departments headed by a board appointee are:

Controller: The county's chief accounting officer, the controller assists in the development and administration of the budget.

Purchasing Agent: An officer responsible for purchasing goods necessary for general county functions. In some counties, this official performs controller-like functions.

Equalization Director: This department head reviews property assessments of cities and townships to try to assure uniformity of assessment practices within the county.

Corporation Counsel: This official serves as legal advisor to the county board, unless the board relies on the prosecutor for this service.

Medical Examiner: Once called coroner, this officer establishes the cause of death if uncertainty exists and investigates deaths occurring in the jail. The office is required by law.

Board of Auditors: Some counties have a three member Board of Auditors. Members serve 3-year terms and perform functions of accounting, budgeting and financial importance. It can become a very independent body, a source of concern to county commissioners.

There are numerous other such departments, as the charts indicate. The county board has very important *supervisory and rule-making powers.* Many of the rules governing county facilities and services are subject to approval by the county board.

Perhaps the most important authority of the county board is in the *budgeting* process. The general fund of the county is controlled by the county board and its use of these monies gives it the ability to affect the operation of nearly every county agency. It is important to note, however, that some agencies secure their funds without county board involvement (e.g., the road commission and social services department) and the control of the county board is thus reduced.

County boards may also exercise *legislative* powers "to pass such laws, regulations and ordinances relating to purely county affairs as they may see fit" (Act 156, 1851). In reality, this power is very limited. As VerBurg (1971, II:15-18) notes, there are important limits on the legislative power of county government:

-an ordinance must relate to "purely county" (not local or state) affairs.

-ordinances must be consistent with state laws - they may not contradict or supplement state laws.

-county ordinances may not interfere with the local affairs of any township, incorporated city, or village within the boundaries of the county.

-counties have not been given (as have cities, villages and townships) the authority to regulate for the health, safety and general welfare of their citizens. Counties lack what is known as the "police power."

-any ordinance which could jump these hurdles must be approved by a 2/3 vote of the county board. The governor has the right to review the ordinance and may veto it, subject to an override by 2/3 of the county board.

Thus, the real local government authority of the county is limited. County boards are more administrative bodies than legislative ones.

OPTIONS AND ALTERNATIVES FOR COUNTY GOVERNMENT

County government is very complex, so one could ask, "Who's in charge? The state? The county board? The voters?" The answer would be either none of the above or all of the above.

County government in Michigan has been criticized for being disorganized. The plural executive-commission form violates principles of simplicity and the principle of separation of powers because it has no clearly identified legislative body, and no single executive official. And, as noted, the authority of the county to actually govern has been limited by the state, which has given much of the "police power" to smaller units of local government.

Generally, the issues surrounding county government today are two-fold: 1) how should counties be internally organized? and 2) what powers should the county have in relation to other local units of government? In the following section the first question will be examined. The second will be examined in Chapter 15.

The "Optional Unified Form"

Recognizing that counties have no single executive with broad responsibilities, the legislature (Act 139, 1973) allowed counties to adopt an "optional unified form" of organization. Under this legislation voters in any county can adopt an *elected executive* or *appointed county manager* form of organization. The county board may place this question on the ballot, or it may be done through citizen initiative. Two urbanized counties- Oakland and Bay-have shifted to the elected executive approach. An important point to note is that the powers

of the county do not change, only its internal organization.

If the elected executive form is chosen by the voters, the executive is elected to a 4-year term in the presidential years, as are all other elected countywide officials. It is a partisan office, with nominations in partisan primaries followed by partisan general elections. Thus the elected executive would be expected to have at least as much political prestige and "clout" as other county officials.

If the appointed manager option is chosen the county board would select the manager, who would serve at the pleasure of the board. The manager is to be selected on the basis of merit. The manager does not have quite as much independence as an elected official.

The principal duties of either the manager or elected executive are to supervise, control and direct the functions of county departments (except those headed by elected officials), coordinate the activities of the county and enforce its rules and ordinances, prepare and submit a budget including any plans for capital improvement and submit recommendations to the county board for the efficient conduct of county business. Finally, with the approval of the county board, the manager or executive may appoint or remove the heads of county departments.

One additional (and important) power is provided the elected executive, but not the manager. An elected executive may veto any ordinance or resolution passed by the county board, and may veto any item in an appropriation resolution. (This veto may be overridden by a 2/3 vote of the board.)

It is important to realize that in these forms - elected executive or manager - nearly all other existing elected officials and appointed boards remain in place. While the executive can initiate appointments to head county departments, the county board would continue to appoint members of the many semi-independent commissions discussed earlier.

Either approach means adding a unified executive to all the county agencies which now exist. Thus, even the more powerful of the two (the elected executive) would have to work very hard to overcome the built-in power of officials like the

WAYNE COUNTY ORGANIZATIONAL CHART

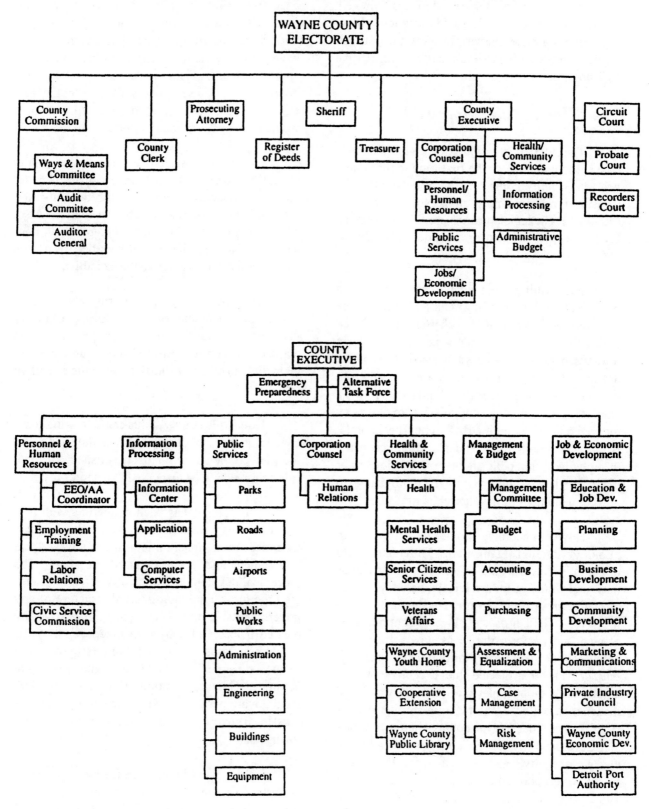

Executive Office, Wayne County, Mich.

171

sheriff and road commission. In either of these approaches a stronger single executive is achieved, but whether the executive could be called "chief" executive is another matter. In short, the optional unified form does not provide as unified an executive as is possible.

The "Home Rule" Approach

The 1963 Constitution extended the home rule concept to counties for the first time in the state's history. County home rule is not detailed in the Constitution, but is simply referred to (See Article 7, section 2.) The legislature has provided the details for "home rule" or "charter" counties in Act 293 of 1966.

Establishing a home rule county follows a procedure similar to drafting a charter for a city. The question of whether to draft a charter can be placed before the voters by the county board or by citizen initiative petitions. If voters decide to have a charter drafted, charter commissioners are elected from districts. Working under time limits set by law, a charter is prepared by the commission, reviewed by the governor, and submitted to the county electorate. If approved, the charter would take effect according to a plan and timetable spelled out in the charter itself. The law requires that there be provisions to allow amendment of the charter as time goes by.

How can becoming a home rule county change a county's internal organization? The county board of commissioners would continue to be elected as now, and would become a legislative body. Other elected county officers required by the state Constitution (e.g., clerk, prosecutor) would continue to be elected and perform duties as now. Except in counties larger than 1.5 million population, a charter *must* provide for an elected chief executive. Wayne county may adopt a manager form, in which the manager is called a chief administrative officer (CAO). In 1980, a Wayne county charter commission developed two charters, one providing for the elected executive and the other for the CAO. Wayne voters chose the executive approach, and in 1982, William Lucas was elected as the first home rule county executive in Michigan.

The elected executive is chosen for a 4-year term through partisan nominating primary elections and a partisan general election. The powers of the executive would include supervision of departments (except if headed by an elected official), and preparing and administering budgets. The executive would have veto powers, including a line-item veto over appropriations, subject to override by a 2/3 county board vote. These powers for the home rule executive are the same as the elected executive would have in the optional unified form.

One way in which the home rule county executive would be strengthened is that many departments, boards and commissions in county government may be reorganized by the charter. Also, power to *appoint* and *remove at pleasure* all non-elected department heads and members of boards and commissions is given to the executive.

Organizationally, the home rule county would not differ too much from the elected executive version of the unified form. It represents some clarification and reorganization of county government, but not complete unification of the executive branch.

Home rule county status can also bring some changes in the relationship between the county and local governments within it. These aspects of home rule counties will be discussed in Chapter 15.

This chapter has been concerned with presenting county government as it is in Michigan today. Counties are obviously important as a weak local government and as an agent of the state. The piecemeal development of county offices has created the most confusing internal structure of any governmental level in Michigan. These are many elected offices, and many semi-independent boards and commissions. There is no single executive, even in the "reformed" optional form and home rule counties. Counties continue to be a rather weak local government, with Michigan choosing to vest most local government powers in cities, villages and townships.

Yet on the whole, counties have grown in importance in the last decades. Some consider the county to be the "wave of the future" in local government. Many seek to continue to reform its internal organization, and some seek to further expand its powers.

Chapter 14

Local School Government in Michigan

A Brief History of Education in Michigan

Today's Local School Districts

Financing K-12 School Districts

Intermediate School Districts

Community College Districts

Private Schools in Michigan

Libraries

"Religion, morality and knowledge, being necessary to good government and the happiness of mankind, schools and the means of education shall forever be encouraged."

Article 3, Northwest Ordinance, 1787
Article 8, Sect. 1, Michigan Constitution

Chapter 14

Learning Objectives

Identify the major steps in the early development of education in Michigan.

What factors encouraged the consolidation of schools in the early 20th century?

Identify the major duties of the local school board.

How are K-12 schools financed in Michigan?

Explain the "charter school" concept in Michigan.

Explain the main programs of an intermediate school district.

Who is eligible to serve on a local school board? How is the board chosen?

What percent of Michigan's school children attend private schools?

How are community colleges organized? What programs do they offer?

Key Terms To Know

sixteenth section
superintendent of public instruction
"rate bills"
consolidation
K-12 school district
foundation/basic grant
intermediate school district
community college district
school board
charter school

A BRIEF HISTORY OF EDUCATION IN MICHIGAN

Michigan's educational system can trace its roots back to the territorial era. Following the Ordinance of 1785 the practice was established that section sixteen of a township would be set aside for school purposes. Though the application of this policy was haphazard, it gradually became common for revenues from the sale of property in the section to be used for school funding. Since this was national policy it has been called the first federal aid to education. In 1817 the territorial legislature began to plan a state-wide school system. Even though the planned system never materialized, such farsighted thinking put Michigan in the forefront of educational development for the time.

The first organized school in the state appears to have been founded in 1828 in Raisinville, near the present village of Maybee on the Raisin river. Initially it was planned that each township would have a single school. However, for many people, having only one school might have required too long a walk on a cold February morning in the early nineteenth century. So, in 1829, a territorial law allowed the formation of school districts in an area smaller than a township. In these original "one room schoolhouses" students usually were taught by one person and received no more than the first eight years of education. This level of primary education was typical of the time.

When the 1835 Constitution was written the state continued its leadership in education. The Constitution created an office of Superintendent of Public Instruction and Michigan became the first state to create such an office in its basic document. Shortly after the Constitution was ratified, Michigan petitioned the national government to turn the revenues from the sale of the sixteenth section of each township over to the state rather than the township as had been the case in Ohio, Illinois and Indiana. The funds from the sale of each sixteenth section went into a state fund instead of remaining with the township. Thus an early form of statewide funding made it possible to equalize educational resources in the state.

In 1837, a state law provided for the establishment of school districts in each township with funding based on the number of pupils in the district. The same law established the University of Michigan and created "branches" of the University. Though short-lived, these branches were the forerunners of modern high schools.

In 1843 a new law provided for the creation of "union schools" where several schools might be combined to form a single larger district. This was usually the beginning of a system of separate grades and also the beginning of a long process of consolidation (merger) of districts. In 1848 the first public high school in the state was established in Detroit.

The Constitution of 1850 provided a system of free basic education to everyone. Prior to this time many districts had charged tuition, called "rate bills." At this time, however, only three months of school was provided at no cost—if one desired more, there was a tuition charge. By 1869 all primary (elementary) education was free. In the early 1860s, about three-fourths of school age children attended school. The school year averaged about 130 days, compared to today's 190.

In 1871 Michigan became one of the first states to adopt a compulsory education policy. Initially, students were required to attend school for 12 weeks a year and this was extended to four months in 1884. Today nearly all children between the ages of 6 and 16 are required to attend school.

Even though Detroit had established a high school in 1848, most high schools of the time were private, not public. The cause of public secondary education received a great boost in 1874 in the *Kalamazoo* case, in which the state Supreme Court ruled that tax dollars could be used to support public high schools.

The Consolidation Movement

By the 20th century, school districts were the most numerous governmental unit in the state. In 1912 there were 7,362 school districts in Michigan. In 2002 there were 519 K-12 districts and 36 non K-12 districts. (The state has also authorized up to 150 charter schools.) Why has the number of school disticts diminished so much?

As more and more was demanded of the educational system it became obvious that the "little one-room schoolhouse" (and larger variations of it) could not offer the full spectrum of specialized courses and training that a larger school district could. Consolidation (merger of one or more districts) also produced savings as facilities were combined. When students had to walk to school, consolidation was often impossible. With the invention and use of the automobile (or more appropriately, the school bus) consolidation of districts became a workable option.

The laws regarding the boundaries of school districts are complex. Four methods are used:

Consolidation of districts. Two or more districts may vote to form a new school district.

Annexation of one district to another. One district can annex a part of another if the school board of the annexing district passes a resolution to annex and the voters of the area being annexed approve.

Transfer of territory between districts. If two-thirds of the resident property owners of an area request a transfer to another district, the intermediate school board may order the transfer.

Dissolution of districts. A school district may be dissolved when its territory is attached to another district and there are not enough persons in the district who are qualified or will accept school board offices.

Today, this consolidation movement has slowed.

THE STRUCTURE AND ORGANIZATION OF TODAY'S LOCAL SCHOOL DISTRICTS

Today many of the major concerns and problems with education come to rest with the local school board. In many communities the organization and politics of the school board is a matter of intense concern to voters, parents and students.

The Powers and Duties of the Local School Board

Each school district in Michigan is governed by a school board consisting of between 3 and 11 members. Board members have the responsibility of keeping their district's schools functioning. To do so, the school board has a number of powers and duties.

Except for Detroit, school board members are chosen by the voters of the school district in non-partisan, at-large elections. Members of the Detroit Board of Education were elected from districts throughout the city. However, in 1999 the state legislature allowed the mayor of Detroit to appoint six members to a new school board in an attempt to improve the Detroit system. The state superintendent of education appointed a seventh member. The appointed board will serve until 2004, when the voters of Detroit will decide on whether to retain the system. Any registered voter who is a resident of the district may seek election as a member of the school board. One must circulate petitions and secure a minimum number of valid signatures, and one's name will appear on the final ballot. There is no primary election, only a general election. School district election administration is reviewed in chapter 5.

Many of the duties of the local school board are set by the elected State Board of Education. This eight-member board has general supervision of all public education except the three constitutionally independent major universities: The University of Michigan, Michigan State University and Wayne State University. The board provides advice to the legislature for educational programs and appoints a State Superintendent of Public Instruction to carry out state educational policy on a daily basis. The board does not make law or have taxing power. (See chapter 7 for more detail on the state Department of Education.)

The state requires that the local school board do several things. For example, each district must provide a kindergarten, and a minimum number of school days each year. The law requires that a district must be in session for a certain number of days and hours per year to receive full state aid. Each district must provide for a state-mandated core

Figure 14.1

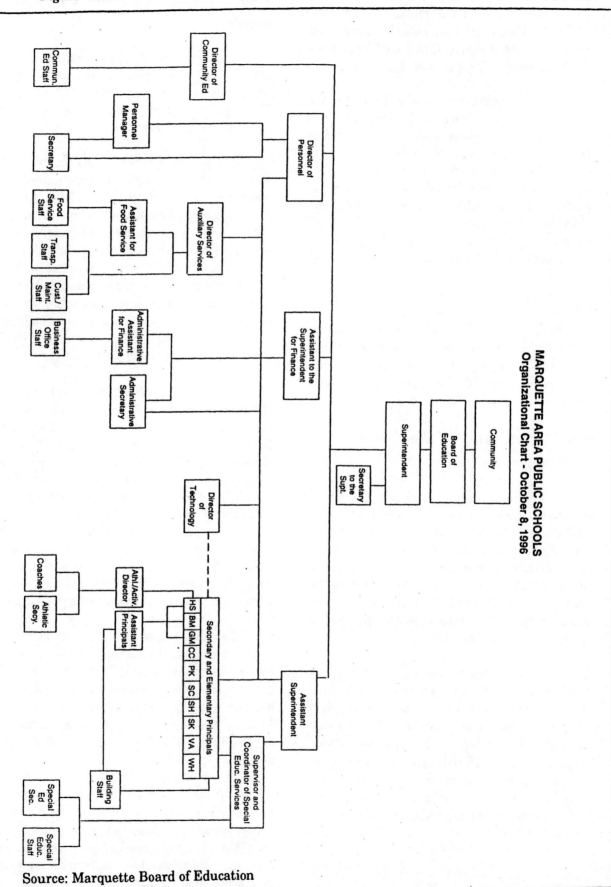

MARQUETTE AREA PUBLIC SCHOOLS
Organizational Chart - October 8, 1996

Source: Marquette Board of Education

curriculum, special education programs and maintain school buildings up to state health and safety standards. Each district must also include a civics course in its graduation requirements, hire certified teachers, and provide a system of teacher tenure.

Many important decisions are left to the local school board's own choice. Within broad limits set by the state, the local board makes policy regarding building design, employee compensation, the school calendar and attendance zones, the specifics of the curriculum, educational standards, adult education, guidance and counseling services, textbooks, employee working conditions and compensation, pupil transportation, graduation requirements, extra-curricular activities and many other matters.

As can be seen from the above list, local school boards have very important powers. The state has permitted local school districts considerable independence by keeping the state requirements rather minimal. With few state-wide standards and much local flexibility, districts are free to differ from each other if desired.

The Organization of the School District

The elected board has the responsibility to operate the school system. The board will hire a professionally trained superintendent to direct the daily affairs of the district. In turn, the superintendent will employ teachers and other employees, subject to the board's approval. As noted earlier, the board has authority to establish policies on many important matters, and these policies will be implemented by the superintendent.

The administrative organization of a school district will reflect the programs offered and the district's size. The activities of a large district might involve much more than K-12 classroom activities. Large districts often operate libraries, have a wide range of after-school activities, engage in lobbying and develop many recreational services for the residents of the district. An example of the organizational structure of a large school district appears in Figure 14.1.

Charter Schools/Public School Academies

Michigan law allows the creation of "charter schools" or "public school academies" to provide instruction in all or part of the K-12 curriculum. These are public schools intended as innovative or experimental approaches to education.

Schools may be chartered (or "contracted" by K-12 district boards of education. Such schools may operate only in that district's boundaries. Likewise the board of an intermediate school district (see below) may charter schools within the ISD boundary. There is no limit on the number of such schools which a K-12 or ISD board may create within its own boundaries. Boards of community colleges may also charter schools but are limited to one within the college district. Finally, any state public university may issue contracts to any number of charter schools, any-where in the state.

As of the fall of 2002, the overall number of charter schools has been capped at 150, but there has been much discussion about raising that number. Since 1995 when Wayne State opened the first charter school, 150 charter schools have been formed, serving more than 65,000 students, about 3.8% of Michigan's nearly 1.7 million students. Nine of Michigan's 15 public universities have chartered 110 schools. Central Michigan University alone has chartered over 40. Intermediate school districts have chartered 15, local school districts have chartered 12 and one by a community college. All these numbers are likely to increase in the years to come.

The governing board of a charter school is not elected, but is organized under the non-profit corporation laws of Michigan. A board of directors will exist and such board's composition and competence must be acceptable to the public body issuing the contract. The contract can, of course, be amended as allowed by law and can be for any period of time desired.

These "academies" or "charter schools" can be formed as non-profit corporations by virtually any entity---parents, teachers, businesses---but may not be affiliated with a religious organization. In general, they are bound by state laws regarding core curriculum, accounting standards, achievement tests and

Figure 14.2

Michigan's Intermediate School Districts

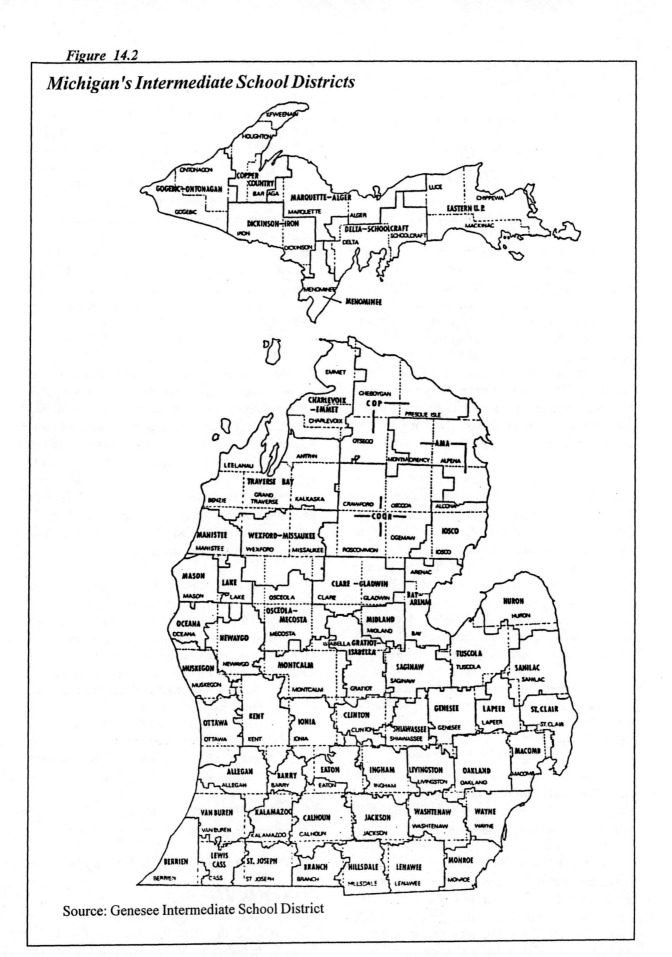

Source: Genesee Intermediate School District

the like. The same labor agreements in place for the authorizing body's employees must pertain for the charter schools as well.

FINANCING PUBLIC SCHOOLS IN MICHIGAN

Historically, financial responsibility for financing the operating costs of K-12 education in Michigan has been a shared responsibility of state government and local school districts. The state does not provide general support for captial (building and sites) improvements. (The national government contributes only about 5% of the total revenue for such schools, usually in specific targeted programs.) At different times since 1960, the state's share had been as great as 60-65% for some districts, or as little as 35-40% for others. Fluctuations in the state share of operating costs were due to recessions and/or changing state priorities. The local share also fluctuated and was based entirely on the property tax.

For at least 20 years prior to 1994, the method of financing schools in Michigan was among the most controversial issues in the state. Many factors contributed to the protracted conflict: the state's share was unreliable and changing; the property tax relied on by local districts had climbed to a state-wide average of about 35 mills, about 2/3 of all property taxes paid; the tax base of districts was very unequal. Even though the state had attempted to make per-pupil revenues more equal through a state aid formula, very wide disparities existed.

Much of this changed in 1994. Faced with a choice between a ballot issue and a legislated change, the voters chose the ballot issue--Proposal A--by a vote of 2 to 1.

Proposal A has the following essential features. It sets the minimum property tax for K-12 schools at 6 mills for "homesteads" (principal residences) and at 24 mills on all other taxable properties. It allows a local millage option for 3 more mills. It raised the state sales tax by 50%, from 4% to 6%, and earmarked the increase for school funding. It cut the state income tax from 4.6% to 4.4% and raised taxes on tobacco products, and real estate transfers (sales). Probably of great importance to its passage, Proposal A restricted future increases in

the taxable value of property to 5% or the rate of inflation, whichever is *less*.

The proposal modified school expenditure patterns as well. Under the terms of proposal A, each district in the state was guaranteed at least as much per-pupil operating revenue as the earlier combined state aid--local property tax total. This "foundation" or "basic" grant is to be approximately $6700 per pupil in 2002-2003. The state plan calls for large increases in funding for at-risk (low-income) students and for pre-school funding as well. Charter schools operating in Michigan receive only a foundation grant and cannot levy a millage. Proposal A did not address capital improvement programs for distsricts.

The anticipated effects of the plan are as follows: most central city school districts saw large property tax rate decreases, and gain considerable per-pupil revenues due mainly to increased funding for at-risk students; per pupil revenues to most school districts rose; inequality of revenues between most districts declined (more than a few well-off school districts still exist), so "equal educational opportunity" might be better realized. Michigan's above-average property tax reliance was dramatically reduced while its sales and income tax burdens moved closer to the average state's.

Many issues remain. Will relying on the state sales tax for revenues hurt schools during recessions? Will the state find other revenues to smooth out such downturns? Will relying on state revenues to finance most schools (the ratio will be about 80% state, 20% local) reduce the incentive for school consolidation? Will state dominance of finance lead to state dominance of policy--a loss of local control of curriculum, standards and the like? Should the state share in capital improvements as well as in operating costs of K-12 education in Michigan as it does for community and 4 year colleges.

We will have to wait and see.

INTERMEDIATE SCHOOL DISTRICTS

In 1962 the state legislature replaced the "county school districts" with the Intermediate School

Figure 14.3

Genesee Intermediate School District

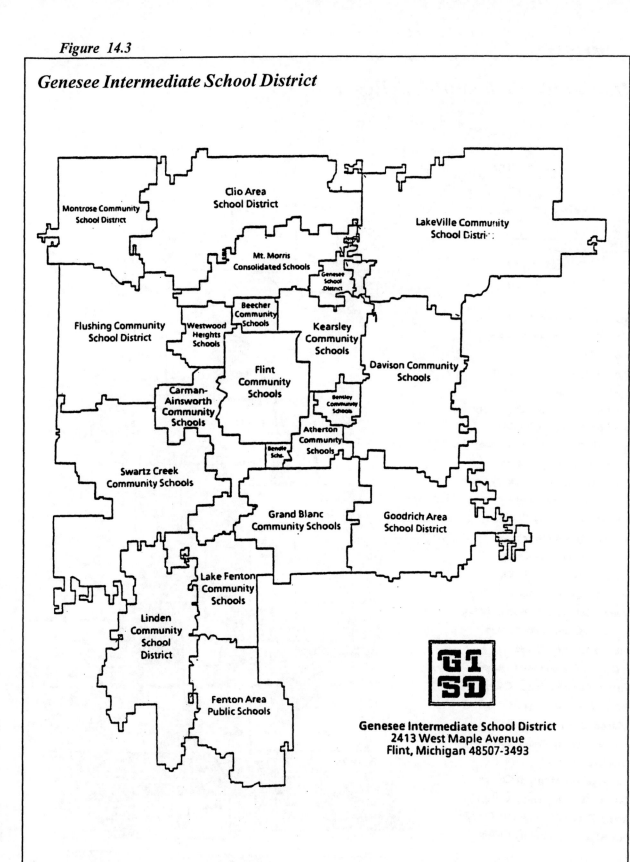

Genesee Intermediate School District
2413 West Maple Avenue
Flint, Michigan 48507-3493

Figure 14.4

Michigan's Community Colleges

1 Alpena Community College
2 Bay de Noc Community College
3 Delta College
4 Glen Oaks Community College
5 Gogebic Community College
6 Grand Rapids Community College
7 Henry Ford Community College
  Highland Park Community College _closed
9 Jackson Community College
10 Kalamazoo Valley Community College
11 Kellogg Community College
12 Kirtland Community College
13 Lake Michigan College
14 Lansing Community College
15 Macomb Community College
16 Mid Michigan Community College
17 Monroe County Community College
18 Montcalm Community College
19 Mott Community College
20 Muskegon Community College
21 North Central Michigan College
22 Northwestern Michigan College
23 Oakland Community College
24 St. Clair County Community College
25 Schoolcraft College
26 Southwestern Michigan College
27 Washtenaw Community College
28 Wayne County Community College
29 West Shore Community College

Organized District

Intermediate District   County District   K-12 District

Not in a district

District. These districts include a number of K-12 districts and usually approximate county lines. Examples appear in the maps in Figure 14.2 and 14.3. In less populous areas of the state several counties may join together to form an intermediate district. There were 57 ISDs in Michigan as of 2000.

The major function of the intermediate districts is to provide services that might not be available or affordable if each separate district had to develop its own. ISDs could be considered regional service centers for the K-12 districts within their boundaries.

Intermediate districts commonly provide data processing facilities, regional media centers, and management and consultant services. ISDs may also establish special education programs and vocational education programs and, if the district voters approve, levy millage to pay for such programs. The programs of the intermediate districts are financed by a small share of local property tax and aid from the state.

State law requires that 5 or 7 members be chosen for the ISD board. These members are usually selected by a committee of set up by the local school boards or by the public at an at-large, non-partisan general election. The term of office is 6 years and terms are overlapping. Any registered voter in the district is eligible to be a member of the intermediate district board. The day-to-day activities of the ISD are overseen by a superintendent of the district, a professional educator selected by the board.

COMMUNITY COLLEGE DISTRICTS

Since 1914 when Grand Rapids Junior College opened, the state has seen a continuing growth of junior and community colleges. The 1963 Constitution states: "The legislature shall provide by law for the establishment and financial support of public community and junior colleges..." (Article VIII, Section 7)

Community and junior colleges offer the first two years of coursework toward a four-year college degree as well as a wide variety of vocational programs leading to an associate degree. Today there are 28 public two-year colleges in the state, and about 90 percent of Michigan's citizens live within commuting distance of at least one such college. (See Figure 14-3)

A community college may be operated as an arm of a K-12 school district. The formation of community college districts independent of K-12 districts is authorized by the Community College Act of 1966. A community college district may be created by one or more adjoining counties, one or more adjoining K-12 school districts or one or more adjoining intermediate school districts. The proposal to form a district and the proposal to levy millage to support the college must be approved by the state Board of Education and by a majority vote of those voting on the questions.

Seven members are elected to community college boards in at-large, non-partisan elections, usually held in June. They are elected for staggered six-year terms. (The Wayne County Community College Board consists of nine members elected from districts for six year terms.) Any registered voter who lives in the district may seek election to the board.

The State Board for Public Community and Junior Colleges is an advisory body within the state Department of Education, and acts to oversee and plan for community colleges and their programs. Community colleges are supported by property taxes, student tuition and aid from the state. In recent years, property taxes provide 30%, student tuition over 30% and state aid provides about 35% of the typical community college's revenues.

PRIVATE SCHOOLS IN MICHIGAN

In earlier years, before public schools were functioning, private schools provided a large proportion of the education available in the state. Today, nearly 12 percent of the K-12 students in Michigan attend private schools, about the same as the national average. Most, but not all, of these private schools are associated with a religious denomination. About 65 percent of the K-12 private school students attend Roman Catholic schools and another 10-15 percent attend a Lutheran-affiliated school.

There has been some controversy about the range of the state's authority over these schools. Most of these issues involve religious schools and deal with the First Amendment guarantees aganist the "establishment" of religion and "free exercise"of religion. Currently, they must operate under state law and meet requirements similar to public schools regarding teacher qualifications, curricula and safety regulations. Though the power of the state to contribute financial aid to these schools is limited by the First Amendment to the U.S. Constitution and the Michigan Constitution (Article 8, section 2), the state may provide transportation, crossing guards, school lunches, and some other services for students attending private schools. Most other types of governmental aid to private schools have been interpreted as unconstitutional.

Private Colleges

Though many students attend private grade and high schools, an even greater proportion of Michigan's college students attend one of the private colleges in the state. These institutions receive no direct financial aid from the state government. Expenses are paid by tuition, gifts and support from private groups and individuals. However, the state has established a program of tuition grants for private college students. This program is viewed as aiding the student, not any particular private school, religious or otherwise.

LIBRARIES

The Michigan Constitution (Article 8, section 9) says: "The legislature shall provide by law for the establishment and support of libraries which shall be available to all residents of the state..." There are a number of kinds of libraries in the state. Townships, cities, villages, counties, school districts and colleges may choose to support libraries. Two or more governmental units may form a district library.

Local libraries are usually supported by local funds that may be supplemented by fines paid to local courts, as specified in the state Constitution. District libraries may levy a property tax to support their activities.

Many libraries receive state aid based on population and may receive funds for special projects. Libraries may join together to form regional cooperatives. The Library of Michigan, located in Lansing, serves the state government and all other libraries in the state. In 2001 Governor Engler made this library a major part of a new department, the Department of History, Arts and Libraries. Any Michigan resident can find library assistance through this facility.

THE FUTURE

As we enter the 21st century, considerable uncertainty exists regarding education in Michigan. Once noted as a leader in education, Michigan's ranking has fallen. The state confronts a mixture of educational problems. Some feel there are too many school districts and colleges. Others blame unionization among public school teachers. Some note the effects of declining birth rates and still others blame TV, video games, poverty, changing family patterns and a resurgence of private schools.

Recently, the quality of education has become a national issue. Many studies, including some in Michigan, have generated many proposals for change. Among the suggestions are stricter graduation requirements, longer school days, longer school years, "choice" of schools within or between school districts, a "voucher" system to provide state funding for both public and private education and higher standards for teachers.

Since educational expenditures are a very large share of total government expenditures the future of education in Michigan is one of the most important issues facing the state's citizens.

Chapter 15

Local Government-
Problems and Prospects

Fragmentation in Local Government

Benefits from Fragmentation

Drawbacks of Fragmentation

Proposals: Coping with Fragmentation

> *"The legislature may establish...additional forms of government or authorities with powers, duties and jurisdictions as the legislature shall provide."*
> Article VII, Sec. 27, Michigan Constitution

Chapter 15

Learning Objectives

What is meant by the term "fragmentation"?

Describe the factors contributing to fragmentation in Michigan local government?

What are some of the benefits of fragmentation?

What are the possible drawbacks of fragmentation?

Identify some major approaches to dealing with fragmentation. Summarize each of these.

How could community resources be made more equal?

How could "growth sharing" work?

Describe what a "federated" metro area might look like.

How could use of the county overcome problems of fragmentation?

Key Terms To Know

fragmentation
annexation
consolidation
duplication
intergovernmental contract
special district
growth sharing
metro federation

The earlier chapters in this part of the book have examined townships, villages, cities, counties and school districts in terms of their origins, forms and powers. The intent of this chapter is to introduce an overall view of local government in Michigan. This chapter will look at the "forest" not just the individual "trees." The chapter will examine the following kinds of questions:

-What are the overall patterns of local government in Michigan?
-What are the origins of these patterns?
-Are there benefits in these patterns?
-Are there costs or problems caused by the patterns?
-What are possible changes to eliminate or reduce these patterns?

FRAGMENTATION IN LOCAL GOVERNMENT

The simplest local government pattern in Michigan occurs in very rural areas. There, a Michigan resident lives in a township, school district and county. Regardless of where they lived in the township, a resident would be no further than three miles from another township. If their own township were surrounded by townships, there would be nine townships within four and one-half miles. Michigan's "simple" government landscape isn't so simple after all! It is not likely that one can avoid the effects of these other governments. Whether to work, shop, worship, hunt, fish, visit friends, attend school or whatever, the chances are good that the actions of neighboring governments have some effects on one's life. How did the landscape get so crowded?

Regional Growth and Fragmentation

Township boundaries were in place as long ago as the original land survey, and county boundaries were set before the 20th century. Many villages and cities were formed long ago by the legislature. Since 1909, the formation of cities and villages by local citizens has been permitted, subject to controls by the state. School districts were developed with an early emphasis on small size. Thus, the basic boundary framework of local government is old, and

emphasizes localism.

Furthermore, the state made it rather easy to form new, smaller-than-township local governments. This occurred because in the early 20th century Michigan was a predominantly rural state. At that time, county and township governments were sufficient for most people. Rural interests dominated the state legislature, and felt that urbanized places in the state should properly have "their own" local governments. Thus the village form was provided as a kind of "middle-level" form to meet urban needs and the city form was intended to give both more self-government and more local powers to those places with the greatest urban needs. The emphasis, then, was on creating more local governments as needs changed.

Coupled with this was a tendency to increase the powers of townships, the most common form of general-purpose local government. Thus, as needs for urban services increased in many densely settled townships near cities, the township government did not attach itself to a city or a village. The city or village boundaries did not expand to match urban needs. Instead, either a new city or village was formed from all or part of the township, or the township itself met the greater needs of an urban society.

It is important to keep in mind that Michigan law makes it difficult for one unit of government to take over the territory of another (annexation). If annexation were easy, the boundaries of local units could be adjusted to changing population patterns.

Consider this map as a beginning point in an illustration of the effects of these policies.

Figure 15-1

Area X—1930

T-1	T-2
C1	
T-3	T-4

It shows, for 1930, a city which had been

formed out of some of the territory of the four surrounding townships. Assume that the population of the city is 80 percent of the total in the area (Let the city have 80 people and each of the townships 5 people). The city would be providing urban-type services to the 80 people in its small boundary, the townships each would provide rural services to the 5 people in their large boundaries. Note that in 1930, 80 percent of the residents were within one governmental unit.

Enter: change and growth. Assume the hypothetical area X grows. Its economy "takes off." New jobs and residences are developed. Eventually, population would spill out of the city, following changing transportation, and later, employment patterns. The region as a whole grows, and (as a whole) probably prospers. Let's say that by 2000 the area has more than doubled in population since 1930. The city no longer contains a majority of the population. All governments would be providing more services because of this urbanization.

In fact, because the incorporation of new cities and villages was fairly easy, our map might have changed. The area might look like this:

Figure 15-2

Area X—2000

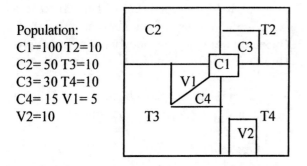

Population:
C1=100 T2=10
C2=50 T3=10
C3=30 T4=10
C4=15 V1=5
V2=10

Obviously, T1 has become a city of 50 people (C2). T2's territory is smaller, as a city of 30 people (C3) has been formed at the expanding edge of the old central city. Likewise, local units have been formed in T3 and T4. Now we have a map of 9 local governments, not 5. While in 1930 the original city had 80 percent of the population, by 2000 no unit of government can claim more than 42 percent, and the smallest have less than 5 percent of the area's total population.

This pattern of growth and additional governments is commonly referred to as "fragmentation." The area is a *whole* social and economic creature, but the governments are over *parts* of it.

What if townships had been kept weak, new cities and villages next to an existing city had been prohibited, and cities allowed to easily expand their boundaries? If all these guidelines had been followed, the 2000 map might look like this:

Figure 15-3

Area X-2000 (option)

Population:
C (C1+C2+C3+C4+V1)=200

T2=	10
T3=	10
T4=	20
V2= (part of T4)	10

Compare Figures 15-2 and 15-3. Clearly, if the above guidelines had been in place the local map would be a bit simpler. One city government would provide urban services to the great majority of residents (over 80% in this example).

Michigan's pattern is not like this. Township powers were expanded, not limited. Forming new cities or villages next to an existing city was permitted, not prohibited, and annexation of smaller units by larger ones was difficult. Furthermore, once a government is in place, numerous pressures exist to keep it. Officials will defend it (and themselves) and citizens will identify with the government and seek to retain it. A whole network of interests and loyalties tends to keep the system as it is.

Schools and Fragmentation

The development of school district boundaries deserves special mention in connection with fragmentation. The earliest school districts in Michigan were quite small, in response to desires for local control and because of transportation limitations. As time went by, transportation allowed larger districts. Educational needs grew in a changing complex society. Citizens desired more and better education, and the legislature required it.

Figure 15-4

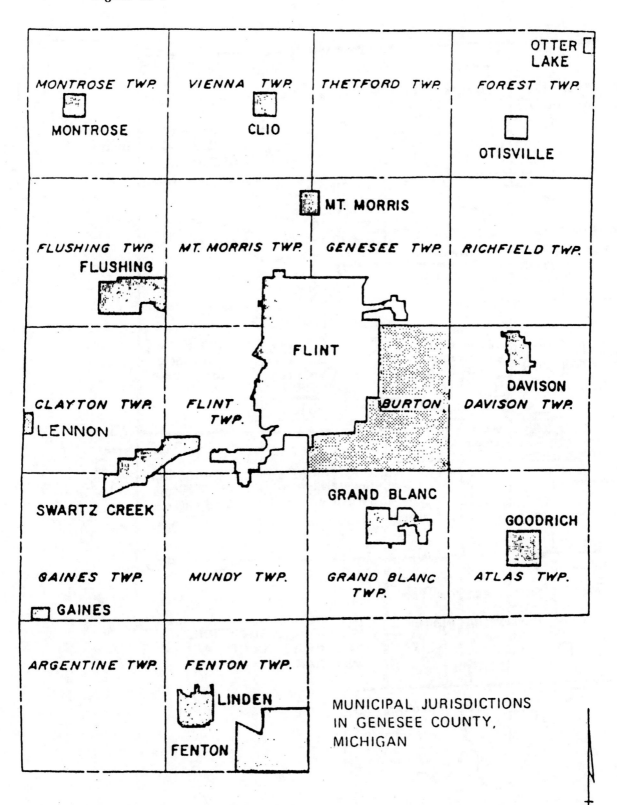

Source: Genesee County Metropolitan Planning Commisson

189

Figure 15-5

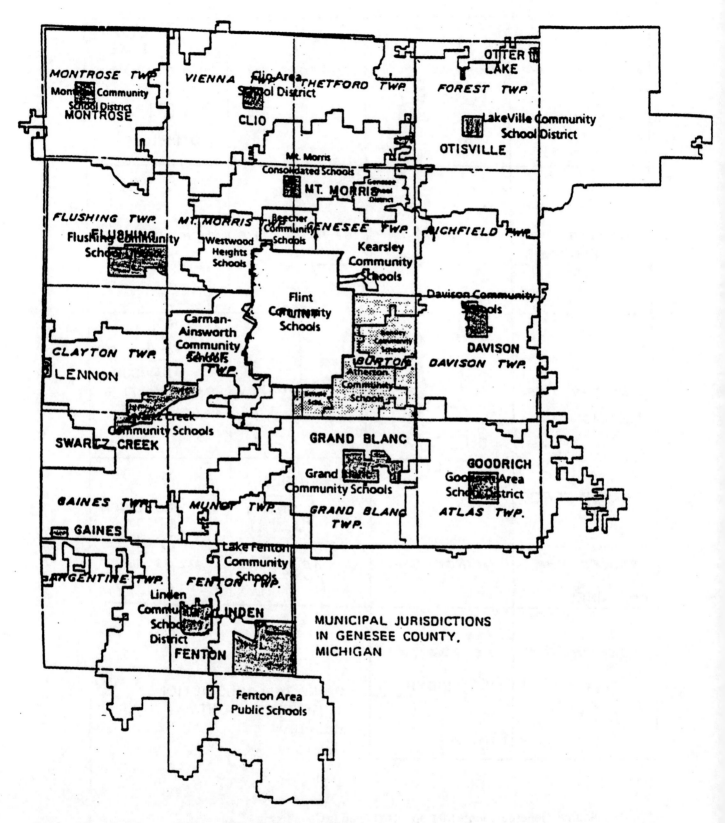

Source: Genesee County Metropolitan Planning Commission.

To afford this increased scale of education, *consolidation* became common (see chapter 14). Thus, throughout the state, in urban and rural areas alike, the number of school districts was reduced. This helped reduce fragmentation because consolidation lowered the number of governments. However, since school boundaries do not necessarily correspond to those of other local governments, they increase complexity. The total effect can be staggering in its complexity. For example, consider Figure 15-4, a map of non-school governments in Genesee county, and Figure 15-5, showing K-12 school districts overlapping these others. That's fragmentation!

BENEFITS FROM FRAGMENTATION

What can be said in defense of having many governments so close to each other?

There is a widespread belief that the pattern contributes to political democracy by giving citizens more direct control of local policy. A citizen's vote is thought to be worth more in elections in smaller communities. If I am one of 100 voters in my town, I have more to say (1/100) over decisions than if my town was merged with others for a total population of 500. There, I would be only 1/500th.

As an extension of this, wouldn't I also have easier access to governing officials, whom I might know personally? Wouldn't officials be more sensitive to citizens who had large shares of voting power?

Another kind of benefit might exist from fragmentation. Since governments provide services, we might expect the services to be different from government to government. Services will vary from unit to unit—units will provide different levels of services and might provide different combinations of services.

From the point of view of individuals, these differences will allow them to pick from different communities. One can't avoid living in a local government and school district but fragmentation

gives one some choices. Living in a fragmented area is a bit like living in a supermarket—within the limits of the money one has, one has a lot of choice as to what one buys. This choice between various combinations and levels of local government services can be considered an important element of personal freedom.

These benefits may be very important but fragmentation does have its critics.

DRAWBACKS OF FRAGMENTATION

Many students of local government have argued that there are many costs to society because of fragmentation. Not all of these alleged drawbacks are easy to prove.

Most critics of fragmentation are quick to point out that the boundaries of local governments are usually old and inflexible, and that the actual social, economic and population patterns are newer and changing. Thus, the boundaries might not match the needs of the people—people with shared needs are not governed by one unit of government, but many. No one government is able to "get its hands on" all aspects of a problem.

Further, it is argued, the pattern of governments is so complex that it confuses citizens. Some people may have a difficult time figuring out which community and school district they live in. Others may be more affected by a neighboring government than their own. What good is a powerful vote in a small community if you aren't sure about which government does what or if a community in which you have *no* vote has important effects on you?

Critics also point out that different communities have different property tax bases and different household income levels. Communities will differ in their ability to provide services. Consider the following kinds of variations in community resources:

Figure 15-6

Variations in Local Resources			
	Property Tax Base		
		High	Low
Income of Residents	High	A	C
	Low	B	D

Community A is able to afford a very high level of services. Community D would have to decide to have very high income and/or property tax rates to provide a high (or maybe even a low) level of services. Thus these differences in communities will likely lead to an inequality of services. How much inequality is too much? Are there some services which should exist for all, equally? If so, a fragmented local system might not be the best way to bring that about.

Another very common criticism of fragmentation is that having so many governments requires a great many elected and appointed officials, and may also require more government employees than necessary. Imagine two neighboring full-service school districts, each with its own officials and administrators for various programs. If the two separate bureaucracies were merged, could the same services be delivered with fewer employees and/or lower tax costs? In other words, isn't duplication costly, and couldn't the same services be delivered as effectively at lower cost?

PROPOSALS: COPING WITH FRAGMENTATION

The arguments between critics and defenders of fragmentation have generated numerous ideas. Those supporting the existing pattern offer modest proposals designed to eliminate the worst aspects of fragmentation. Those who find great fault with the existing pattern tend to propose more radical change. Here is a brief tour through the land of possibilities.

In deciding how modest or radical a proposal is, keep the following questions in mind:

Does the proposal reduce the number of governments in a area?

Does the proposal reduce local authority?

Does it call for the creation of a new level of government?

Would resources and/or services become more equal?

The following discussion will outline the possibilities for change from the more modest to the more radical.

Voluntary Cooperation

Many proposals suggest that local officials sit down together, recognize each other's concerns, and cooperate to the maximum extent possible. Such discussion can be encouraged by citizens or perhaps by the state. For example, the state could (as Michigan does) allow local governments to contract with each other for services (Michigan Constitution, Article 7, section 28). In a contract relationship, one community "hires" another to provide a service at an agreed-upon price. For example, if a township is growing, it may desire police protection. Rather than create a police department the township might contract with a village, city, another township, or the county to provide police service. The contract determines service levels and price. It can tailor the services to need and it can be changed or terminated.

Often, cooperating means coordinating. If one community is preparing to zone some land at its border, it might take into account the wishes of the community "across the road."

Voluntary agreements between governments do not threaten the existence of any government and can be targeted to problems of mutual concern. For these reasons, they are not unusual. One the other hand, these agreements typically cover only one problem and may lead to problems if a special district or authority is created.

A *special district* or *authority* as a more permanent form of interlocal agreement than a contract. Such a district could be created by local governments or by the state. Usually, a special district has its own taxing authority and governing body, and provides a specialized service to the communities within its boundaries. It should be noted, however, that such districts often represent an additional government in an already fragmented area. Furthermore, such districts are often very obscure to the voters and thus might not be accountable to the citizens. Examples of the special district (authority) approach to shared needs are the Huron-Clinton Metropolitan Authority (which operates regional parks in southeastern Michigan), the Detroit Port Authority, the Southeastern Michigan Transportation Authority (SEMTA) and a great number of small scale authorities for water and sewer purposes.

Annexation and Consolidation

Neither *annexation* (the taking of some of one government's territory by another) nor *consolidation* (the merger of two or more units) is easy or common in Michigan. (A notable exception is the case of school districts.) Essentially, annexation or consolidation occur only when both parties favor it. Communities are given veto power over whether all or part of their territory will be joined with another government.

Some observers propose that annexation and consolidation be used more, and perhaps without the consent of all those involved. For example, the state could provide financial incentives by providing more state aid to the new combined community. In the case of annexation, the state could subsidize annexation by continuing a high level of support for the community which lost territory.

Another approach might be for the state to simply allow a larger population community to take territory from a smaller. Thus, as population within a city spilled into sparsely settled communities, the city could expand its boundaries (and resources) at its own initiative.

A strong role for the state is not an absolute requirement before annexation or consolidation can occur. In the 1980's a combination of declining enrollments, reduced state aid, lower property tax growth, increased salary and utility costs and high (especially computer) equipment costs caused many school districts to consider consolidation.

In 1982, voters in the city of Battle Creek and adjacent Battle Creek township each voted to merge into a single city government. The major incentive for doing so was provided by the Kellogg Corporation. It threatened to locate new headquarters outside Michigan unless consolidation put an end to local government duplication, conflict and bickering.

Making Community Resources More Equal

So far, this chapter has identified approaches that deal with cooperation or with boundary changes. Many observers of fragmentation are concerned more with community resources than with boundaries. Their emphasis is on the fact that different communities have different abilities to pay for services, not boundaries, and they propose changing this inequality.

One approach is to have the state share its money with local communities in such a way that the resources of the communities are more equal. This principle is applied in Michigan's school aid program. The state distributes money to local governments (K-12 school districts) based partly on their willingness to help themselves. This program does not make school districts perfectly equal in the amount of spending per pupil, but it makes them much less unequal than they would be if they each had to depend only on their own resources.

The state also has "revenue-sharing" programs for cities, villages, townships and counties. Some of these programs are based on formulas which take community need and ability to pay into account. (More detail on these state programs is found in chapter 16.)

In short, one way to reduce the inequality of community resources is to have the state act as a redistributor. Another approach would be to have the national government do the same kind of equalizing on a large national scale.

As another means of reducing inequalities between local governments, some have suggested *growth-sharing*. Supporters of growth-sharing point out that not only are communities usually unequal, but that the inequality often increases over time. Some communities grow much faster than others, widening the gap.

Why do some parts of a region grow more rapidly than others? Some have more open land available than others, and it can be developed at less cost than land with existing structures. Some communities are in the path of population spillover from other older communities. Some communities pursue new growth very aggressively, offering tax incentives for development. Some are able to take advantage of the location of major public facilities like highways and airports. Such major facilities are usually not developed at the communities own expense, but can give it an economic advantage.

Whatever the causes, growth advantages some more than others. Growth may mean that the personal income level of the community rises. It may mean that the property tax base of the community increases. It may mean both, and it can lead to increased inequalities between school districts and between local governments.

The advocates of growth-sharing would not allow a community to keep all of its new property tax base. They suggest creating a regional pool of tax base, consisting of some or all of the new growth. A typical proposal would set aside one-half of all new commercial and industrial tax base. The local community would tax only half the value of its new growth in those categories. The other half would be set aside as an area-wide tax base, taxed at an area-wide rate. The proceeds from the area-wide tax base could then be distributed to area governments based on need. Poorer communities would receive larger shares than richer ones. Thus, part of the new tax base would benefit the community in which it occurred, and part of it would be used to offset inequalities between communities.

Thus, growth-sharing might prevent government inequalities from widening. It might also reduce some of the willy-nilly competition for new property tax base. Since residents of communities in which little or no growth occurs pay highway taxes and utility bills which help others to grow, sharing growth is a way of compensating them.

"Federate" the Fragmented Area

Another approach to reducing the effects of fragmentation is to introduce a "federal" arrangement. Remember (from chapter 2) that federalism involves establishing at least two governmental levels—one dealing with problems in *parts* of the whole, another with problems of the *whole*. At the local level, this concept can be applied—different levels of government can be assigned different functions.

Suppose that careful analysis can determine which problems and services are "local" and which are "regional." Then, one could assign those local functions to local government—the existing cities, villages and townships. Those problems which were area-wide would be assigned to an area-wide government—say, the county. Thus, strong local governments for local matters could be combined with a strong regional government for regional matters. The trick in all this, as you may have guessed, is deciding which powers go to which level. Another issue is who would decide these matters. Would each community have to vote its consent? Would a majority of the whole area's population decide? Would the state government establish this federation?

Use the County Government as a Regional Government

Since county boundaries are so large, a county usually encompasses most of a metropolitan area's fragmented governments. For many metro areas in Michigan, except Detroit, one county surrounds the metro area. Some have suggested the county as an appropriate scale for dealing with fragmentation--the county is small enough to be "local" and large enough to be effective.

A proposal to use the county as a regional government might read as follows. The state would reduce the powers of local governments over almost everything, and increase the powers of the county. Counties would become true "home rule" governments with broad powers, a charter, and flexibility of internal organization. These ordinances of the county would supercede those of any local unit within it. Obviously, area-wide problems would be dealt with by the county. A single county-wide tax base would exist.

Many current features of county government would have to change in order to have the county become a strong regional government. Today's "home rule" county in Michigan really isn't that strong. Its taxing power is no greater than that of an ordinary county, and it does not have broad ordinance authority. Today's Michigan home rule county law does not allow a county ordinance to supercede a local ordinance without the consent of the local government affected, unless the county is carrying out activity under the state law, rather than its own charter.

Have The State Take Over Local Services

In a fragmented setting, many believe, the biggest problems are policy differences between units of government and/or inequalities of tax base. Either of these kinds of problems could be eliminated if powers now exercised by local governments were transferred to the state. Thus, policy would become standardized, and all could share equally in the state's resources.

This idea has received attention in Michigan in terms of the K-12 school system. It has been suggested that the state assume the full cost of the schools. This would still allow local boards of education to set policy within the various districts, but it would eliminate the inequalities of finance between districts. An obvious criticism of this approach is that people value differences in policy and tax base. Those who would lose under this approach would be quick to say that local control would be threatened.

The above proposals are not the only ones which have been advanced to cope with fragmentation but they are a sample of possible solutions. In most cases, the proposals involve significant change and thus are not likely to meet with quick success. The pattern of fragmentation has grown slowly over time and has created a network of interests, loyalties, and rivalries. Thus, the pattern is likely to persist, and the issues surrounding fragmentation will also likely remain.

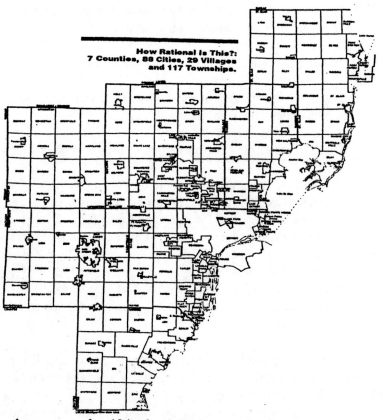

How Rational Is This?:
7 Counties, 88 Cities, 29 Villages and 117 Townships.

*Within the boundaries of the area on the map are also 124 school districts.

Reprinted with permission: of *Metro Times*, Nov. 7, 1990

THE STATE BOUNDARY COMMISSION
INCORPORATION AND ANNEXATION

The State Boundary Commission has the power to approve or disapprove both incorporations and annexations for cities, villages and townships. Three of the five commission members are appointed by the governor and two "temporary" members are appointed by the presiding judge in the county where the annexation or incorporation proposal was initiated. Decisions of the commission are made by a majority vote.

The decision to incorporate or to annex territory is important to those living in the areas affected and often is surrounded by great controversy. Though there are many exceptions and qualifications, the basic procedures are as follows:

To *incorporate* a city or village:

-petitions signed by one percent of those living in the area must be presented to the Boundary Commission. At least 100 landowners must sign.

-the Boundary Commission may approve, disapprove or amend the proposed incorporation. In making its decision, the Boundary Commission must consider the population density, the land area, natural boundaries, future growth, need for organized community services, cost of those services, and the effect of the proposed incorporation on the entire area.

-once the incorporation is approved, those living in the area affected must also approve the incorporation and elect members to a charter commission.

-a charter must be drafted, approved by the governor and passed by the voters in the area.

The *annexation* of territory is a more complex process. For home rule cities annexation may occur by action of either the city council or citizen petition.

Citizens may directly initiate annexation:

1) with a petition signed by landowners equal to one percent of the population of the "affected territory." The "affected territory" includes the governments from which territory is taken and to which territory is to be annexed.

2) with a petition signed by 20 percent of the voters in the area to be annexed. This area is smaller than the "affected territory."

3) with petitions filed by those who own 75 percent of the land to be annexed. This is often the method used for nonresidential areas.

The city council may also initiate annexation by council resolution.

Once the action is initiated, the State Boundary Commission may approve, disapprove or alter the proposed annexation. The criteria for approving annexations are the same as that used for incorporations (i.e., population density, need for organized community services, general effect on the area etc.). A local referendum is not required if the area to be annexed contains less than 100 residents. However, a public referendum must take place if 25 percent of the voters in any or all of the following areas request it:

1) The area to be annexed.

2) The township from which the area is being taken.

3) The city to which the area is being annexed. Each area must file separate petitions to have a referendum in that area.

These are some of the general principles of annexation. There are several special methods that make it easier for a city to annex adjoining property. Villages have similar annexation powers to those described above but the county Board of Commissioners has greater involvement in the process. Similarly, a fourth class city may petition the county commission for permission to annex.

Part 5

Financing Government Services in Michigan

Introduction

Government Revenues and Spending in Michigan

Introduction to Part 5

Learning Objectives

How does the role of the government differ between socialist and capitalistic economies?

What is an example of a pure public good?

How does a progressive tax differ from a regressive tax?

Compare the state and national governments in terms of their borrowing power.

Why are interest rates important to the economy of a state like Michigan?

Key Terms to Know

socialism
capitalism
mixed economy
pure public goods
progressive tax
regressive tax
proportional tax
subsidy

This part of the book will examine state and local government revenues and services in Michigan. More attention is paid to these matters here than in most introductory books of this kind. The attention reflects the times, for concern about the economic aspects of government is very great as we enter the 21st century. At the national level, the level and composition of taxing and spending are changing.

In good times or bad, the economic roles of government are powerful forces in society. Revenues will be required to operate governmental institutions and programs. Choices will always need to be made about how to raise those revenues. Choices will always need to be made about which programs governments should provide. There will nearly always be political conflict about these choices.

GOVERNMENT AND ECONOMY

An economy is a system for the production and distribution of goods and services. Some economies are owned and controlled by governments. These are commonly called socialist or "command" economies. In some of them the government is democratically selected, in others it is not. In the United States the scope of governmental economic activity is not as broad. Most Americans seem to value placing limits on government's role in the economy, so that decisions of individuals as to ownership, purchase, sale, wages, savings and investment are given greater weight. Thus the U.S. is said to be capitalistic.

While government roles in a capitalistic economy are more limited than in socialism, those roles are important. In fact, there will be some aspects of economic life which will require a role for government. For example, the private economy will require a system of enforceable rules governing ownership and contract obligations. There will probably be some goods or services (benefits) desired by all people which the private economy will not produce. For example, assume that nearly everyone desires protection against sudden air attack by outsiders. Such protection is very costly to

provide and once its exists for one person, all would have it. The private economy is not likely to produce such a benefit. Without government, no person would have what all want. In other words, in a capitalistic economy there are important roles for government in setting the framework for private exchange and providing services which otherwise would not exist, but are desired by all.

Roles for government can extend far beyond these basics, however, and much political conflict can surround the options. There are few aspects of the private economy which are immune from governmental influence. In fact, in the United States, governments do much more than the minimum economic activities mentioned above. Governments, because of choices made in the political process, touch nearly every aspect of economic life. For this reason, the United States is not considered a pure capitalistic economy but rather a "mixed" economy—combining much private ownership and decision-making with many governmental influences.

Government Goods and Services

As noted earlier, an economy, among other things, produces and distributes goods and services. Governments may have direct and indirect impact on the goods and services available in society.

Some goods and services, like clean air, national defense, lighthouses, and the basic legal system (laws, courts etc.) can be considered pure public goods. This term refers to those goods whose benefits cannot be divided between individuals. Once these public goods exist, everyone can consume them whether they have paid for them or not. Such a good will not likely be produced by profit-seeking businesses. Who would buy such a good if once they had bought it, all others could benefit from it? If such goods are to exist at all, they must be produced by government, with the authority to make all pay a share of the cost.

Bringing about pure public goods is the essential, most basic function of government. This function has grown in the U.S. As society has changed, we can call more and more benefits "public." Defense needs have grown, thus has defense spending. Urban societies need public water and sewer systems instead of private wells and septic tanks to guarantee health. The transport systems necessary to support modern living require governmental roles in finance and planning. Thus, modern societies require a larger role for government in the delivery of public goods.

Providing public goods is not the only economic role of government, however. Government has the ability to influence the production and distribution of private goods and services as well. In doing so, the public sector (government) offsets or changes the actions of the private sector. Some examples (a very incomplete set) follow.

Suppose that a desired benefit was being under-produced by the private economy. Could the government change that situation? Yes! How? The government could make the costs of production lower by paying some of the costs of production. The good could then be sold at a lower price and in larger quantities. Government could pay people to consume the good (through a tax credit or rebate scheme) and thus increase consumption. Such public sector actions (lowering costs and prices) are commonly known as subsidies.

The opposite effects are also within government's grasp. If a product is being over-consumed, a tax might be imposed on its production or consumption. The tax would effectively raise the price of the good and might reduce consumption.

Governments and Income

As noted earlier, an economy generates income and distributes it among individuals. Even in a capitalistic economy, the distribution of income can be affected by the public sector in a variety of ways, through both revenue and spending policies.

Taxes, charges and other forms of government revenue devices are seldom neutral. They usually affect different people differently and can be designed to do so. If, for example, one wished to take a larger share of the income of high income people than lower income people when raising revenue for government, one would design a progressive tax. Here, the highest percentage rates are paid by those at the top income levels. Such a tax, in itself, would narrow the after-tax income gap

between rich and poor. Suppose one wanted to encourage saving and investment—then lower the rates on high income persons, who save and invest at a higher rate, and raise them on lower incomes to make up the difference. Revenue systems which take a larger share of the income of lower income individuals are called regressive tax systems. If a revenue system takes the same percentage of income from all income groups, it is called proportional.

Government revenue systems can thus have different effects on different people. So can public sector spending patterns. Any given governmental spending program can benefit a wide spectrum of society or a narrow group and can exclude any group from benefits. This is the case whether the spending takes the form of cash payments to individuals, or providing services which are used by individuals.

Another powerful impact of government's economic decisions can be seen with respect to borrowing. The national government may borrow to finance any of its activities—whether construction of buildings which will last for many years or to pay for a current program. Generally, state and local governments do not have as much flexibility. Their long term borrowing is usually restricted to capital outlay projects—roads, sewers and the like.

Yet whenever a government borrows (for whatever purpose) it is shifting costs from some people to others. The current generations will pay some of the cost of the debt but so will future generations of taxpayers.

Clearly, the ability of government to bring about changes in the private economy is a powerful force in society. Much political activity involves groups seeking government action (subsdies, regulations, tax and spending changes) to change some aspect of the private economy so as to benefit themselves.

GOVERNMENT, ECONOMY AND FEDERALISM

In federal system such as the United States, the economic impact of governments becomes very complex. There will be many interrelationships between the different governmental levels.

First, there will likely be conflicts about which level should provide which services. For example, as things stand now, education is essentially a state and local responsibility. Should this change? Since many cities exist in every state, should sewers be paid for by the state, the nation, or the local governments?

Second, in a federal system, forces beyond the control of a state or locality can cause the effects of its policies to be altered or offset. Suppose I desire progressive taxation and am successful in changing Michigan's state tax structure to achieve that. Could changes at the national level offset that? Yes, if the national tax structure became more regressive! Would well-to-do residents leave the state to avoid the higher tax rates?

Further, consider the fact that state and local governments' revenues are affected by the performance of the national economy. A state like Michigan, which depends heavily on the export of expensive durable goods (autos), is especially vulnerable. If national economic policy forces interest rates up, consumption of goods like cars, which rely on borrowed money, will decline. Purchases will be deferred. Unemployment in Michigan will rise and revenues to its governments will decline. Some state service costs will rise (layoff benefits) and others will need to be cut. A community seeking to borrow for a new water system will find its interest costs rising. Thus, in a federal system, while governments have some economic independence, they are also interdependent.

With all these factors in mind, let us turn to a summary of recent economic changes in state and local finance in Michigan.

RECENT ECONOMIC CHANGES IN MICHIGAN

In the past 20 years, because of the major role that manufacturing plays in Michigan's economy, the state reacted more strongly than the norm to national economic shifts. When economic times were good the state would experience high employment and high wages. When times were bad the state faced higher than average unemployment rates and a rapid drop in income levels.

Since 1970, reliance on the auto industry has declined and more and more workers have shifted to the service industries. With this shift has come a decline in the state economic position relative to other states. In the future, job growth will be led by the service area and employment in the auto industry and similar manufacturing areas will decline.

Changes in Employment

Since 1970, total wage and salary employment in Michigan increased from 3 million to 4.9 million jobs. There have been dramatic changes in employment levels as a result of Michigan's cyclical economy.

Until the early 1990s Michigan had an unemployment rate above the national average. Since then the state jobless rate has been below the nation's average. However, by mid-2002 the state's unemployment rate was 6.2 %, slightly higher than the national average.

Manufacturing Employment

At the end of the 1970s jobs in manufacturing were about 1.2 million. Since then, however, the manufacturing job loss has been much greater in Michigan than in the nation as a whole. As of 2002, there were approximately 920,000 manufacturing jobs in the state.

Motor Vehicle Employment

In 1970, Michigan had 42 percent of the total national motor vehicle and equipment employment. By 1990, Michigan's share had dropped to 35 percent. In Michigan, motor vehicle related jobs declined from a 20 year high of 410,000 jobs in 1978, to 269,000 jobs in 2002, the lowest total in 20 years.

Service Industry Growth

In the past 20 years service jobs, such as retail or wholesale trade, finance, insurance and real estate, health and social service have increased in both Michigan and the nation. Between 1970 and 1990, Michigan's service sector jobs more than doubled, adding more than 530,000 new jobs. Such jobs have increased in the first years of the 21st century and now total over 1,300,000 jobs.

In 1970, manufacturing industries comprised 36 percent of the total wage and salary jobs in Michigan while service jobs were about 14 percent. By 1990, service jobs and manufacturing jobs were equal in number-each was about 25 percent of total wage and salary jobs in Michigan. By 2002, service industries in Michigan comprised almost 26 percent of the total, as manufacturing jobs declined to about 20 percent of the state total.

The Impact on Income

During the 1970's Michigan's per capita personal income was above the national average. However, during the 1980's Michigan per capita income equaled or dropped below the national average. In the 1990s the state's per capita income grew 28.2% from 1992 to 1997, above the 24.1% increase nationwide. By 2001, Michigan's per capita income of $29,788 was slightly below the national average of $30,472 but higher than most other Great Lakes states. Michigan ranked 18th among the 50 states in per capita income.

Economic Diversity

Whenever Michigan faced economic declines in the past the often heard cry was "Diversify...Michigan needs to rely less on the auto industry." That has happened--to a degree. After being hit hard by the recessions of the 1970s and 1980s, Michigan is less dependent on auto manufacturing than it used to be.

Auto workers made up about 10 percent of Michigan's work force in 1977 and less than 6 percent today. Factory workers were 23 percent of the work force in the late 1970s. Today they are about 14 percent. Income from auto sales has also declined. It made up 20 percent of the state income in 1977 and is about 13 percent today. Income from manufacturing in general is also down ---from about 40 percent of the state's income in 1977 to about 26 percent today. However, while Michigan has diversified, so have most other states, and we remain slightly below the national average as measured by an "Industrial Diversity Index" published in the Detroit News recently.

*This section on recent economic changes adapted from "Michigan Key Indicators" researched by Citizens Research Council of Michigan and published by the Council of Michigan Foundations, Nov. 1992 and the Detroit News Website (detnews.com) article by Peronet Despeignes, "Autos still dominate Michigan economy: Other industries needed." (July 11, 1999)

Chapter 16

Government Revenues and Spending in Michigan

State Revenues

Local Revenues

State and Local Borrowing

Overview of Spending Patterns

> *"The governor shall submit to the legislature at a time fixed by law, a budget for the ensuing fiscal period setting forth in detail, for all operating funds the proposed expenditures and estimated revenue for the state."*
>
> ArticleV, Sec.18 Michigan Constitution

Chapter 16

Learning Objectives

When Michigan became a state, what was the main source of government revenue?
Approximately what percentage of the state budget comes from the federal government?
How much did Michigan's state and local governments spend in a typical year?
What is the Single Business Tax?
What is the source of most local government revenues?
Describe the process of equalization.
How does a general obligation debt differ from a limited obligation debt?
What is the main source of school revenue?
Compared to other local forms of government, what unique revenue raising method do cities have?
What arguments are used to justify borrowing to finance government projects?
Generally, how does Michigan's state and local tax burden compare to that of other states?
What is the major purpose of local spending in Michigan?
How does Michigan's state and local spending compare to that of other states?
What are some of the reasons that will cause the "spending mix" to vary among local units of the same type?
Generally, do governments share in spending programs or are they kept separate?
How does Michigan rank in receiving federal funds? Why?
What are the major stages in the budget process?
What is the purpose of the Budget Stabilization Fund?

Key Terms to Know

progressive tax	regressive tax	Homestead Property Tax
exemption	tax base	Transportation Fund
General Fund	tax credit	Categorical Grants-in-aid
equalization	audit	matching funds
mill	bond	general obligation debt
Headlee amendment	budget	limited obligation debt
Tax Allocation Board	general fund	agency budget
Budget Stabilization Fund (BSF)		State Equalized Value
executive budget		

204

At the time of statehood, the major source of governmental revenues in Michigan was the property tax, administered by a network of county treasurers and township officials. As time went by, methods of financing governments changed. In the latter part of the 19th century, taxes on liquor were established and were an important source of state revenue until the Prohibition era of the 1920's. At that time, state taxes on doing business were instituted.

The Depression era reduced revenues from business taxes, and led to changes in the property tax as well. Depression-era taxpayers faced property foreclosure and government faced slow property tax collection. A state constitutional amendment was passed limiting property tax rates, effectively preventing the state from using that tax. The legislature adopted a 3% sales tax as a substitute, and other taxes on consumption followed.

During World War II the state prospered, and voters forced a sharing of the state sales tax with local governments to keep property taxes down. As a result, dwindling state revenues led the legislature to develop new taxes on consumption (cigarette taxes, for example) and business activities.

A recession in the late 1950's severely hurt Michigan. Stopgap tax hikes and fund transfers were used to narrowly avoid fiscal disaster. The 1963 Constitution liberalized borrowing power and permitted a state income tax. Beginning in the 1930's the national government established programs of aid to states and localities, which grew significantly in the 1960's and 1970's.

Thus, Michigan's revenue patterns have changed over time, toward a greater variety of revenue sources and a decline in the importance of the property tax. Also, as time has passed, the various levels of government have become more financially interrelated. Finally, on the whole, government spending has increased, not only in dollar amounts, but also in terms of its share of total spending in society.

STATE REVENUES

Table 16-1 shows a breakdown of the sources of the state's revenue. Some important overall patterns should be noted. First, the state receives revenue from a variety of sources—its revenues are diversified. Federal aid, income taxes and sales taxes are of the greatest importance. Together, these three sources represent about 60% of the state's revenues. Second, the state raises revenue from personal income and from use of that income through consumption. Third, the sales tax share of total revenues has recently increased. The sales tax rate increased from 4% to 6% in 1994. Finally, state property tax revenues have also increased, as a 6 mill state-wide property tax took effect in 1994-95. This tax replaced a share of local education millages as part of the 1994 "Proposal A" finance reforms.

Federal Aid

About one-fourth of Michigan's revenues come from the national government, about the same as the average state. It is important to realize that nearly all of these federal funds are restricted as to use. Most are categorical grants-in-aid, and the services for which the funds are spent are largely determined by the national government. Among the uses to which these funds are put are pollution control programs, food inspection, highway maintenance, payments to citizens such as the school lunch and Medicaid programs. In some cases, these federal funds are available to the state only if it provides "matching" funds, picking up some part of the costs of the particular program.

The State Income Tax

Prior to the 1960s, state taxation of income was thought to be prohibited by the state Constitution. The 1963 Constitution removed doubt as to the use of income taxation. In 1967 the state established a personal income tax. Today, this tax is very important to state government.

The Constitution (Article 9, section 7) prohibits a "graduated" (or progressive) income tax. Thus the rate of the tax is "flat"—the same regardless of income level. The rate of the tax changed over time and is now 4.2% and is scheduled to drop to 3.9% by 2004.

Table 16.1

STATE OF MICHIGAN

TOTAL
REVENUE BY SOURCE

FY 2001-02

TOTAL RESOURCES: $36,757.0 MILLION
(Chart dollars in millions)

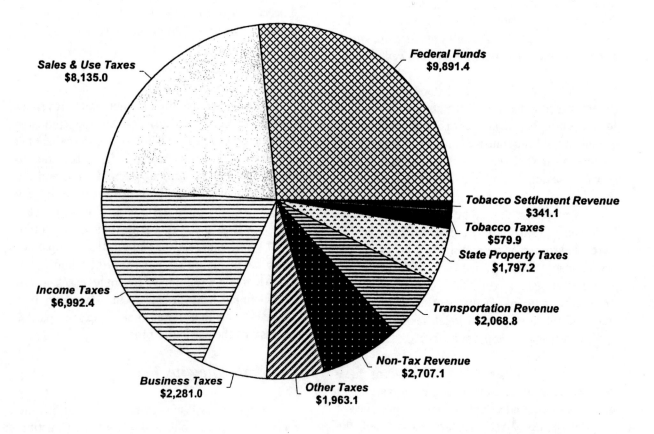

Sales & Use Taxes
$8,135.0

Federal Funds
$9,891.4

Tobacco Settlement Revenue
$341.1

Tobacco Taxes
$579.9

State Property Taxes
$1,797.2

Income Taxes
$6,992.4

Transportation Revenue
$2,068.8

Non-Tax Revenue
$2,707.1

Business Taxes
$2,281.0

Other Taxes
$1,963.1

Table 16.2

2001 MICHIGAN
Individual Income Tax Return

2001
MI-1040

Issued under P.A. 281 of 1967. Filing is mandatory.

This return is due April 15, 2002. Please type or print clearly in blue or black ink.

▶ **1.**

Filer's First Name and Middle Initial	Last Name		▶ **2.** Filer's Social Security Number
If a Joint Return, Spouse's First Name and Middle Initial	Last Name		▶ **3.** Spouse's Social Security Number
Home Address (No., Street, P.O. Box or Rural Route)			Office Use
City or Town	State	ZIP Code	▶ **4.** School District Code (see p. 45)

Check this box if someone else prepares your return and you DO NOT need a book mailed to you next year (see p. 6). ⟶ ☐

▶ **5. STATE CAMPAIGN FUND** — Check this box if you (or your spouse, if filing a joint return) want $3 of your taxes to go to this fund. This will not increase your tax or reduce your refund.

		YES	NO
▶ **5.**	a. You	☐	☐
	b. Spouse	☐	☐

▶ **6. FARMERS, FISHERMEN OR SEAFARERS** If 2/3 of your income is from farming, fishing or seafaring, check this box................. ▶ **6.** ☐

▶ **7. FILING STATUS**
  a. ☐ Single
  b. ☐ Married, filing jointly
  c. ☐ Married, filing separately. Complete item 3 and enter your spouse's name here: _____

▶ **8. RESIDENCY**
  a. ☐ Resident
  b. ☐ Nonresident
  c. ☐ Part-Year Resident

If you check box "b" or "c," you must complete and attach Schedule NR.

9. EXEMPTIONS

If someone else can claim you and/or your spouse as a dependent, check the box, and complete the worksheet on page 12.

	You	Spouse	
	▶ a. ☐	▶ b. ☐	c. ☐ .00

d. Number of exemptions you claimed on your 2001 federal return .... ▶ **9d.** ___ x $2,900   .00

e. Number of individuals 65 or older who qualify for a special exemption................ ▶ **9e.** ___ x $1,900   .00

f. Number of individuals who qualify for the following special exemptions: deaf, blind, hemiplegic, paraplegic, quadriplegic, or totally and permanently disabled .... ▶ **9f.** ___ x $1,900   .00

g. Number of children claimed as Michigan exemptions: Ages 18 and under................ ▶ **9g.** ___ x $600   .00

h. Unemployment Compensation. Unemployment compensation must be 50% or more of AGI (amount entered on line 10).................. ▶ **9h.** ☐ $1,900   .00

Add lines 9c, 9d, 9e, 9f, 9g and 9h. Enter here and on line 15 .... **9.**   .00

10. **Adjusted gross income** from your U.S. *1040, 1040A, 1040EZ or 1040NR* (see p. 12)............ ▶ **10.**   .00

11. Additions (from MI-1040 Schedule 1, line 7)...................................... ▶ **11.**   .00

12. *Total.* Add lines 10 and 11... **12.**   .00

13. Subtractions (from MI-1040 Schedule 1, line 19)............................... ▶ **13.**   .00

14. *Income subject to tax.* Subtract line 13 from line 12........................ **14.**   .00

15. Exemption allowance. Enter the amount from line 9 or Schedule NR, line 20.......... ▶ **15.**   .00

16. *Taxable income.* Subtract line 15 from line 14.............................. **16.**   .00

17. *Tax.* Multiply line 16 by 4.2% (.042). Enter here and carry amount to line 18 .... **17.**   .00

www.treasury.state.mi.us

Continue and sign on page 2.

207

While the rate of the tax is "flat" its effect is actually progressive. ("Things aren't always what they seem" goes the old saying.) The progressivity is brought about by the existence of some exemptions and credits. An exemption is an amount of income not subject to tax which thus reduces taxable income. A credit is a reduction in tax due. In Michigan, an exemption of $2900 is currently allowed for the taxpayer and each dependent. An additional exemption may be taken for all over age 65 and some disabled individuals. Credits are allowed for a share of city income taxes, contributions to public radio and TV stations, colleges, universities and public libraries, property tax and a share of home heating costs for low income taxpayers.

The overall effect of these exemptions and credits is to reduce the rate of tax for all, especially for lower income households. The most powerful factor in the reduction of the tax burden on low income households is the $2900 personal exemption. A four person household with a $22,400 income would face an income tax on only half of that. Obviously, the greater the household income, the less important the per person exemption, and the greater the real tax rate. Figure 16.1 demonstrates how the Michigan income tax compares to other Great Lakes states and the U.S. in general.

About three-quarters of the revenue from the income tax goes into the state's general fund. The remainder goes to the school aid fund.

The State Sales Tax

Since the 1930s, the sales tax has played an important role in state finances. The rate of the tax is constitutionally limited to six percent. The tax is not levied on prescription drugs, food purchased for home consumption and is limited to 4% on household utility costs. The tax is officially paid by the seller, but in practice is passed on to buyers.

Note that a sales tax is not a tax on income as such, but rather a tax on certain uses of income. If one saved all one's income, one could avoid this tax entirely. That's unlikely, of course, but understanding that may help explain why sales taxes are usually considered regressive. Lower income households consume (rather than save) a larger share of their income. Taxes on consumption will thus tend to take a larger share of their income.

The distribution of sales tax revenues is restricted by the state Constitution and state laws. Nearly 75 percent of the tax goes to the School Aid Fund and about 25 percent of the tax is set aside for state aid to cities, villages and townships, which can be spent as they choose.

The state uses another form of consumption tax-the use tax. It is imposed on the value of services like hotel and motel accomodations and telephone use. The tax also applies to used car sales or rentals. The rate of the use tax is also 6 percent. Two-thirds of this revenue goes to the general fund, one-third to the School Aid Fund.

Figure 16.1

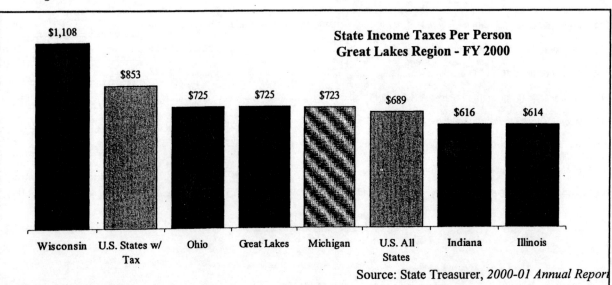

State Income Taxes Per Person
Great Lakes Region - FY 2000

Wisconsin	U.S. States w/ Tax	Ohio	Great Lakes	Michigan	U.S. All States	Indiana	Illinois
$1,108	$853	$725	$725	$723	$689	$616	$614

Source: State Treasurer, *2000-01 Annual Report*

Other consumption related taxes imposed by the state are taxes on beer, cigarettes (75 cents per pack), liquor (a variety of levies totalling about 14% of retail price) and wine.

Transportation-Related Taxes

The state imposes many taxes on transportation. Aircraft must be registered and a fee per pound is charged. Aviation fuel , diesel fuel , and liquefied petroleum gas used in motor vehicles are all taxed. Marine fuel is taxed. Commercial vehicles must pay a registration fee. Watercraft are licenced for three years at fees depending on length. All the aforementioned charges and fees are restricted as to use. Revenues are placed in the Aeronautics Fund, Waterways Fund, or the Transportation Fund.

All these revenue sources together are only a small share of Michigan's transportation-based revenues. The major transportation taxes are the gasoline tax and the motor vehicle weight tax. The gasoline tax was first levied in 1925. The current rate of the tax is 19 cents per gallon set in 1997. All of the revenues from the gasoline tax are placed in the Michigan Transportation fund.

The motor vehicle weight tax dates to 1905, and is the second major source of transportation revenue in Michigan. In late 1983, the weight tax was phased out and replaced with a value tax. As the size of autos has diminished, so did their weight. This caused a decline in weight-based revenues. The shift to value bolstered Transportation Fund revenues.

Business Taxes

Michigan imposes many taxes on business. Taxes on boxing and wrestling matches, in place since 1919, are based on ticket sales. Horse- race wagering has been taxed since 1933. Taxes on insurance premiums, levied since 1913, are set at 1.3% of receipts. Taxes on oil and gas retrieved from the ground have existed since 1929, and now are set at 5 percent on gas and 6.6 percent on oil. Most of these revenue sources contribute to the general fund of the state.

By far, the most significant tax on business at the state level is the single business tax, (SBT) in effect since 1975. This tax modified or replaced 11 separate taxes which had been effect before then. The tax is levied on all forms of business—individual, firm, partnership, trust and corporation. Essentially, the SBT is imposed on the total compensation paid to labor and capital by the business, not on profits. The rate is currently 2.30%. There are some exemptions in calculating business cost or tax base. All the proceeds of this tax become part of the state's general fund. The SBT is gradually being phased out over the next 23 years, with a rate reduction of .1% a year.

Another important tax paid by business in Michigan is the tax to support the state's Unemployment Compensation Fund. Both the state and national governments tax employers for this purpose. The rate varies depending on the unemployment record of the firm. Proceeds of the tax go into the Unemployment Compensation Fund, and benefit levels are set by law.

There are many controversies over business taxation. One major question is: Who really pays the taxes on business? The owners, with smaller profits and dividends? The workers, with lower wages? The consumers, with higher prices? Since these questions are hard to answer it is difficult to know whether taxes on business are progressive or regressive.

One last point about state revenues. Article 9, section 26 of the state Constitution sets a state revenue limit. Generally, the requirement is that the state's revenues (excluding federal aid) may not exceed just under 10 percent of the personal income of all Michigan residents in the preceding year. Excess revenues are to be refunded to taxpayers if they are greater than 1 percent of the total state revenues.

Non-Tax Revenues

While it provides revenue to the state, the lottery is plainly not a "tax", for it can be avoided. (In fact, some of the other "taxes" can also be avoided—the cigarette tax, for example.) The lottery has existed in Michigan since 1972 when Michigan citizens removed a constitutional barrier to such activities. Fifty percent of sales are required to be prizes and 11 percent is used to cover administration

Table 16.3

COLLECTIONS FROM MAJOR MICHIGAN TAXES, 1997-2000

(In Millions)

	State Taxes	1997	1998	1999	2000	Data Sources
Income Taxes	Personal Income	$ 5,935	$ 6,397	$ 6,939	$ 7,247	A
Business Privilege	Single Business	2,270	2,373	2,421	2,363	A
	Unemployment Compensation	1,113	1,024	987	1,024	B
	Oil & Gas Severance	40	33	24	41	A
	Insurance Company Retaliatory	201	139	192	155	A
	Horse Race Wagering	12	13	13	13	A
	Subtotal[7]	$ 3,636	$ 3,582	$ 2,650	$ 3,596	
Sales-Related	Sales	5,376	5,566	5,918	6,241	A
	Use	1,096	1,151	1,294	1,328	A
	Tobacco Products	546	559	599	592	A
	Beer and Wine	48	49	49	50	A
	Liquor	76	82	86	93	A
	Liquor Markup	83	88	96	110	E
	Subtotal	$ 7,225	$ 7,495	$ 8,042	$ 8,414	
Property	Utility Property	148	102	214	157	A
	Intangibles	77	45	1	1	A
	Estate	78	100	175	163	A
	State Real Estate Transfer	187	224	254	251	A
	State Education	1,130	1,237	1,245	1,337	A
	Subtotal	$ 1,620	$ 1,708	$ 1,889	$ 1,889	
Transportation	Gasoline	714	901	924	931	A
	Diesel Fuel	82	120	86	87	A
	Motor Vehicle Weight or Value	594	665	710	757	A
	Other	24	22	26	27	A
	Subtotal[7]	$ 1,414	$ 1,708	$ 1,746	$ 1,802	
	Total State Taxes[7]	$19,830	$20,890	$21,266	$22,968	
	Local Taxes					
Income	City Income	$ 517	$ 546	$ 538	$ 550	C
Sales-Related	Utility Users	$ 54	$ 50	$ 49	$ 53	C
Property	General Property[7]	$ 6,737	$ 7,159	$ 7,565	N/A	D
	Total Local Taxes[7]	$ 7,308	$ 7,755	$ 7,746	N/A	
	Total State and Local Taxes[7]	$27,138	$ 28,645	$ 30,405	N/A	

Data Sources:
[A] Annual Reports of the State Treasurer (state fiscal year basis).
[B] Michigan Unemployment Agency (state fiscal year basis).
[C] State Tax Commission (calendar year basis).
[D] State Tax Commission (local fiscal year basis).
[E] Michigan Department of Consumer and Industry Services, Liquor Control Commission (state fiscal year basis).

[7] Omits collections from certain minor taxes.

Source: Citizens Research Council, *Outline of the Michigan Tax System* 2001

expenses and to compensate ticket agents. Lottery proceeds are usually less than 5% of the state's revenues. Such revenues are required by the state constitution to be placed in the School Aid Fund and make up less than 10% of its total.

In addition, the state receives other non-tax revenues. Of course, U.S. aid is one such example, as is interest the state receives on investments, permit and license fees (as for camping and fishing) and court fines. One might consider tuition at state colleges and universities as another form of non-tax revenues.

LOCAL REVENUES

Understanding local government revenues is a challenge. Local units receive revenues from many sources. The combinations of revenue sources vary with the different forms of local government.

Approximately half of all money received by governments in Michigan is received by local units. In general local governments in Michigan depend on the property tax, aid from the state, charges for services and aid from the national government. (This is the overall pattern—the picture for any one local government, or any one form of local government may vary, as we will soon see.) In the following sections, these major local revenue sources will be outlined.

The Property Tax

As of 1994, the property tax was the largest local revenue source. When the Proposal A reduction in property tax for schools (see chapter 14) took full effect, overall property tax use declined. All local governments make some use of the tax, and all households are affected by it, whether buying a home or not. (Renters are considered as paying the tax as part of the rent and may receive a tax credit for part of their rent.)

Defining the Tax Base. The first step in property taxation is the determination of the tax base—the value of the property in question. Generally, land and improvements are subject to the tax, with some exceptions. The state Constitution exempts property "owned and occupied by non-profit,

religious or educational organizations and used exclusively for religious or educational purposes" (Article 9, section 4). State law exempts a great many other categories, including nearly all household goods, and the state allows local communities to grant tax exemptions to businesses in an attempt to encourage them to locate or expand in the community.

Those properties subject to the tax are assessed. The process is very localized—city and township officials are responsible for assessment. Assessors must meet state certification requirements. An assessment roll is prepared by early March, reflecting the values of property on the preceding "tax day"—December 31 of each year.

An initial assessment would be at 50% of market value, and another assessment is done every year with reference to market value trends. However, as a result of 1994's Proposal A, the actual taxable value of the property (excluding any new construction) can increase by only 5% per year or the rate of inflation, whichever is less. If ownership of the property changes, the current assessed value (also called "state equalized value") will become the new basis for the future taxable value calculations.

There are many levels of review of the assessment. The first is local. All cities and townships are required to have a Board of Review. Generally, this board meets in March, at times and places made known to all property owners whose assessment has been increased. Appeal to the Board is a necessary first step—one can't appeal to higher boards unless one has begun at the local level. The review board consists of three property owners in townships and in cities the number varies according to the charter. It is free to make adjustments to the assessed value of individual properties or to all properties in the community.

The next stage in setting the official taxable value is a county-level process of equalization. Here, county officials review the value of local community property of all types. Within each class of property (i.e. commercial, agricultural, industrial, residential etc.) the county determines whether the local unit's assessment is accurate. If not, the county Board of Commissioners assigns a factor or multiplier to the value set by the local unit so as to change that value. This is done for each *class* of property. (If a class of property was deemed to be under-assessed, a multiplier greater than 1.0 would be used to raise the assessment on all properties in that class. Over-assessed classes would be assigned a factor less than 1.0 to reduce their values.) The purpose of county review is to guarantee equity between classes and between local units of government. It will not, however, correct disparities between individual properties. Since 1994's Proposal A sets an assessment increase cap of the lesser of 5% or the rate of inflation, until an individual property is sold, such disparities between individual properties will likely increase.

The next stage is at the state level. In May, the State Tax Commission reviews the values set by the board of commissioners in each county. It may adjust values for each class of property and thus seek to bring about fairness by class of property to each county. Thus, the final state equalized value is set. Another state body, the State Tax Tribunal, hears appeals of individual taxpayers not satisfied with the decision of their local board of review. Decisions of both state bodies may be appealed to the Court of Appeals. As an incentive for local units to assess properly, state laws require that if the equalized value as determined by the state is greater than that set by the county or local community, the maximum authorized tax rate is to be reduced. This penalizes the community for low assessment.

Setting the Tax Rate. After the value of the property has been established, the next step is the levying of a tax rate. Multiplying the base by the rate will determine the amount of tax due.

The rate of the property tax is stated in mills. A mill is one-tenth of a cent, or, one dollar per thousand dollars. Or, one can say that each ten mills is equal to one percent of value. The following example will illustrate:

Figure 16.2

Calculating Property Tax	
Taxable Value of Home	$40,000
Millage Rate	30
Tax Rate ($30 for each $1000 of value:) 30 X 40 =	$1200

The millage rate applied to any one property is an aggregate (or total) of the millage rates levied by the various units of government in which the property is located. At a minimum, a property will be taxed by the county, a township, an ISD, a K-12 school district and the state, which- after Proposal A-levies a 6 mill tax for K-12 school district operating purposes. A village tax might be added to this. In a city, a property tax would be paid to the city, but not to the village or township. Further, a property tax might be paid to a community college, library district or one or more of a variety of special districts. The statewide average millage is about 40 mills.

Local Unit Tax Rates. The state Constitution allows up to 15 mills of property tax to be levied without a vote of the people. This millage is allocated among K-12 school districts, the county, non-charter townships, ISDs and in some cases, community colleges. These units each receive a guaranteed share of the 15 mills if they can demonstrate need. (The shares are 4 mills-schools, 3 mills-counties, 1 mill-townships, .10 mill ISDs; the community college share varies.) The county tax allocation board (see chapter 13) divides the millage up. The millage can be raised to 18 mills by a vote of county residents, and its distribution between units must then be fixed. Over 40 counties have done this.

Millage levied in addition to the 15 or 18 mills must be either allowed by charter, voted on on by the residents of a unit, or levied to pay off debt. A city or village may exceed the 15 mill limit. By adopting a charter, city residents can allow a millage up to 20 mills. Home rule village charters may go to the same level, and general law villages may levy up to 12 mills. A charter township may have 5 mills levied by the board and up to 5 additional mills by a vote of the public. K-12 school districts may also levy operating millage up to 18 mills, only on non-homestead property, with approval of the voters. Note that for school operating purposes, the maximum property tax for a principal residence (homestead) is the 6 mill state property tax levy. For all other property classes, the maximum is 24 mills--the 6 mill state levy and an 18 mill local levy.

The total of allocated and extra-voted millage of unchartered units may not exceed 50 mills unless the tax is levied to meet payments on debt incurred before 1979. For this kind of debt, the millage may be levied "without limit as to rate and amount" according to the state Constitution (Article 9, section 6). Since the passage of the (Headlee) Tax Limitation Amendment in 1978 (Article 9, sections 25-34), local units may not enter into debt backed by property tax payments, or raise millage rates for other purposes, without a vote of the residents. An exception would exist if a city or village were to levy a rate below that set in its charter—taxes could be raised up to the charter rate without a vote.

The Headlee amendment has another important effect on local unit tax rates. If the property value of a unit (excluding new construction) increases as a rate faster than the national inflation rate, the authorized millage rate must be reduced ("rolled back") so that the percentage increase in property tax revenue is not greater than the inflation rate. Voters may restore the rate if they desire. If a community's growth rate was less than the inflation rate, the allowed millage rate could increase.

By law (Act 5, 1982) any local government's property tax rate is reduced if its total assessed value (excluding new growth) increases, unless its governing body votes to keep the millage rate at the old level. If that is done, the tax rate will yield more money because of the increased tax base.

Collecting the Tax. Generally, local unit treasurers collect the property tax. After the bills are mailed out and after the appropriate "grace period" unpaid bills are turned over to the county for collection. Properties with taxes unpaid over a three year period are offered for sale. A government or individual may buy such a property for the tax owed, or the title goes to the state. An owner may redeem property within one year.

Property Tax Relief. Over the years, the property tax has been severely criticized. Among the objections to the tax are: the assessment process doesn't guarantee fair treatment; improvements are taxed; since the tax is on the value of the property, those with low or fixed incomes are hard pressed to keep up with increases; farmland at the edge of urban areas soars in value while farm income might not; local units with open land and low taxes attract new business, and larger cities are hurt by the fact that so much of their land is property tax exempt (roads, churches, hospitals, schools etc.). In re-

sponse to criticism, many property tax relief schemes have been proposed, and quite a few adopted. This section will review some of these.

Property taxes paid by owners are deductible on one's federal income tax return and reduce the federal income tax due. As noted earlier, many kinds of property are exempt, a form of tax relief. The 1974 Farmland and Open Space Law permits owners of some agricultural lands to reduce state income tax obligations if local property taxes exceed 7 percent of household income, and if the owner has agreed to keep the land in agricultural use for 10 years. As noted earlier, city, village and township governments may extend property tax reductions to business firms.

One of the more important forms of property tax relief in Michigan is the so-called "circuit breaker" or Homestead Property Tax Credit Program. Over one third of Michigan's households receive tax relief from this program. One is eligible for this tax credit if the property taxes on one's principal residence exceed 3.5% of household income. (Renters can get relief for the amount by which their annual rent exceeds 20% of their household income.) The state allows a reduction in one's state income tax obligation if property taxes exceed the 3.5% burden. The state pays 60% of the excess burden (or overload) back to the taxpayer. The credit is phased out for households with incomes between $75,000 and $80,000. Seniors, veterans and disabled persons receive greater benefits.

The property tax is considered by many to be a regressive tax. Although all in a community pay the same millage rate, the percentage of income devoted to housing is thought to decline as income increases. Thus, the percent of one's income allocated to the property tax would decline as income increased. It is clear that analyzing this is difficult because of factors like income tax deductibility and community differences. Programs like Michigan's "circuit breaker" rebate can offset this regressivity if designed properly.

State Aid

Aid from the state is the second major source of local government revenues. There are a great many state programs which provide funds to various local governments. This section will review these, which represent about one-half of total state expenditures. Some of the state aids to local government are required by the Constitution, others by law. The (Headlee) Tax Limitation Amendment requires that at least 42 percent of the state's revenues (not counting U.S. aid to the state) be shared with local governments (see p. 130). While there are numerous state aid programs, a few deserve special attention.

In 2002, state aid in support of local governments was over 60% of state spending from its own sources--about $16 billion. Almost 70% of this total was spending through the School Aid Fund (see below). Another 10% of this was for a program of "revenue sharing" with cities, villages, townships and counties. The remainder is distributed through special targeted grants, mostly in the area of transportation.

Revenue Sharing. Public Act 532, 1998 established a program of revenue sharing with local non-school units based entirely on state sales tax revenues. Michigan's constitution requires that 15% of such revenues be sent to cities, villages and townships. This share of the sales tax amounts to about 40% of shared revenues. Payments are made to the locals on a per captia basis.

The P.A. 532 portion (60% of the total) includes counties as well as the other locals. Counties receive about one-fourth of these dollars, and the remainder is distributed to other locals, based on a formula. the formula elements include taxable property per person in each unit, its population, and an analysis of tax rates. This plan replaces an earlier revenue sharing scheme and will not be fully phased in until 2007.

Transportation Funding. Another important form of state aid to counties, villages and cities is the distribution of transportation tax revenues to local units, primarily for road construction and maintenance. All revenues from the state-imposed transportation taxes (discussed above) go to the Michigan Transportation Fund, and are divided between the state and some localities. Ten percent of the fund is set aside as a comprehensive transportation fund for use in public transit programs. The remainder is divided as follows: almost 40% to the state for road uses, about 20% to cities and villages

and just about 40% to county road commissions for use in maintaining roads in townships. The precise amount each local unit receives is determined by statutory formulae: counties receive money based primarily on the taxes on vehicles in the county and road mileage. Cities and villages receive funds based mainly on their population and road mileage.

School Aid Fund. The single largest state aid to local governments is the School Aid Fund, established in the 1963 Constitution. This fund consists of revenues from a variety of sources. Most taxes on tobacco, all the liquor excise tax, all net proceeds from the lottery and about 75% of the sales tax revenues are "earmarked" for this fund, as are the funds from the state-wide property tax of 6 mills. In addition, the legislature appropriates money from the general fund to the School Aid Fund.

Revenues to this fund are distributed to K-12 districts. State policy sets a "basic foundation" standard ($6700 per pupil in 2002) This amount is to increase every year, and districts whose total spending (state aid and local taxes combined) would fall below this standard are to receive greater year-to-year increases. Thus, the spending gap between districts should narrow. K-12 districts also receive money through some categorical grants, restricted to special purposes, such as adult education and special grants for "at-risk" students. Charter schools receive only the basic foundation grant.

The School Aid Fund is of great significance to K-12 schooling in Michigan. Since Proposal 1A, the state's share of school finance has risen from 45% in 1993 to about 80% in 2002, and appears to have brought about more spending equality from district to district. It is important to note, however, that the state only aids in the operational costs of K-12 districts. The state does not support the capital outlay ("brick and mortar"), needs of local districts. (It does do so for community colleges and 4-year colleges and universities.) Thus, K-12 districts with need for new buildings and/or the upgrading of old buildings are at the mercy of the voters controlling millage levies for capital outlay purposes. (See the later discussion about borrowing.)

Local Unit Patterns

As mentioned earlier, the combination of revenue sources varies a bit between the different forms of local government. Combinations of sources will also vary between units of the same governmental form! Two cities, for example, might have very different revenue patterns. Obviously, the local money landscape is very complicated. Generalization is difficult and risky, but this section will attempt to describe the revenues of each major local government.

Counties. County governments receive their funds from local property taxes, unrestricted state aid, restricted state aid for transportation and mental health programs, and charges for services. Counties also receive federal aid in the form of categorical grants and revenue sharing.

Townships. While townships receive some federal aid, the major sources of a township's revenue are likely to be state aid, local property taxes, and charges for services.

Villages. Villages rely heavily on local property taxes, state aid and charges for services.

Cities. Cities depend on local property taxes, state aid, and charges for services. Many (especially larger) cities receive federal categorical aid funds for a variety of purposes.

Cities are unlike all other local forms in one respect: any Michigan city may adopt an income tax. It may be imposed on residents (including corporations) and non-residents who work in the city. The rate is limited to one percent (residents) and 1/2 percent (non-residents). Detroit may set rates of 3 and 1.5 percent respectively. Just over 20 Michigan cities (both large and small) have adopted this tax, which is controversial, especially among non-resident workers. In theory, the city income tax is justified by the fact that much city property, used by non-residents, is exempt from property taxation—colleges, superhighways and so forth. The half-rate tax on non-residents is justified, in theory, by their consumption of vital services (streets, police, fire) while at work. What do you think?

K-12 Schools. On a statewide average, only about 5% of K-12 revenue is from U.S. aid. School districts do not receive federal revenue-sharing, only special grant funds. Thus, school revenue comes

from two sources: state aid and the local property tax.

Other Local Schools. Intermediate school districts receive revenues from local property taxes and state categorical program aid. Community colleges receive revenues from local property taxes, state aid from the general fund, and charges in the form of tuition and fees paid by the students. These sources are usually approximately of equal importance in the college budget.

Special Districts. Special districts and authorities have varying methods of finance. Some are supported by local property taxes, some by charges for services and some receive some of their revenue from the state.

STATE AND LOCAL BORROWING

Governments do not always depend only on a particular year's revenues to pay the cost of all that year's spending. They may also borrow to do so.

Most Americans are aware of borrowing practices at the national level. The national government is a frequent borrower, and may borrow with few restrictions. The U.S. Constitution does not require that the national government's budget be "balanced". The nation may borrow both for long-term projects (dams, buildings, harbors and park development) and to meet its current program costs, even if no long term capital improvement results. Furthermore, if the national budget is in deficit one year, the debt represented by that deficit does not have to be paid off the next year. If such a choice is made, the national government may operate with a deficit, covered by borrowing, year after year. Up until just recently it did this, and the accumulated deficits grew. The total of all these deficits is the "national debt."

Borrowing by governments is easily defended. Costly projects which will last a long time should be partly paid for by all who will use them. Paying off debt over a long time through taxes or charges on many generations helps accomplish this. Deficit spending by government during an economic recession can help stimulate the economy by keeping spending levels high.

Critics of borrowing argue that government borrowing forces interest rates up for all borrowers and depresses private spending. They also are more critical of borrowing to meet today's operating costs, because such borrowing puts a debt burden on future generations without providing them any clear benefits. While many of these pros and cons of borrowing are focused on the nation, the same issues exist regarding state and local borrowing.

In Michigan, as in most American states, there are many limits on the borrowing power of governments. A most important difference between governments in Michigan and the national government is the fact that Michigan's governments are not permitted to have a year-end deficit in operating funds. Also, a distinction is made between operating funds and capital improvements. Generally, long-term borrowing may be done only for capital improvements, not for current operations.

A government may have a surplus in its operating budget. Surpluses can be used as revenue the following year.

Only short-term borrowing is permitted for operating expenses. If a government is "short" one month, and expects a state aid payment in, say, three weeks, it may borrow to tide itself over. But all such short-term debt must be eliminated by the end of the government's accounting year—commonly known as the fiscal year (FY).

Types of State and Local Debt

In general, state and local governments may enter into two types of debt. The main difference between them is the method of repayment.

A "general obligation" debt is one in which the entire resources of the borrower are pledged as collateral. The "full faith and credit" of the borrower is pledged toward repayment.

The state may enter short-term general obligation debt agreements to cover a fiscal year's costs, if the debt is repaid within that year, without a vote of the people. The state may also enter into

long-term general obligation debt if proposed by a 2/3 vote of both houses of the legislature and approved by a majority of those voting on the proposal in a statewide general election. Over the past 30 years, Michigan voters have approved general obligation debt for bonus payments to Vietnam veterans (1974), constructing facilities to reduce water pollution (1968), to construct public recreational facilities (1968 & 1988) and to finance a wide variety of environmental cleanup and park improvements (1998). The voters have rejected long-term borrowing for low income housing (1968), Vietnam veteran bonuses (1970), and public transport systems (1974). Likewise, at the local level, entering into general obligation debt is approved by the voters at a referendum.

A government in Michigan may also enter into limited obligation indebtedness by issuing "revenue bonds." This is the most common form of borrowing. Here, the revenues pledged to pay off the debt usually come from the project developed with the borrowed money. The "full faith and credit" of the government is not pledged in repayment. Limited obligation borrowing does not require a vote of the people.

Examples of the kinds of projects for which such borrowing might be used are highway bonds (paid back from gas and weight taxes) borrowing for a college dormitory (paid from room and board charges) and special assessment bonds (paid back from charges to homeowners who received, say, a new sidewalk).

Frequently, limited obligation borrowing is done by "authorities"— state and local agencies empowered to issue limited obligation debt. At the state level, prominent examples are the Michigan State Housing Development Authority, State Building Authority and the Hospital Development Authority. Local governments use building authorities and other forms for specialized borrowing.

Local unit borrowing is monitored by the state's Municipal Finance Commission. This body consists of the state treasurer, attorney general and superintendent of public instruction. It reviews the financial condition of local units and must approve most of the borrowing of the governmental subdivisions of the state. The commission is responsible for enforcing state laws regarding forms of indebted-

Table 16-4

General Obligation Bond Payment Schedule (In Thousands of Dollars)

For Period Ended September 30	Principal	Interest	Total
2001	$ 42,392	$ 49,108	$ 91,500
2002	44,321	47,299	91,620
2003	46,786	45,140	91,926
2004	46,121	43,198	89,319
2005	48,123	41,057	89,180
2006	50,458	37,392	87,850
2007	48,690	37,346	86,036
2008	52,339	33,604	85,943
2009	51,997	33,894	85,891
2010	53,624	31,573	85,197
2011	59,986	24,523	84,509
2012	59,501	24,514	84,015
2013	61,975	14,278	76,253
2014	42,160	11,404	53,564
2015	43,435	9,103	52,538
2016	46,140	6,686	52,826
2017	33,490	4,560	38,050
2018	35,215	2,761	37,976
2019	16,270	1,391	17,661
2020	17,200	472	17,672
Total [a]	$ 900,223	$ 499,303	$ 1,399,526

(a) Does not include $44.5 million in General Obligation school loan notes issued on April 24, 2000, and maturing on April 23, 2001.

Bonds and Notes Payable by Fiscal Year (In Thousands of Dollars)

Item	Outstanding on September 30				
	1996	1997	1998	1999	2000
GENERAL OBLIGATION DEBT					
School Loans	$180,000	$174,445	$328,670	$322,650	$360,870
Water Resources	14,000	9,000	4,000	-0-	-0-
Environmental Protection	377,823	368,914	450,727	439,851	421,652 *
Recreation	113,160	102,825	90,675	76,876	65,341
Clean Michigan Initiative					96,860
Total General Obligation Debt	$684,983	$655,184	$874,072	$839,377	$944,723
NON-GENERAL OBLIGATION DEBT					
Michigan Department of Transportation Tax Dedicated Bonds	$ 854,196	$ 873,701	$ 866,018	$ 827,870	$ 801,829 *
Special Authorities-Revenue Bonds and Notes					
International Bridge Authority	5,905	3,380	2,805	1,818	-0-
Mackinac Island State Park Commission	2,520	2,360	2,200	2,980	2,805 *
Michigan State Housing Development Authority	1,987,286	2,068,424	2,088,563	2,026,541	2,058,321
Michigan State Hospital Finance Authority	2,777,024	2,887,783	3,586,525	3,569,311	3,735,500 *
Michigan Higher Education Facilities Authority	179,135	174,745	218,190	220,395	228,845 *
Michigan Higher Education Student Loan Authority	625,424	672,949	817,425	782,360	835,595
Michigan Municipal Bond Authority	1,368,035	1,591,875	1,685,997	2,243,566	2,555,130
Michigan State Building Authority (a)	1,478,896	1,616,717	1,996,787	1,945,086	1,957,803 *
Michigan Strategic Fund	1,991,591	2,088,621	2,182,659	2,011,684	2,322,470 *
Michigan Underground Storage Tank Financial Assurance Authority	216,600	205,950	193,555	180,540	166,870
Michigan Family Farm Development Authority	1,659	1,108	1,008	505	410
Total Non-General Obligation Debt	$11,488,271	$12,187,613	$13,641,732	$13,812,656	$14,665,578

* All or part of the principal amount not presented, and not represented in the totals due to the advance refunding of all or part of this obligation.

Source: *Annual Report of the State Treasurer, FY 2000-01, p.23*

Table 16-5

Local Government Unit Bonds and Notes (In Thousands of Dollars)

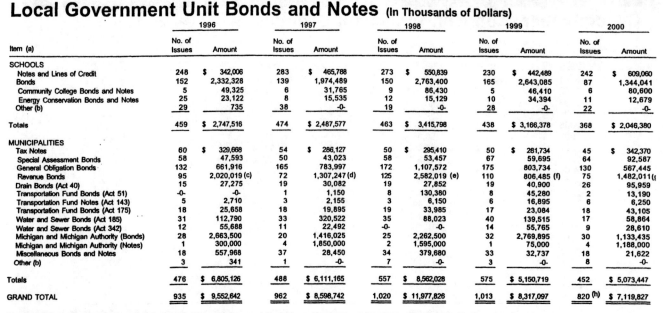

Item (a)	1996 No. of Issues	1996 Amount	1997 No. of Issues	1997 Amount	1998 No. of Issues	1998 Amount	1999 No. of Issues	1999 Amount	2000 No. of Issues	2000 Amount
SCHOOLS										
Notes and Lines of Credit	248	$ 342,006	283	$ 465,788	273	$ 550,839	230	$ 442,489	242	$ 609,060
Bonds	152	2,332,328	139	1,974,489	150	2,763,400	165	2,643,085	87	1,344,041
Community College Bonds and Notes	5	49,325	6	31,765	9	86,430	5	46,410	6	80,600
Energy Conservation Bonds and Notes	25	23,122	8	15,535	12	15,129	10	34,394	11	12,679
Other (b)	29	735	38	-0-	19	-0-	28	-0-	22	-0-
Totals	459	$ 2,747,516	474	$ 2,487,577	463	$ 3,415,798	438	$ 3,166,378	368	$ 2,046,380
MUNICIPALITIES										
Tax Notes	60	$ 329,668	54	$ 286,127	50	$ 295,410	50	$ 281,734	45	$ 342,370
Special Assessment Bonds	58	47,593	50	43,023	58	53,457	67	59,695	64	92,587
General Obligation Bonds	132	661,916	165	783,997	172	1,107,572	175	803,734	130	567,445
Revenue Bonds	95	2,020,019 (c)	72	1,307,247 (d)	125	2,582,019 (e)	110	806,485 (f)	75	1,482,011 (g
Drain Bonds (Act 40)	15	27,275	19	30,082	19	27,852	19	40,900	26	95,959
Transportation Fund Bonds (Act 51)	-0-	-0-	1	1,150	8	130,380	8	45,280	2	13,190
Transportation Fund Notes (Act 143)	5	2,710	3	2,155	3	6,150	6	16,895	6	6,250
Transportation Fund Bonds (Act 175)	18	25,658	18	19,895	19	33,985	17	23,084	18	43,105
Water and Sewer Bonds (Act 185)	31	112,790	33	320,522	35	88,023	40	139,515	17	58,864
Water and Sewer Bonds (Act 342)	12	55,688	11	22,492	-0-	-0-	14	55,765	9	28,610
Michigan and Michigan Authority (Bonds)	28	2,663,500	20	1,416,025	25	2,262,500	32	2,769,895	30	1,133,435
Michigan and Michigan Authority (Notes)	1	300,000	4	1,850,000	2	1,595,000	1	75,000	4	1,188,000
Miscellaneous Bonds and Notes	18	557,968	37	28,450	34	379,680	33	32,737	18	21,622
Other (b)	3	341	1	-0-	7	-0-	3	-0-	8	-0-
Totals	476	$ 6,805,126	488	$ 6,111,165	557	$ 8,562,028	575	$ 5,150,719	452	$ 5,073,447
GRAND TOTAL	935	$ 9,552,642	962	$ 8,598,742	1,020	$ 11,977,826	1,013	$ 8,317,097	820 (h)	$ 7,119,827

(a) Figures reflect approvals granted as of September 30 of the respective year. Approved issues may or may not have been sold by the unit of local government.
(b) Includes transfer of debt service funds remaining after final maturity of original debt; use of excess bond proceeds and derivative products.
(c) Includes 1 issue of Industrial Revenue Bonds.
(d) Includes no issues of Industrial Revenue Bonds.
(e) Includes 2 issues of Industrial Revenue Bonds.
(f) Includes 3 issues of Industrial Revenue Bonds.
(g) Includes 3 issues of Industrial Revenue Bonds.
(h) Includes 89 Prior Approval Orders and 731 Exception From Prior Approval Orders issued.

Special Revenue Debt, Bond and Note Payments (In Thousands of Dollars)

Item		Issue Date	Maturity Dates	Amount issued	Principal Payments	Interest Payments	Outstanding Principal as of 9-30-00
Michigan Department of Transportation							
Tax Dedicated Bonds Michigan							
Comprehensive Transportation	Series 1985	1985	2011	$57,830	$ 400	$ 1,260	$ -0- *
	RF. SR. 1988-I	1988	2009	73,155	-0-	-0-	-0-
	Series 1992-A	1992	2022	37,655	775	1,653	29,015 *
	RF. SR. 1992-B	1992	2011	127,310	7,045	6,889	113,395
	RF. SR. 1996-A	1996	2014	22,650	75	1,207	22,435 *
	RF. SR. 1998-A	1998	2010	38,640	-0-	1,901	38,640
State Trunkline Fund	Series 1989-A	1989	2019	135,780	-0-	-0-	11,195 *
	Series 1992-A	1992	2021	253,618	6,765	4,901	115,658 *
	RF. SR. 1992-B I & II	1992	2021	99,592	2,675	2,043	40,136 *
	Series 1994-A	1994	2024	150,000	2,525	1,427	25,780 *
	RF. SR. 1994-B	1994	2002	90,990	4,995	957	16,565 *
	SR. 1996-A	1996	2026	54,500	785	680	11,120 *
	RF. SR. 1998-A	1998	2026	377,890	-0-	19,455	377,890
Total Special Revenue Debt					$26,040	$42,373	$801,829

* All or part of the principal amount not presented and not represented in the totals due to the advance refunding of all or part of this obligation. The table below summarizes the advance refunding activity by issue.

Series	Advanced Refunded From Series	Amount Refunded	FY 00 Paid From Escrow Principal	FY 00 Paid From Escrow Interest	FY 00 Escrow Balance
Comprehensive Transportation:					
1985	1988-II & 1992-B	$ 27,176	$6,091	$21,405	$ -0-
1992-A	1996-A	5,305	-0-	299	5,100
Trunkline Transportation:					
1989-A	1992-B, 1994-B & 1998-A	111,245	-0-	-0-	-0-
1992-A	1998-A	131,195	-0-	7,241	131,195
1992-B I & II	1998-A	56,780	-0-	3,171	56,780
1994-A	1998-A	112,815	-0-	6,443	112,815
1996-A	1998-A	41,170	-0-	2,297	41,170
Totals			$6,091	$40,856	$347,060

Source: *Annual Report of the State Treasurer FY 2000-01, p.24*

ness, borrowing procedures and debt limits set for local governments.

Tables 16.4 and 16.5 present some detailed information on the outstanding debt of state and local governments in Michigan. Note that most of the debt of Michigan governments is at the local level. Note also that the typical form of debt (state or local) is of the limited obligation variety.

Borrowing Procedures

When a government has decided to borrow, its intention to do so is publicized in newspapers and among banking and financial institutions. Potential lenders may consult a number of sources to advise them on the financial strength of the borrower. Moody's and Standard and Poor's are investment centers which evaluate a government's ability to pay loans off. They issue "credit ratings" for governments. The better a unit's credit rating, the more easily it can attract lenders, and the lower the interest rate it will pay.

The government will have determined the method of repayment it wishes to use. Lenders will thus know the amount sought and the schedule of repayment planned. The interest rate paid on the bonds is usually the subject of bidding by potential lenders. The borrowing government will solicit bids from lenders. Lenders will submit bids indicating the interest rate they expect, and the government will then select the lender(s). Banks and investment companies are the major purchasers of such debt and an entire industry of attorneys and finance experts is involved in the process.

The debt of a government is physically represented by a bond or note, a form of I.O.U. The "evidences of indebtedness" are usually sold in large dollar denominations, are numbered and contain a statement of the interest rate and maturity (payment) schedule. When the details are completed, the borrowing government issues the bond or note, and receives the cash it needs.

Interest rates paid by the government will vary with overall economic conditions, and will differ according to the method of repayment and the financial condition of the government. Generally,

units pay higher interest on revenue bonds than on general obligation bonds. The national government subsidizes state and local borrowing. Income received from interest on such loans is tax exempt, while interest and dividends from loans to private corporations is not. A lender can thus loan money to a state or local government for a lower interest charge and still receive a satisfactory return on their investment.

REVENUE ISSUES

One of the most important issues is how revenues in Michigan compare to those in other states in terms of the burden they place on incomes. Table 16.6 presents information on this question.

Table 16.6

Tax Burdens in the U.S. -2000

Total Tax Burden
(National/State/Local)

Connecticut	39.9%	HIGHEST
Alaska	29.2%	LOWEST
Michigan	34.7%	(11th)
Average	33.8%	

State/Local Tax Burden

Maine	13.6%	HIGHEST
Alaska	6.3%	LOWEST
Michigan	10.6%	(16th)
Average	10.2%	

Ideally, a state and local tax system should meet a number of basic standards. For example, it is generally agreed that revenue sources should be diversified, or balanced between many sources. This helps stabilize the flow of revenues to government. It seems generally agreed that state revenues in Michigan are balanced—many sources are used. Some local units, however, (especially schools) tend to rely heavily on just one or two sources.

Taxes should be convenient to administer and pay, and differ quite a bit in these respects. While the administration and payment of the income and sales taxes would seem quite clear and efficient, that of the property tax is very cumbersome.

Another major revenue issue can be stated: "who should pay what share of their income to government?" This is the issue of whether taxes and charges should be progressive, regressive or proportional. As noted above, the state income tax is somewhat progressive. Taxes or charges based on the value of consumption (sales taxes on electricity use or weight taxes on autos, for example) are probably regressive. In Michigan many rebate schemes reduce the regressivity of taxes, but there are still many political conflicts. Furthermore, we see tax burden issues cropping up in terms of factors other than income levels. Should senior citizens— regardless of their income—be given tax deductions? Should veterans?

Revenues, of course, may affect different people differently. So may the spending of governments, to be examined next.

AN OVERVIEW OF SPENDING PATTERNS

This section presents an overview of government spending in Michigan. The emphasis is on spending by state and local governments, although some attention is paid to national government expenditures. This examination of spending will not present details on spending for all the various governmental functions. Instead, it will present the overall pattern of expenditures at the state and local level and outline the stages in the spending process.

If this book had been written 70 years ago, it would have been possible to survey government spending in three neat, separate categories—national, state and local. Then, with few exceptions, each level of government raised its own money with its own taxes and spent its own money on programs which the other levels had little to do with. The three levels were characterized by little sharing of responsibilities.

Today, the levels are more interwoven. As was seen earlier, state government receives many funds from the national, and local governments typically receive funds from the nation and the state. For almost every policy area, each level of government spends money. An exception would be defense spending, paid for almost entirely by the nation, or street light repair, usually paid for with local funds. But for most government services today, more than one level is involved in spending, directly through its own agencies or indirectly by giving funds to other governments for them to administer.

Analyzing this intricate pattern is very difficult. Perhaps it can be approached through raising some basic questions and attempting to answer them.

How much money is spent by the state governments in Michigan? How is it divided up among major purposes? Tables 16.8 and 16.9 present answers to these questions.

Does each level of government contribute equally to each program area? No, not necessarily. Table 16-7 shows that the "mixing" of responsibilities differs from program to program.

Table 16.7

Estimated State and Local Expenditures in Michigan-2000

Purpose	Percent Financed by:		
	U.S.	State	Local
Education	7	73	20
Public Welfare	24	63	14
Health,Hospitals	30	40	20
Highways	10	60	30

Source: Author's estimates

Table 16-7 clearly indicates the extent to which "shared responsibility" has developed in the U.S. federal system.

Table 16.8

Adjusted Gross Appropriations: FY 2000-01

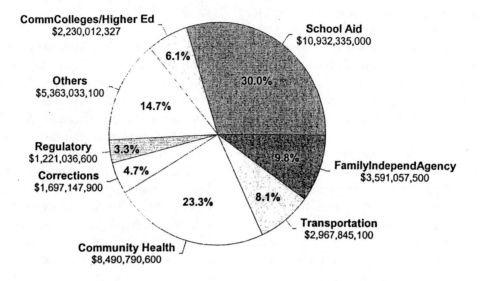

CommColleges/Higher Ed
$2,230,012,327

School Aid
$10,932,335,000

6.1%

Others
$5,363,033,100

14.7%

30.0%

Regulatory
$1,221,036,600

3.3%

9.8%

FamilyIndependAgency
$3,591,057,500

Corrections
$1,697,147,900

4.7%

23.3%

8.1%

Transportation
$2,967,845,100

Community Health
$8,490,790,600

Total Adjusted Gross Appropriations = $36,493,258,127

GF/GP Appropriations: FY 2000-01

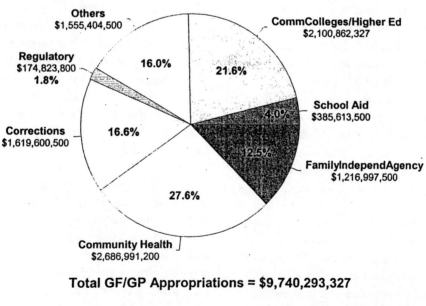

Others
$1,555,404,500

CommColleges/Higher Ed
$2,100,862,327

Regulatory
$174,823,800
1.8%

16.0%

21.6%

4.0%

School Aid
$385,613,500

Corrections
$1,619,600,500

16.6%

12.5%

FamilyIndependAgency
$1,216,997,500

27.6%

Community Health
$2,686,991,200

Total GF/GP Appropriations = $9,740,293,327

*NOTE: Higher Education Conference Committee report awaits Senate and House approval;
amounts used for calculation are those appearing in the conference report.*

Source: House Fiscal Agency, FY 2000-01 Appropriations summary.

If we look just at state government spending, what patterns would we find? We would see two categories of spending dominating the "pie." Table 16.8 summarizes state spending during fiscal year 2000-01. Education and social services account for 60% of the total. Keep in mind that much of this state spending is for aid to individuals (e.g. social services) and that much of it is for aid to local governments. Much of the transportation, health and education spending is actually carried out by local governments with money received from the state.

If we examine local spending, what patterns would exist? Plainly, expenditures for schools are the single most important locak government cost, although 80% of the total spent by locals for education is from the state school fund. Also interesting to note is that, in Michigan, local governments spend very little on public welfare, since such programs are mainly a national-state responsibility..

How do types of local governments compare with each other—which local governments spend how much and what do they spend it on? Some interesting patterns emerge. Highway expenditures are mainly county and municipal (city and village). The small local amount of welfare expenditure is nearly all county-level. Municipalities dominate police and fire service spending. Spending on health and hospitals shows counties, municipalities and special districts (authorities) all having strong roles. All forms of local government have some debt, although debt payment spending is a small share of their total spending in each case. Municipalities dominate the "other" category, an indication that urban-type services are being provided by these cities and villages.

One might also ask: "Will each unit of government in a particular category (each township,say) spend its money in the same mixture? The answer would be "no". The individual units of each type will differ in their spending patterns. More urbanized townships, for example, are likely to spend a larger share of their budget on police-fire services than rural townships. Small cities might not own and operate a city hospital. Some school districts are not in debt.

Keep in mind that the sources of these funds are often state and/or national programs. Just what

is the pattern of national government spending in Michigan? It is clear that most national spending in Michigan consists of aid to individuals, not to governments. The largest of these programs is spending for social security.

In terms of federal aid, Michigan's rank is low compared to other states. In most cases, Michigan received less per person than the average. Why? Part of the reason for Michigan's low rank is the fact that national taxes per person in Michigan are above the national average. This is because of the state's high income levels and the progressivity of the national tax structure. Another reason is the low level of defense spending in Michigan compared to other states. The defense share of national spending is large, and Michigan does not receive much of it. Finally, there are few federal employees in Michigan, compared to the average state.

THE SPENDING PROCESS

This section attempts to introduce the process of developing spending decisions in government. Much of what has been said elsewhere in this book is relevant to this discussion. The spending decisions of governments are often surrounded by interest group pressures and party differences. There is often disagreement as to whether, and how much, to spend, and about which agency or government should administer the funds. Needless to say, there is also conflict as to how government will raise the money it spends.

It is helpful to view spending as related to budgeting. A budget is a plan for both raising money and spending it. Budgets reflect decisions about taxes and spending. For every government, the budget is a plan for the fiscal year—the government's accounting year. (Fiscal years are not usually calendar years but other 12 month periods.)

Grover Starling (1982:p.272ff) has described several stages in the budget process. Step one would be *perceiving public needs*. Officials make evaluations of what programs citizens want. Surveys, interest groups and the officials' own goals may be of great impact at this stage. The government's agencies themselves may influence this process by encouraging spending on their own programs. This stage is central to the budget process because the conflicts at this stage affect all later stages.

The second step is to *develop preliminary revenue estimates* which can serve as guidance to officials as to how much is available for spending. This step involves analyzing any surplus from the existing year, and attempting to forecast the yield from existing revenue sources. This stage is usually dominated by officials with major financial responsibilities, most of whom are in the executive branch of the government (the treasurer, controller, and/or budget director, for example). Naturally, forecasts take into account the performance of the economy and the actions of any other governments which are a source of revenue. This is clearly a difficult endeavor, and much of the later budget stages depend on the assumptions made here. Whether a tax hike or reduction is suggested will depend largely on assumptions; whether programs are created or cut will do so as well.

Based upon these preliminary estimates, and guidance from the executive, agencies will *submit their plans and requests.* These agency budget requests are usually quite detailed. They would contain expenditures the agency would seek to make on personnel, materials, contracts with outside suppliers and any payments made to individuals. A government's personnel costs are usually the largest share of its costs since individuals usually deliver government services. Thus wages, salaries and fringe benefits (including payment for retirement programs) make up most government costs. Material costs may be important for some departments— asphalt, say, for a road department. The precise mix of costs will vary with the agency.

Based on these agency requests, political forces, and refined estimates of revenue, the *executive budget proposal* is developed. This document is a synthesis of revenue estimates and spending proposals. The executive budget will typically include a summary with special references to any important changes proposed in revenues or spending. It will also include a detailed presentation of revenue estimates and an agency-by-agency spending plan, including precise figures in each category of cost for each agency. Details can be mind-boggling, as the official proposal may be 2 or 3 inches thick!

Once the executive budget has been proposed, conflicts shift to the legislature. *Hearings on the proposed budget* are held, as the legislature begins to consider spending levels, tax hikes or cuts, program cuts or changes. This process at the state level was summarized in chapter 8, and a similar one exists in all governments. Keep in mind that the executive in many governments has a veto over legislative action. This stage of legislative review and action leads to approval of a budget, which might differ in many respects from that proposed by the executive.

As a result, programs have been established, funding types and levels set, and a detailed plan put in place. Obviously, the next step is *execution or administration of the budget.* Budget administration aims (in theory, at least) at efficiency and accountability. Program goals are to be met within the budget, and a variety of procedures must be followed. The budget managers must establish controls on employment practices, purchasing operations, the receipt and disbursement of all funds devoted to the program(s) under their supervision. Agency managers are accountable to the chief executive and ultimately the legislature.

By the mid-point of the spending year, plans are usually underway for the following year's budget proposal. However, a year's spending isn't complete until the *review and audit* stage is reached. Most governments have internal controls designed to prevent (or discover) fraud and many other forms of mismanagement. For example, more than one official may have to sign checks, or an internal audit staff may review all, a sample of, or unusual transactions. Citizens and/or employees may also "blow the whistle" on illegal or questionable practices.

Furthermore, independent external auditors are often used. The state legislature employs the Auditor General to examine executive branch spending. Local governments commonly employ private accounting firms to audit the government's receipt and disbursement of funds, and the state treasury department also audits local governments from time to time.

Finally, a spending year isn't over until *oversight and evaluation* of programs is accomplished. This is an ongoing process, involving interest groups, executive agencies, the media, the legislature and others. Was the budget adequate? Did the program "work"? Would more spending accomplish more? Would less? Should the agency be reorganized? In effect, we return to stage one—the perception of public needs!

Cutting Spending

As was clear to Michigan residents in the 1980's and 1990's, governments frequently need to reduce spending levels. In 2003 the new governor also be faced a significicant deficit in the state budget. Anytime one spends less one year than than the last, a cut has clearly occurred. Even spending more can mean spending less if the increase does not keep up with inflation. From the perspective of this chapter, spending reduction illustrates many spending issues.

Why would spending be reduced? The needs to be met by a program might no longer exist. A program might have been shown to be ineffective. A program might lose the political competition for more dollars. Earmarked revenues might fall short and decision-makers might not vote supplements. Revenues in general might be reduced because of tax cuts and/or an economic downturn, but state and local budgets will still have to be "balanced". Spending on discretionary programs might be cut in order to fund required programs. Commonly, spending reductions generate as much intense conflict as spending increases. Many vested interests will seek to protect themselves and shift the burden of cuts to others.

These are some general ground rules for spending reduction, however. Only about 30% of all state government spending can be said to be up to the full discretion of the legislature. National government restrictions on the spending of U.S. aid and state constitutional limits set the framework for spending many funds. Thus, when the time arrives to cut budgets, the "ax" might fall more quickly on some, not others.

Another important factor is whether cuts can be avoided by drawing upon past surpluses, or reserves, if any exist. In the mid-1970s, the Budget Stabilization Fund (BSF) was created at the state level. Known as the "rainy-day fund", its purpose was to cushion the ups and downs of state government revenues. According to a formula set by the law (Act 76, 1977), state revenues are placed in the fund when the state's personal income growth is greater than 2%, and may be transferred back to the general fund when the state's economy is not growing or unemployment exceeds 8%. Michigan's BSF grew during the late 70's, was used to avoid some spending cuts in the 1980s and 1990s, and grew again in the late 1990s. By 2002 the economy slowed down and the state was again facing a deficit and was forced to draw from the fund. Of course, when the state's economy recovers from recession, the law requires that money otherwise available for spending be set aside in the fund.

Spending reductions can be made at the beginning of a fiscal year by lower budgets, but may need to be made in the middle of a fiscal year as well. When this occurs, the usual practice is similar to that used at the state level (see chapter 8). Commonly, the executive proposes reductions through "executive orders", which are subject to the approval of the legislature.

Once made, spending reductions are not necessarily permanent. There will likely be pressure to re-establish spending levels as the state economy improves or higher taxes are levied. Clearly, policy makers will have a difficult time determining whether today's increased spending will have to be cut tomorrow if another downturn occurs.

As this chapter and part of the book end, what conclusions can be drawn? The topics of revenues and expenditures are very complex. There is an interplay of forces and decisions on revenue systems, programs, actions of other governments and the performance of the economy. These chapters have attempted to organize this complexity, provide an overview of Michigan's public finances and compare Michigan to other states. The attention paid to these topics indicates their importance. While many public issues do not directly involve money, most do.

Table 16.9

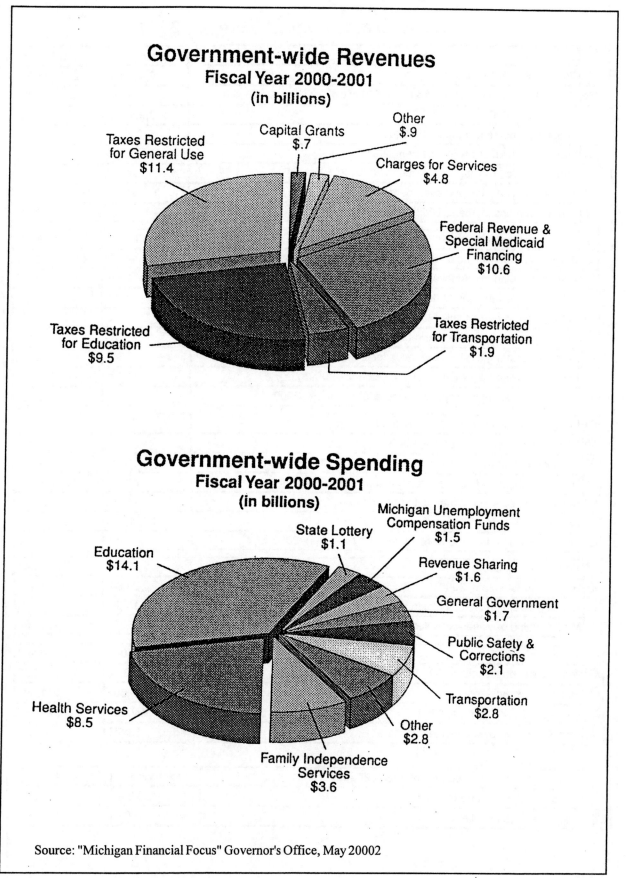

Government-wide Revenues
Fiscal Year 2000-2001
(in billions)

Taxes Restricted for General Use $11.4

Capital Grants $.7

Other $.9

Charges for Services $4.8

Federal Revenue & Special Medicaid Financing $10.6

Taxes Restricted for Transportation $1.9

Taxes Restricted for Education $9.5

Government-wide Spending
Fiscal Year 2000-2001
(in billions)

Education $14.1

State Lottery $1.1

Michigan Unemployment Compensation Funds $1.5

Revenue Sharing $1.6

General Government $1.7

Public Safety & Corrections $2.1

Transportation $2.8

Other $2.8

Family Independence Services $3.6

Health Services $8.5

Source: "Michigan Financial Focus" Governor's Office, May 20002

Basic Census Data, Michigan, 2000

People QuickFacts	Michigan	USA
Population, 2001 estimate	9,990,817	284,796,887
Population percent change, April 1, 2000-July 1, 2001	0.5%	1.2%
Population, 2000	9,938,444	281,421,906
Population, percent change, 1990 to 2000	6.9%	13.1%
Persons under 5 years old, percent, 2000	6.8%	6.8%
Persons under 18 years old, percent, 2000	26.1%	25.7%
Persons 65 years old and over, percent, 2000	12.3%	12.4%
Female persons, percent, 2000	51.0%	50.9%
White persons, percent, 2000 (a)	80.2%	75.1%
Black or African American persons, percent, 2000 (a)	14.2%	12.3%
American Indian and Alaska Native persons, percent, 2000 (a)	0.6%	0.9%
Asian persons, percent, 2000 (a)	1.8%	3.6%
Native Hawaiian and Other Pacific Islander, percent, 2000 (a)	Z	0.1%
Persons reporting some other race, percent, 2000 (a)	1.3%	5.5%
Persons reporting two or more races, percent, 2000	1.9%	2.4%
Persons of Hispanic or Latino origin, percent, 2000 (b)	3.3%	12.5%
White persons, not of Hispanic/Latino origin, percent, 2000	78.6%	69.1%
Living in same house in 1995 and 2000, pct age 5+, 2000	57.3%	54.1%
Foreign born persons, percent, 2000	5.3%	11.1%
Language other than English spoken at home, pct age 5+, 2000	8.4%	17.9%
High school graduates, percent of persons age 25+, 2000	83.4%	80.4%
Bachelor's degree or higher, pct of persons age 25+, 2000	21.8%	24.4%
Persons with a disability, age 5+, 2000	1,711,231	49,746,248
Mean travel time to work, workers age 16+ (minutes), 2000	24.1	25.5
Housing units, 2000	4,234,279	115,904,641
Homeownership rate, 2000	73.8%	66.2%
Housing units in multi-unit structures, percent, 2000	18.8%	26.4%
Median value of owner-occupied housing units, 2000	$115,600	$119,600
Households, 2000	3,785,661	105,480,101
Persons per household, 2000	2.56	2.59
Median household money income, 1999	$44,667	$41,994
Per capita money income, 1999	$22,168	$21,587
Persons below poverty, percent, 1999	10.5%	12.4%

Geography QuickFacts	Michigan	USA
Land area, 2000 (square miles)	56,804	3,537,438
Persons per square mile, 2000	175.0	79.6

226

MICHIGAN'S CONSTITUTION

This Appendix presents the 1963 Constitution of Michigan. The following summary of the state's past Constitutions might be of interest to many readers. It is adapted from *The State We're In* published by The League of Women Voters of Michigan.

Since Michigan became a state it has had four different constitutions. The Constitutions of 1835, 1850, 1908 and 1963 had many aspects in common yet each revealed the needs and demands of their own times.

Two years before becoming a state, Michigan adopted the Constitution of 1835. The governor and lieutenant governor were the only executive officers elected under this Constitution. They were elected to serve two year terms. All other executive appointments, except the treasurer, were made by the governor. This was a document that provided for a strong executive. The legislature was a bicameral body with an upper and lower house. The state court system consisted of a Supreme Court, circuit courts, a Probate court for each county and four justices of the peace for each township. This Constitution also specified the officials to be elected at the county level.

Fifteen years later, in 1850, a new basic law was written and adopted. This was a longer and more detailed document than the first. Under the Constitution of 1850 many details of the legislature's operation were spelled out. The powers of the governor were also reduced. The legislature was limited in its power to spend and borrow money. Under this Constitution the judges of the Supreme Court and five state administrators were to be elected. For the first time in the state's history, this Constitution required that the question of calling a new constitutional convention be placed before the voters every 16 years, though the issue could be dealt with at other times by either the legislature or public petition. This 16 year rule has appeared in all subsequent Michigan constitutions. There were several attempts to revise the Constitution in the 1860's and the 1870's but they were unsuccessful.

In response to the Progressive movement the Constitution of 1908 gave the public a greater voice in the affairs of government. Citizens gained the right to initiate state constitutional amendments and to circulate petitions for the recall of elected officials. The legislature was also allowed to submit any law that it passed (except appropriations bills) to a vote of the people. The governor was given the power of an "item veto" in appropriations bills. (This is the power to veto a single item and accept the rest of the bill.) Home rule was provided for cities and allowed them to have greater flexibility in their own governance.

On several occasions the Michigan Supreme Court ruled that before a constitutional convention could be called by the voters, a majority of those voting in the election had to vote in favor of the proposal. This type of majority was often difficult to secure because not everyone who voted in the election voted on the proposal for a constitutional convention. (Many voters often skip or ignore ballot proposals.) In 1960 a citizen petition drive resulted in the adoption of the so-called Gateway Amendment, which allowed a proposal for a constitutional convention to pass if supported by a majority of those voting on the question. This made proposals much easier to approve. In 1961 the voters approved the calling of a new constitutional convention. The state's current Constitution was approved two years later.

The 1963 Constitution

Michigan's present Constitution, ratified in 1963, went into effect on January 1, 1964. This document, like every new constitution, reflects the needs of its own time. The major new provisions of the Constitution of 1963:

-Guarantee equal protection of the laws in the Declaration of Rights and prohibit discrimination on the basis of religion, race, color and national origin. A Civil Rights Commission was created to investigate cases of discrimination.
-Prohibit the death penalty, forbidden by state law since 1846.
-Provide for a unified court of justice and the creation of a new Court of Appeals.
-Create a bi-partisan Apportionment Commission to decide legislative district boundaries.
-Set four year terms for the governor and lieutenant governor and require their election as a team.
-Give the lieutenant governor the power to vote in case of a tie in the state Senate.
-Require that administrative departments, bureaus and agencies be combined into no more than 20 major departments.
-Prohibit a graduated income tax. (The 1908 Constitution did not mention an income tax at all. Inclusion of the prohibition of a graduated tax had the implied effect of making a flat rate income tax legal.)
-Require an annual executive budget.
-Outline state responsibility for public community and junior colleges.
-Create authority for local civil service systems.
-Give greater flexibility to local units of government.
-Create authority for long term borrowing by the state, for specific purposes, subject to a 2/3 vote in each house of the legislature and a vote of the people.
-Require that property be assessed at no more than 50% of the true cash value, equalized.

The current Constitution also provides for an automatic vote on a new constitutional convention every 16 years. In 1978 and 1994, voters refused to call a new convention. Any constitution, however, must adapt to change and Michigan's Constitution provides several ways to do this.

Changing Michigan's Constitution

Ideas about the basic law of society—the law that governs government— do change. If the state's Constitution could not be modified it could become an obstacle to meeting new needs and problems.

In Michigan, there are a number of ways to change the Constitution. One method is general revision (a complete rewriting). This is done by a constitutional convention, and voter approval of the finished product. The process operates the following way.

Since 1978, the question of calling a constitutional convention must be put on the ballot every 16 years. The next automatic vote for a new convention will be in 2010. The question may also be placed on the ballot by the legislature or by citizen initiative.

-If the majority voting on the question approve, an election of delegates must be held within six months. The delegates, one from each existing legislative district, convene at the state capitol on the first Tuesday of October following their election.

-Any proposed constitutional revision or amendments adopted by the convention must be submitted to the voters in a manner and at a time provided by the convention, but no sooner than 90 days after their final adjournment.

-If the majority of the qualified voters approve the revision or amendments, the changes become effective as provided by the convention.

A second approach is to amend (or change part of) the document. In Michigan there are two ways to do this. The first is by legislative proposal and a vote of the people. In this procedure an amendment to the Constitution may be proposed by legislators in the state Senate or the state House.

-The proposed amendment must be agreed to on a roll call vote by 2/3 of the members elected to and serving in each house.

-Within 60 days the proposal must be submitted to the electorate at the next general or special election as the legislature shall direct.

-If a majority of those voting on the proposal approve, the amendment becomes part of the document 45 days after the date of the election.

The Constitution can also be amended by citizen initiative and a vote of the people. In this method, an amendment may be proposed by qualified voters of the state in a petition directed to the secretary of state.

-All petitions must include the full text of the proposed amendment, and may be signed only by registered voters.

-The number of valid signatures must equal at least 10% of the total votes cast for all candidates for governor in the last election.

-Petitions must be filed with the secretary of state at least 120 days before the election at which the proposal is to be voted upon.

-The secretary of state must declare the validity and sufficiency of the signatures on the petitions at least 60 days prior to the election.

If a majority of those voting on the issue approve the amendment, it becomes effective 45 days after the election.

There are other ways, not spelled out in the state Constitution, whereby it can be changed. It can be interpreted by the courts. A legal case might arise in which the meaning of part of the document is challenged. In settling this case a court might change an older interpretation of the words to a newer version. The United States courts, and those of the state, are responsible for making sure that Michigan's Constitution and laws do not conflict with the national Constitution or laws. If they do, they are null and void—no longer a part of the state's law.

Even though Michigan's Constitution is fairly specific it does not spell out each and every detail in the operation of state and local government. Sometimes it uses vague language or is silent on a matter. Whenever this is the case, the actions of government officials—judges, legislators, and executives—are very important in determining the meaning of the state's Constitution and how it will be applied.

CONSTITUTION OF THE STATE OF MICHIGAN OF 1963

TABLE OF CONTENTS

PREAMBLE

BIBLIOGRAPHY

GENERAL REFERENCE

A guide to materials on Politics and Government in Michigan

Barfknecht, Gary, *Michillaneous*. Davison, Mich.: Friede Publications, 1982. A collection of curious and unusual facts about the state.

Brown, William and Ken VerBerg, *Michigan Politics and Government*. University of Nebraska Press, 1995.

Conot, Robert, *American Odyssey*.New York: William Morrow & Co.Inc. 1974. An interesting history of Michigan, with an emphasis on Detroit, inter-group relations, and economic development.

Council of State Governments, *The Book of the States*. Lexington, Ky. 1979. (Published every two years.)

Fenton, John H., *Midwest Politics*. New York: Holt, Rinehart & Winston, 1966.

Fischer, Floyd C., *The Government of Michigan*. Boston: Allyn & Bacon Inc., 1965.

Institute for Public Policy and Social Research, Michigan Database (MIDB). A computer based data base providing demographic data, population trends and maps for researchers. Brendan Mullan , director, Michigan State Univ.

League of Women Voters of Michigan, *The State We're In*. Lansing, Mich.: 1986. Revised periodically. The League is one of the most prominent organizations devoted to the study and analysis of public issues. It publishes extensively. Its address: League of Women Voters of Michigan, 202 Mill St. Lansing, Mich. 48933. There are many local chapters of the organization—check your phone book. By the way, men may join.

Lewis, Ferris E., *State and Local Government in Michigan*. Hillsdale, Mich.: Hillsdale Educational Publishers, 1979.

The Mackinac Center for Public Policy, Midland, Mi. A conservative/Republican "think tank" that distributes many publications on Michigan government and policy.

May, George S., *A Most Unique Machine: The Michigan Origins of the Automobile Industry*. Grand Rapids, Mich.: Eerdmans, 1975.

McHargue, Daniel S., *Michigan Government in Brief*. Ann Arbor, Mich.: University of Michigan Press, 1961.

Public Sector Sector Consultants, *Michigan Government Directory,* Lansing Mich., Biennial.

State of Michigan, *Michigan Manual*. The Department of Administration, Lansing Michigan: . (Published every two years.) Contains many current details about the Michigan state government.

Peirce, Neal R., *The Megastates of America.* New York: W.W. Norton & Co., 1972.

Peirce, Neal R. and John Keefe, *The Great Lakes States of America.* New York: W.W. Norton & Co., 1980.

Reichley, James, *States in Crisis: Politics in Ten American States, 1950-1962.* Chapel Hill: University of North Carolina Press, 1964.

Santer, Richard A. Michigan, *Heart of the Great Lakes.* Dubuque, Iowa: Kendall/Hunt Publishing Co.1977. An excellent survey of the state's history, geology, climate, population, economy and many public issues.

Senninger, Earl J. Jr., *Atlas of Michigan.* 3rd ed. Flint, Mich.: Flint Geographical Press, 1970. A collection of maps of the state outlining the economic, historical and geographical patterns of Michigan.

Sommers, Lawrence, *Michigan, A Geography,* Boulder, Colorado, Westview Press, 1984.

Thomas, T., *Michigan Government and You.* Hillsdale Publ Co.

Verway, David I. ed., *Michigan Statistical Abstract*, Wayne State Univ. Detroit.

Part One Michigan: History and Place in the Federal System

Bald, F. Clever, *Michigan in Four Centuries.* New York: Harper & Bros., 1961. One of the best standard histories of the state.

Bransky, James A., "Tribal Court Jurisdiction," Michigan Bar Journal, May 1988, p.370-76. Lansing, Mich.

Carter, James L., *Superior: A State for the North Country,* Marquette, Mich. The Pilot Press, 1980.

Catton, Bruce, *Michigan, A Bicentennial History.* New York: W.W. Norton & Co., 1976.

Cooley, Thomas McIntyre, *Michigan, A History of Governments.* Boston: Houghton Mifflin & Co., 1885.

Dunbar, Willis F., *Michigan: A History of the Wolverine State.* Grand Rapids, Mich.: William B. Eerdmans Publishing Co., 1970. (Revised Edition) May, George S., *Michigan: A History of the Wolverine State.* Grand Rapids, Mich.: William B. Eerdmans Publishing Co., 1980. Long considered the premier Michigan history text.

Graff, George P., *The People of Michigan.* 2nd ed. Lansing, Mich.: Michigan Department of Education, 1974.

Lewis, Ferris E., Michigan, *Yesterday and Today.* Hillsdale, Mich.: Hillsdale Educational Publishers, 1967.

May, George and Brinks, Herbert eds., *A Michigan Reader: 11,000 B.C. to A.D. 1865.* Grand Rapids, Mich.: William B. Eerdmans Publishing Co., 1974.

Quaife, M.M. and Glazer, Sidney, *Michigan-From Primitive Wilderness to Industrial Common-wealth.* New York: Prentice Hall, 1948.

Rubenstein, Bruce A. and Ziewacz, Lawrence E., *Michigan: A History of the Great Lakes State.* St. Louis: Forum Press, 1981.

Rubenstein, Bruce, and Ziewacz, Larry, *Payoffs in the Cloarkroom.* Michigan State Univ. Press. 1995.

Warner, Robert and Vanderhill, C. Warren, eds., *A Michigan Reader: 1865 to the Present.* Grand Rapids, Mich.: Eerdmans Publishing Co., 1974.

The Michigan Department of State publishes many informative bulletins and short papers on Michigan history. Contact the History Division of the department.

Part Two Power-Seeking in Michigan

Both of the major political parties in the state publish newsletters and other information relevant to state politics. Their addresses:

Democratic Party of Michigan 606 Townsend, Lansing,Mich.48933
Republican Party of Michigan 223 North Walnut,Lansing,Mich.48933

The Michigan Department of State publishes information related to candidate committee operations, interest group registration and campaign spending. Contact the Elections Division, Campaign Finance Reporting Office at P.O. Box 20126, Lansing, Mich. 48901.

Groop, Richard E. et. al. *Michigan Political Atlas,* East Lansing, Mich. Center for Cartographic Research and Spatial Analysis, Michigan State University, 1984.

Hrebenar, R. and Thomas, C., *Interest Group Politics in the Midwestern States.* Iowa State Univ. Press. 1993.

Inside Michigan Politics, 2029 S. Waverly Road, Lansing Mi.; Editor William Ballenger. An "insider" newsletter that deals with many current aspects of Michigan politics, elections and public opinion.

LaPolombara, Joseph, *Guide to Michigan Politics.* East Lansing, Mich.: Michigan State University Press, 1960.

League of Women Voters of Michigan, *Green Grass Roots: A Political Notebook for People Who Want to Participate.* Lansing, Mich.,1980.

——————————————,*Citizens Handbook,* Information on voting, elections and citizens action. Published Periodically.

——————————————,*Legislative Action Handbook.* Lansing, Mich. 1982. Information on the Michigan legislature, how to lobby, write testimony and conduct a legislative interview.

Michigan Secretary of State, *Laws Relating to Elections.* Lansing,Mich.1978. Contains the elections laws of the state. Revised periodically.

Sarasohn, Stephen B. and Vera H., *Political Party Patterns in Michigan.* Detroit: Wayne State University Press, 1957.

Sawyer, Robert Lee, *The Democratic State Central Committee in Michigan, 1949-1959: Rise of the New Politics and the New Political Leadership.* Ann Arbor, Mich.: Institute of Public Administration, University of Michigan, 1960.

Staebler, Neil, *Out of the Smoke-filled Room: A story of Michigan Politics.* An insiders view of Michigan politics from the 1940's to the 1980's. Ann Arbor: George Wahr Publ. Co. 1991.

State of Michigan, *A Citizen's Guide to Lobbying.* Lansing, Mich.:Published every two years. A good guide to the legislature--lists current members and committees and gives suggestions on how to lobby the legislature.

Streeter, Floyd Benjamin, *Political Parties in Michigan.* Lansing, Mich.: Michigan Historical Commission, 1918.

Part Three   State Government in Michigan

Berthelot, Helen, *Win Some-Lose Some; G. Mennen Williams and the New Democrats,* Wayne State Univ. Press, 1995.

Carr, Robert W., *Government in Michigan Under the 1964 Constitution.* Ann Arbor, Mich.: University of Michigan Press, 1965.

Constitutional Convention, 1963; "What the Proposed New State Constitution Means to You—A Report to the People", Lansing: State Constitutional Convention Office: 1963. Contains the proposed 1963 Constitution with explanation of the changes. Copies of the Constitution (as amended) are available from the Department of Management and Budget, General Services Section, P.O. Box 30026, Lansing, Mich. 48909. There is a small charge.

Citizens Conference on State Legislatures, *The Sometimes Governments.* New York: Bantam Books, 1971.

Citizens Research Council of Michigan, Michigan Constitutional Issues- 1978. Report No. 256. Detroit,Mich. 1978.

Council on Michigan Foundations, Grand Haven, Mich. A coalition of private foundations in Michigan. Studies current issues in the state.

Friedman, Robert B. *The Michigan Constitutional Convention and Administrative Organization: A Case Study in the Politics of Constitution Making.* Ann Arbor, Mich.: Institute of Public Administration, University of Michigan, 1963.

Fuller, Richard C.,*George Romney and Michigan.* New York: Vantage Press, 1966.

Hauge, Vincent and Hill, Spencer, *Major Issues in Michigan Politics,* Houghton Mich. Politics Press of Michigan, 1986.

Holmes, Grace W. and George, B.J. Jr., *An Introduction to Michigan Civil and Criminal Procedure.* Detroit: Center for the Administration of Justice, Wayne State University Law School, 1976.

League of Women Voters of Michigan, *Reapportionment/Redistricting: The Michigan Focus.* Lansing, Mich., 1981.

Michigan Compiled Laws Annotated (MCLA), St. Paul, Minn.: West Publishing Co., Published periodically. Available in major libraries together with Michigan Statutes Annotated, a basic reference on Michigan statutes.

Michigan Statutes Annotated (MSA), Willmette, Illinois: Callaghan Publishing, published periodically, a basic reference on Michigan law. Available in major libraries. Can be used in conjunction with the Michigan Compiled Laws Annotated.

Morris, Susanne R., *The Legislative Process in Michigan.* Hillsdale, Mich.: Hillsdale Educational Publishers, 1979. An excellent case study of the legislative process in Michigan. Has a good bibliography on the legislative process.

Office of the Governor, *Budget Message of the Governor.* Lansing: State of Michigan, Published yearly, the message and accompanying Executive Budget proposal provide a thorough review of state spending and executive organization.

Official Michigan, (weekly newspaper) published by Sanilac Publishing Co. 432 S. Sandusky Rd. Sandusky Mi. 48471.

Pollock, James K., *Making Michigan's Constitution, 1961-1961.* Ann Arbor, Michigan: G. Wahr Publishing Co., 1962.

Public Sector Consultants, *Michigan in Brief: An Issues Handbook*, Lansing, Mich. (annual).

Public TV, "Off The Record" Tim Skubik, host. Weekly review of major issues and personalities in Michigan Politics..

Stieber, Carolyn, *The Politics of Change in Michigan.* East Lansing: Michigan State Univ. Press, 1970. A good look at issues in Michigan in the 1950s and 1960s with a special focus on the parties, the constitutional convention, and the new 1963 Constitution.

Steingold, Fred S., *The Practical Guide to Michigan Law.* Ann Arbor: The University of Michigan Press, 1983.

Stollman Gerald H., *Michigan: State Legislators and Their Work.* Washington, D.C.: University Press of America, 1979. A good survey of the Michigan House and Senate at work.

Sturm, Albert L., *Constitution Making in Michigan, 1961-1962.* Ann Arbor, Mich.: Institute of Public Administration, University of Michigan, 1963.

Weddon, Willah, *Michigan Governors: Their Life Stories,* NOG Press, Lansing, 1994.

Weeks, George, *Stewards of the State: The Governors of Michigan,* Ann Arbor, Mi. The Detroit News and the Historical Society of Michigan, 1987.

Part Four   Local Government In Michigan

Organizations representing local governments are among the best sources of information. Among those which might be contacted are:

The Michigan Townships Association
3121 W. Saginaw St., Lansing.

The Michigan Municipal League
1675 Green Rd., Ann Arbor.

The Michigan Association of Counties
319 Lenawee, Lansing

Bauckham, John, *Authority and Responsibilities of Michigan Township Officials, Boards and Commissions.* Lansing: Michigan Townships Association, 1976.

Citizens Research Council of Michigan, "A New Approach to the Organization of Wayne County Government." Detroit: Citizens Research Council of Michigan, 1971. A report expressing concern about the roles and organization of county government in Michigan.

Citizens Research Council of Michigan, "A Bird's Eye View of Michigan Local Government at the End of the Twentieth Century." Detroit: Citizens Research Council of Michigan, August 1999. A good survey of the structure, powers and financing of Michigan local governmental units.

Goldman, Barbara Kukes (ed.), *Oakland County Government.* League of Women Voters, Birmingham, Mi, 1982.

Gluck, Peter R. and Meister, Richard J., *Cities in Transition,* New York: New Viewpoints, Division of Franklin Watts. 1979.

Office of the Lieutenant Governor. *Report of the Governor's Special Commission on Local Government. Lansing:* 1972. A survey of many local government issues.

Michigan Municipal League, *Annexation Procedures in Michigan,* Technical Topic 34. Ann Arbor, 1980.

——————————————, *Village Primary Elections and Village Charter Amendments,* Technical Topic 10. Ann Arbor, Mich., 1980.

——————————————, *Significance of City Incorporation of Unincorporated Areas,* Technical Topic 12. Ann Arbor, Mich., 1979.

——————————————, *Cost and Effect of Changing from Village to City,* Technical Topic 24A. Ann Arbor, Mich., 1977.

——————————————, *Organization of City and Village Government in Michigan,* Technical Topic 32. Ann Arbor, Mich., 1981.

State Board of Education, *State of Michigan General School Laws and Administrative Rules.* Lansing, 1977. (The School Code.)

VerBurg, Kenneth, *Guide to Michigan County Government:Third Edition,* East Lansing, Mich.: Institute for Community Development, Continuing Educational Service, Michigan State University, (1997)

———————————, *A Study of the Legal Powers of Michigan Local Governments.* East Lansing, Mich.: Institute for Community Development and Services, Michigan State University, 1969.

———————————, *Managing the Modern Michigan Township.* East Lansing,: Community Development Lifelong Education Programs, Michigan State University, 1981.

Part Five   Financing Government Services in Michigan

Advisory Commission on Intergovernmental Relations, *Significant Features of Fiscal Federalism, 1992.* Washington, ACIR, 1992. This national agency publishes many excellent reports on relations between levels of government in the United States.

Brazer, Harvey,(ed.) and Laren, Deborah (ass't ed.) *Michigan's Fiscal and Economic Structure.* Ann Arbor: University of Michigan Press, 1982. A thorough technical analysis of Michigan's economy in the early 1980s.

Citizens Research Council of Michigan, *Outline of the Michigan Tax System.* Published yearly. This private organization publishes excellent information on many current issues in the state. Its emphasis is the economy and government revenues and spending patterns. Its address: 500 Guardian Building-South, Detroit, 48226.

League of Women Voters of Michigan, *Social Services System.* Lansing, 1982.

———————————————, *Financing Government Services in Michigan.* Lansing, Mich., 1979.

Michigan Department of Management and Budget, Office of Revenue and Tax Analysis, *Michigan Tax Structure.* Lansing, 1983.

———————————————————, *State and Local Finance Guide-Resource Notebook.* Lansing, 1982.

Michigan Department of Treasury, *Annual Report of the State Treasurer,* (FY2000-01), Lansing.

Michigan Futures, *Crossing to the New Economy*, Bingham Farms, Mi.

Starling, Grover, *Managing the Public Sector.* (Revised Edition), Homewood, Ill.: Dorsey Press, 1982.

Taylor, Milton C., *Michigan Tax System: Equity or Rip-off?.* East Lansing, Mich.: Institute for Community Development, Continuing Education Service, Michigan State University, 19

VerBurg, Kenneth, *Michigan Local Property Tax Primer.* (Technical Bulletin B25). East Lansing, Mich.: Institute for Community Development, Continuing Education Series, January 1978.

Websites

Many offices and levels of Michigan's governments are accessible on the Internet and the World Wide Web and are often linked to other sources of information on Michigan government and politics. A few of the more useful follow:

Gongwer News Service: http://www.voyager.net/gongwer
> A source of much curent information and news on Michigan government and politics.

State of Michigan Website: //http.www.Mighigan.gov. This will connect you to all the state websites as well as many "non offical" related sites.

Governor's Office: http://www.migov.state.mi.us
> Current news on the governor and information on the executive branch. Links to many agencies and departments in the executive branch.

*Of particular note is the "Voters Information Center" under the Michigan Secretary of States office. Voters can simply type in their name and address to find their voting location and the candidates in their area as well as other election information.

State Senate: http://www.coast.net/~misenate/senhp.html
> Current information on the State Senate and its members.

State House of Representatives: http://www.house.state.mi.us
> Current information on the State House and its members.

Citizen's Research Council of Michigan: http://www.crcmich.org
> A great deal of research on many current issues in Michigan politics and policy.

Many government agencies, local governments and associations of governments also maintain websites. Most can be accessed through the above sites.

INDEX